CAMBRIDGE SURVEYS OF ECONOMIC LITERATURE

THEORIES OF INFLATION

CAMBRIDGE SURVEYS OF ECONOMIC LITERATURE

The literature of economics is expanding rapidly, and many subjects have changed out of recognition within the space of a few years. Perceiving the state of knowledge in fast-developing subjects is difficult for students and time-consuming for professional economists. This series of books is intended to help with this problem. Each book will be quite brief, giving a clear structure to and balanced overview of the topic, and written at a level intelligible to the senior undergraduate. They will therefore be useful for teaching but will also provide a mature yet compact presentation of the subject for economists wishing to update their knowledge outside their own specialism.

Theories of inflation

HELMUT FRISCH

Professor of Economics
University of Technology, Vienna

CAMBRIDGE UNIVERSITY PRESS

CAMBRIDGE

LONDON   NEW YORK   NEW ROCHELLE

MELBOURNE   SYDNEY

Published by the Press Syndicate of the University of Cambridge
The Pitt Building, Trumpington Street, Cambridge CB2 1RP
32 East 57th Street, New York, NY 10022, USA
296 Beaconsfield Parade, Middle Park, Melbourne 3206, Australia

First published 1983

Printed in the United States of America

Library of Congress Cataloging in Publication Data
Frisch, Helmut.
Theories of inflation.
(Cambridge surveys of economic literature)
Based on: Die neue Inflationstheorie. Göttingen:
Vandenhoeck und Ruprecht. 1980.
Bibliography: p.
1. Inflation (Finance)   I. Title.   II. Series.
HG229.F723   1983   332.4'1'01   83-1871
ISBN 0 521 22470 5   hard covers
ISBN 0 521 29512 2   paperback

CONTENTS

v

PREFACE

The purpose of this book is to summarize and evaluate the inflation literature of the two decades 1960–80. In this context two important questions arise: Did we learn anything? and What did we learn? The answer to the first question is undoubtedly yes; we try to answer the second question in Chapter 3, "The Phillips Curve," in Chapter 4, "Monetarist Inflation Theory," and in Chapter 5, "The Hypothesis of Structural Inflation."

Because of the absence of a generally accepted paradigm in today's macroeconomics, it is not possible to develop contemporary inflation theory as a succession of models of increasing complexity. Rather, the models are developed chronologically as in the Phillips curve chapter, or in adherence to a particular school of economic thought, as in the chapter on monetarism.

The book is an expanded version of my article, "Inflation Theory 1963–1975: A 'Second-Generation' Survey," in the *Journal of Economic Literature,* December 1977. Since the appearance of the article, inflation literature and macroeconomic theorizing have advanced considerably. These recent developments in inflation theory and related macroeconomics are also covered in the book.

In 1980 my book *Die neue Inflationstheorie* appeared in German. The present volume differs from it in that most of the chapters have been substantially revised and new material has been added – for example, Chapter 6 on stagflation.

The book is written for students at the advanced undergraduate level and for professional economists who are looking for a reference text. The emphasis is on the basic concepts of the inflation models and their economic content.

In preparing this volume I have benefited from attending a series of international conferences on inflation theory in the years 1974–9 and from discussions with distinguished scholars, especially O. Aukrust (Oslo), W. Branson (Princeton), M. Bronfenbrenner (Durham), K. Brunner (Rochester), E.-M. Claassen (Paris), R. Dornbusch (MIT), R. Gordon (Northwestern University), H. König (Mannheim), D. Laidler (London/Ontario), M. Parkin (London/Ontario), D. Patinkin (Jerusalem), A. Lindbeck (Stockholm), F. Machlup (New York), A. Meltzer (Pittsburgh), and P. Kouri (New York).

I would like to express my thanks to the members of the Institute of Economics at the University of Technology in Vienna, A. Guger, G. Hanappi, H. Otruba, and A. Wörgötter, who have read and commented on the entire manuscript. I owe a special debt to J. Maurer and F. Hof, who subjected the drafts at all stages to their searching, unrelenting, and useful criticism. Their observations and suggestions have helped to clarify various issues and have led to significant improvements. I am very grateful to Th. Huertas (Citibank, New York) for translating an earlier draft of the manuscript and for many useful suggestions and revisions. I would like to acknowledge the help of L. Kaplan (Vienna) for his stylistic improvements and editorial work.

I wish to thank Mrs. R. Tomaschek for typing and proofreading the text at various stages of preparation and for her patience in preparing the book for publication.

Finally I would like to express my deep gratitude to Mark Perlman for having encouraged me to write this book, for many discussions on the state of the art, and for having pushed me to finish the manuscript at several critical stages.

After having expressed my thanks to some of the many colleagues who have helped me, I should add that any mistakes and limitations of the book must, of course, be "charged" to my account.

Helmut Frisch

Vienna
February 1983

INTRODUCTION

This book offers a survey of the developments of inflation theory during the two decades 1960–80, developments that reflect the economic history of this period. The process of inflation began in the early 1960s in a moderate way, accelerated at the end of the decade, and reached a peak just before the world recession in 1973–74. Since then the inflation process seems to have lost its dynamics in most of the industrial countries; that is, inflation rates show a tendency to decrease. These events have stimulated economic theorizing and model building designed to shed some light on the inflation process as experienced by the Western countries in these two decades.

The beginning of the new debate in inflation theory can be characterized by the attempt to explain the inflation process as "causal": Does inflation originate in the labor market or can it be explained by the rate of growth of the money supply? Later, with the acceleration of inflation, the emphasis shifted to explaining inflationary expectations. The treatment of expectations distinguishes the new inflation models from the traditional theory.

Since the end of the 1960s the widely accepted view based on the "neoclassical synthesis" (P. Samuelson) has been increasingly challenged. The consensus has disappeared. Two schools have emerged and they both emphasize the difference between their approaches: neo-Keynesian macroeconomics versus the

1

monetarist approach. Neither school is homogeneous; both encompass a spectrum of views. Monetarism as discussed in Chapter 4 is defined by the following four propositions:

1. Stability of the private sector
2. Long-run neutrality of money
3. Acceptance of the short-run Phillips curve
4. Dislike of activist economic policy

Acceptance of all four propositions makes one a monetarist "Mark I" along with Milton Friedman. If one rejects proposition 3 and replaces it with the proposition of the short-run neutrality of money, one espouses monetarism "Mark II" as do the proponents of the rational expectations school.

What, then, constitutes neo-Keynesianism? Acceptance of the following propositions:

1. Instability of the private sector or slow adjustment processes to return to equilibrium
2. Long-run neutrality of money
3. Existence of a trade-off between inflation and unemployment
4. Preference for a countercyclical policy

For a long time the Keynesian inflation theory was identified with the Phillips–Lipsey model of inflation, implying a stable trade-off between inflation and unemployment. Recently J. Tobin (1980), a proponent of neo-Keynesian theory, has accepted the view of a short-run and a long-run Phillips curve, according to which a trade-off between inflation and unemployment is only temporary. With this twist the neo-Keynesian theory and monetarism Mark I approach each other. Neo-Keynesian macroeconomics can be interpreted as disequlibrium economics in which the emphasis is on price and wage "stickiness" rather than on instantaneous market clearing.

The book begins with some problems of definition. As the student soon discovers, the problem of inflation starts with the attempt to define it. Although there is no lack of definitions of inflation, a generally accepted definition does not, in fact, exist. Therefore we shall use a pragmatic definition: "Inflation is a process of continuously rising prices, or continuously falling value of money" (Laidler and Parkin, 1975).

The following problem might also surprise the student. Although the whole world speaks about inflation, measuring inflation is not a simple exercise. One is immediately confronted with the problem of calculating a price index. No single approach to index construction yields the "optimal" index. Chapter 1 therefore describes the construction and characteristics of the two most important price indexes: the Laspeyres Index and the Paasche Index.

As mentioned, the development of a theory of inflationary expectations can be considered the essential difference between the new theory of inflation, explained in Chapters 3 and 4, and the traditional theory, described in Chapter 7. In Chapter 2 the two central concepts of expectation formation are introduced and interpreted: (1) adaptive expectations and (2) rational expectations.

According to the model of adaptive expectations, the forecast for the next period is a weighted average of past inflation rates. Expectations are corrected by some fraction of the past period's expectations error. The adaptive expectations mechanism emphasizes the "learning behavior" of the agents. This approach was challenged by the rational expectations school, which argues that agents are aware of the structure of the economic system; the rational way for them to form their expectations is to base them on the predictions of the economic model. An implication of this approach is that agents use their information efficiently (i.e., do not waste information) and do not make systematic forecast errors. At this point the discussion of the model of expectation formation in Chapter 2 ends. The far-reaching implications of the two different models of expectations appear in the discussion of the Phillips curve (Chapter 3) and in the discussion of the monetarist inflation theory (Chapter 4).

Despite all the criticism of the Phillips curve model, it can be considered one of the central models of the new inflation theory (Chapter 3). The Phillips curve was first interpreted by R. Lipsey as the neo-Keynesian inflation theory. It identified the labor market as the source of inflation and led to the notion of a stable trade-off between inflation and unemployment. This concept dominated the discussions on inflation in the 1960s. However, at the end of the 1960s M. Friedman and E. Phelps differentiated between the short-run and long-run Phillips curves. This theory became known as the "natural rate of unemployment hypothesis." This hypothesis, which has been generally accepted almost everywhere, says that the rate of unemployment can deviate from its equilibrium in the short run but will return to its natural rate level in the long run after an adjustment for inflationary expectations. The natural rate hypothesis was challenged by the rational expectations school, which argues that economic agents use their information efficiently and do not make systematic forecast errors, as implied in the adaptive expectations model (see Chapter 2). Rational expectations together with the further assumption that markets always clear lead to the result that not even a short-run Phillips curve exists. The criticism from the school of rational expectations has livened the discussion, but the power of this theory's logic is greater than its value as a description of the real world.

The Phillips curve model is thus compatible with various interpretations: with the neo-Keynesian interpretation (Phillips–Lipsey) and with the neoclassical–monetarist interpretation (Friedman–Phelps). In the school of rational expectations, however, and only in this school, the Phillips curve disappears as a systematic connection between the rates of inflation and unemployment.

The chapter on the Phillips curve also contains an analysis of the forms of unemployment rates, in which the results of the New Microeconomics (Phelps et al., 1971) are compared with the Keynesian concept of "involuntary unemployment." This section clarifies several concepts as well as criticizes the tendency of the New Microeconomics to reduce the total rate of unemployment to frictional or search unemployment.

In the new standard textbooks of macroeconomics, such as R. Dornbusch and St. Fischer (1978) or R. Gordon (1978), the Phillips curve is introduced into the IS-LM system and is interpreted as a supply curve. An analysis of this expanded IS-LM model ends the chapter on the Phillips curve. It is followed in Chapter 4 by a detailed discussion of the inflation theory of monetarism. M.

Friedman's dictum "Inflation is a monetary phenomenon" is the motto of this theory.

What is monetarism? It is first of all the summation of various theoreticians who were united in their criticism of the Keynesian orthodoxy that ruled at the end of the 1960s. It is furthermore the attempt to create a new paradigm to stand against Keynesian macroeconomics. Although various authors have made important contributions, the central role of Friedman in the formulation of monetarist theory or, more precisely, of monetarism Mark I is unchallenged. Section 4.3, "From the Quantity Theory to the Monetary Theory of Nominal Income," is therefore devoted to a more detailed discussion of the Friedman version of monetarism. Afterward a standard model of monetarism is developed, which rests on three bases: (1) the quantity theory, (2) the "expectations-augmented" Phillips curve, and (3) Okun's law. In this model, changes in the rate of growth of the money supply generate real effects (i.e., they influence the rate of real growth and the rate of unemployment); in the long run, after the expectations adjustment process has terminated, the real effects disappear and only a permanent increase in the trend rate of inflation remains. This type of model, which combines monetarism with an expectations-augmented Phillips curve, was labeled monetarism Mark I earlier in the discussion.

The transition from monetarism Mark I to monetarism Mark II can be made easily in the context of the monetarist model. One has only to replace the adaptive expectations mechanism with rational expectations. In the new model the role of monetary policy is different. Changes in the rate of growth of the money supply – if they are anticipated by the agents – influence only inflation and not real output or employment. A generalization of this result is the policy ineffectiveness postulate, which states that a systematic economic policy changes only the rate of inflation and does not exert any influence on the real part of the economy. The difference between monetarism I and monetarism II is, in brief, the neutrality of money. According to monetarism I, money is neutral only in the long run; according to monetarism

II, money is neutral even in the short run. A short summary of the debate about the policy ineffectiveness postulate and a critique of the least plausible assumptions of monetarism Mark II close this section.

The last part of Chapter 4 is concerned with the monetarism of the open economy. H.G. Johnson (1976) argued that a small, open economy in the face of excess demand does not have an inflation problem but rather a problem of balance of payments. In contrast to the theory of the closed economy, an increase in the money supply does not increase the rate of inflation (since prices are determined by the "world market") but leads to a deterioration in the balance of payments. Another group of models of the monetary approach sketches a theory of world inflation in which the world price level depends on the world money supply.

In Chapter 5 the view is entirely different. The Phillips curve model and the monetarist inflation theory consider inflation a problem of short-run stabilization policy. Inflation reflects excess demand in the goods and labor markets or excess supply in the money market. The hypothesis of structural inflation attempts to link the long-run tendency toward inflation in the industrialized economies to structural factors. A variant that has become very popular in European discussion is called the Scandinavian model. According to this model the economy is divided into two parts: an "exposed" sector producing "traded goods" and a "sheltered" sector producing "nontraded goods." Both sectors grow at different rates of labor productivity. A wage spillover effect results in the money wages in the sheltered sector growing at approximately the same rate as the money wages in the exposed sector. The model relies on the small-country assumption, which implies that the country is a price taker in the world market. Given fixed exchange rates, the model leads to the so-called Aukrust equation with the simple message that the domestic rate of inflation is explained by the world rate of inflation and a component that depends on the difference in productivity growth between the exposed and the sheltered sectors. This model was explicitly (or implicitly) used by a number of smaller European economies

(such as Austria, Norway, Sweden, Finland, and the Nether-
lands) to explain their inflation problem and to serve as a model
for antiinflationary policy (especially incomes policy).

Chapter 6 discusses stagflation – a state of the economy that is
as inconvenient as the word itself is inelegant. It is a condition in
which inflation is combined with substantial unemployment. Two
types of stagflation are distinguished: (1) stagflation as an adjustment process following a previous demand inflation, and (2)
stagflation resulting from an autonomous shift in the supply function (supply inflation).

One specific type of supply inflation, the "oil shock," is discussed in detail. Given the assumptions of the model, the supply
curve becomes a vertical line on the horizontal axis. The oil
shock moves the supply curve to the left in the direction of the
origin. Stagflation phenomena result from this shift in the supply
curve. Finally it is shown that in the situation in which the output
is determined by supply, demand policy influences only the price
level and has no effect on output and employment.

The final Chapter 7 provides a survey of the traditional concepts of inflation. We begin with the quantity theory of money but in
the context of the neoclassical model. In this model the relative
prices and the quantities demanded and supplied are determined
in the real sector of the economy, whereas the general price level
is determined in the monetary sector. Doubling the money supply
doubles all nominal prices but leaves the relative prices and the
volume of transactions constant. The quantity theory in the context of the neoclassical model explains inflation causally: The
quantity of money determines the level of prices and the rate of
change in the money supply determines the rate of inflation.

In 1939 J.M. Keynes wrote two long articles in the British daily
newspaper *The Times,* which became the basis for his famous
essay *How to Pay for the War.* Keynes investigated the relationship among inflation, taxation, and the distribution of income
that results from an unanticipated increase in nonconsumption
expenditures. The government's need to finance the war manifests itself in excess demand in the goods market – the "inflation

gap.'' The inflation process described in *How to Pay for the War* is basically a redistribution process in which income from wage earners with a low propensity to save and a low marginal tax rate is transferred to the entrepreneurial sector with a higher propensity to save and a higher marginal tax rate. Recently Keynes's inflation gap model has received renewed attention by S. Maital (1972) and J.A. Trevithick (1975).

B. Hansen's model of the double inflation gap is a straightforward extension of the Keynes model. Hansen differentiates between a goods gap (excess demand in the goods market) and a factor gap (excess demand in the labor market).

A central topic in the discussion of inflation in the 1960s was the classification of inflation into demand-pull and cost-push. Using the aggregate demand curve and the aggregate supply curve, we try to distinguish the two concepts. Although this distinction has its place in the literature of inflation, it has lost most of its significance in contemporary models of inflation.

By comparing the new theories of inflation as set out in Chapters 3, 4, and 5 with the traditional theory, we can easily see the difference: The traditional theory explains changes in the price level, whereas the new models focus on the inflationary process per se. The traditional inflation literature manages to do without inflationary expectations, whereas the new inflation models consider inflationary expectations the core of the inflationary process.

1

Inflation: definition and measurement

This book describes the most influential concepts of traditional and recent theories of inflation. In the discussions of the various models, the reader will probably notice that the concept of inflation is used without further explanation. The problems associated with inflation do not begin with the explanation of it, however; they start with the attempt to define it. In fact, there is no generally acceptable or satisfactory definition. In the literature, a pragmatic definition has the widest acceptance. Although it lacks precision, the following definition has an advantage in that it corresponds to common usage: "Inflation is a process of continuously rising prices, or equivalently, of continuously falling value of money" (Laidler and Parkin, 1975, p. 741). It refers to the symptoms of inflation but tells nothing about the causes and effects of inflation.

Some comments may make the definition of inflation more precise.

   a. The definition states what inflation is not; that is, it is not a one-time or short-run increase in the general price level. Similarly, one cannot label as inflation price increases during the recovery phase of the business cycle that are rescinded through price reductions during the recession. Only when price increases are irreversible can one speak of inflation without qualification.

b. One must emphasize that inflation does not concern increases in the prices of individual commodities; it refers to an increase in the general price level, the weighted average of all prices.
c. One should hesitate to label as inflation increases in the general price level at a rate of less than 1 percent per year. The rate of increase in the general price level that merits the title "inflation" depends on the sensitivity of economic agents to inflation. This is necessarily a subjective criterion.

In addition to the symptom-based definition of inflation, one finds in the literature more specialized definitions that take into account either the causes or the effects of inflation or refer to some particular characteristic of the inflation process. M. Bronfenbrenner and F.D. Holzmann distinguish four types of definitions of inflation:

1. Inflation is a condition of generalized excess demand, in which "too much money chases too few goods."
2. Inflation is a rise of the money stock or money income, either total or per capita.
[Bronfenbrenner and Holzman, 1963, p. 599]

Both these definitions are causal. In the first case inflation is traced to demand in the goods market; in the second inflation is explained as the result of a change in the money supply. In recent discussions M. Friedman has popularized the monetarist causal definition: "Inflation is always and everywhere a monetary phenomenon . . . and can be produced only by a more rapid increase in the quantity of money than in output" (Friedman, 1970b, p. 24).

3. Inflation is a rise in price levels with additional characteristics or conditions: It is incompletely anticipated; it leads (via cost increases) to further rises; it does not increase employment and real output; it is faster than some "safe" rate; it arises "from the side of money"; it is measured by prices net of indirect taxes and subsides; and/or it is irreversible.
[Bronfenbrenner and Holzmann, 1963, p. 599]

This is an extended version of the symptom-based definition of inflation that requires the increase in the general price level to have certain characteristics.

Table 1.1. *Types of inflation*

Classification	Criterion for classification
a. Open or suppressed inflation	Working of the market mechanism
b. Creeping, moderate, or galloping inflation, hyperinflation	Rate at which prices increase
c. Anticipated and unanticipated inflation	Expectations of inflation
d. Cost-push or demand-pull inflation	Causes of inflation

4. Inflation is a fall in the external value of money as measured by foreign exchange rates, by the price of gold, or indicated by excess demand for gold or foreign exchange at official rates. [Bronfenbrenner and Holzmann, 1963, p. 599]

The fourth definition emphasizes external developments in the general price level. Inflation is measured by movements in the exchange rate, a method appropriate for open economies under certain conditions.

Along with these definitions of inflation, there are at least as many classifications of inflation. In Table 1.1 we describe only a few categories:

a. If inflation is open, the market economy basically continues to function as a process in which prices are set. Any excess demand (the goods or factor gap) leads to an increase in prices and money wages. Suppressed inflation occurs when government controls prevent goods prices and money wages from rising, so that excess demand is not reduced but suppressed. If controls are lifted, one must reckon with increases in the general price level and in money wages (Hansen, 1951, p. 3).

b. The criterion underlying this classification is the rate of the observed increase in the general price level. Inflationary processes in which the increase in prices does not exceed 2–3 percent and in which there are no expectations of inflation to speak of may be characterized as "creeping" inflation. Higher rates of price increase are labeled "moderate"; a further acceleration of the increase in prices merits the epithet "galloping." However, one cannot set exact boundaries between any two of these categories. Extraordinarily high rates of price increases, which in general are also accelerating, can be called "hyperinflation." P. Cagan (1956, p. 25) defines this as a condition in which the general price level is increasing at a rate of more than 50 percent per month. In hyperinflations money loses its function as a store of value and at least partly as a medium of exchange. In the period after World War I hyperinflation occurred in various European countries such as Germany, Poland, Austria, Russia, and Hungary. After World War II it occurred in some South American countries.

c. In this case expectations are the criterion used to classify inflation. In its emphasis on the difference between anticipated and unanticipated inflation, the new theory of inflation differs significantly from the traditional theory. The classification is relevant in determining the effects of inflation. Only unanticipated inflation produces real effects; that is, only unanticipated inflation affects output and employment.

d. The differentiation between demand-pull and cost-push inflation hinges on the cause of inflation. The former is considered to result from excess aggregate demand; the latter from a shift in the aggregate supply function. In the recent literature on inflation, however, this dichotomy has lost the central role with which traditional theory endowed it. This is a consequence of the failure to identify empirically the two types of inflation.

The symptom-based definition of inflation formulated at the outset leads directly to the problem of how to define the price level. Two questions must be resolved:

1. How does one calculate the general price level from the prices of individual commodities and services?
2. Which price index measures inflation appropriately?

1. The calculation of the general price level and the attendant difficulties form part of the so-called index number problem (Sam-

uelson and Swamy, 1974; Allen, 1975). Let us examine an economy that has n goods. Although we can empirically observe the development of n individual prices p_i and quantities x_i as well as the development of the sum of their nominal values ($\sum_{i=1}^{n} x_i p_i = y$), we cannot separate y into a price component p (price index) and a real component x (quantity index) without confronting the problem of building an index. Since no single approach to index construction yields the "best" index formula, one cannot theoretically establish that any one particular decomposition of y is superior to any other.

The following linear approach is the basis for the indexes most commonly used to measure the level of prices and the changes in that level.

$$P_t = 100 \sum_{i=1}^{n} g_i \frac{p_i^t}{p_i^0} \tag{1}$$

where $\sum_{i=1}^{n} g_i = 1$, P_t is the general price level in period t, p_i^t is the price of good i in period t, and g_i is the weight of the ith ratio of prices in the overall index. The price level of the base period is assumed to be 100. The price level in period t may be represented as the sum of the price level in the base period and a weighted sum of the rates of changes in the prices of individual commodities. This is shown in the following calculation:

$$
\begin{aligned}
P_t &= P_0 + 100 \sum_{i=1}^{n} g_i \frac{p_i^t}{p_i^0} - P_0 \\
&= P_0 + 100 \sum_{i=1}^{n} g_i \frac{p_i^t - p_i^0}{p_i^0} \\
&= P_0 + 100 \sum_{i=1}^{n} g_i \frac{\Delta p_i}{p_i^0}
\end{aligned}
\tag{2}
$$

The Laspeyres Index

The Laspeyres Index formula is based on the principle used in constructing equation (1). As weights it uses the base-period share in the nominal expenditures of the individual goods:

$$g_i = \frac{p_i^0 x_i^0}{\sum\limits_{j=1}^{n} p_j^0 x_j^0} \tag{3}$$

By using equations (1) and (3), we can write the Laspeyres Index formula as follows:

$$L_P = \frac{\sum\limits_{i=1}^{n} p_i^t x_i^0}{\sum\limits_{i=1}^{n} p_i^0 x_i^0} \cdot 100 \tag{4}$$

Thus, the Laspeyres Index L_P shows the relative change in the cost of a basket of goods originally purchased in a base period. Although this index is most often used in statistics, it has a significant weakness – namely, that the base-period bundle of goods is held constant. If the relative prices of goods change during the period of inflation, then firms and households will demand smaller quantities of goods that have become relatively more expensive and larger quantities of goods that have become relatively less expensive. The effect of this demand shift is suppressed in the Laspeyres Index. It accords too much weight to goods that have become relatively more expensive and too little weight to goods that have become relatively less expensive. In relation to the "actual" change in prices, therefore, the Laspeyres Index overestimates the rise in the general price level.

Finally, the Laspeyres Index does not take into account new goods that appeared on the market for the first time after the base period. Correspondingly, the index contains goods that have become obsolete in the current period.

The Paasche Index
The Paasche Index differs from the Laspeyres Index in its system of weights used for equation (1). These weights are defined as

$$g_i = \frac{p_i^0 x_i^t}{\sum\limits_{j=1}^{n} p_j^0 x_j^t} \tag{5}$$

A simple transformation yields

$$P_P = \frac{\sum\limits_{i=1}^{n} p_i^t x_i^t}{\sum\limits_{i=1}^{n} p_i^0 x_i^t} \cdot 100 \tag{6}$$

The Paasche Index therefore takes the basket of goods purchased in the end period as a point of reference. In contrast to the Laspeyres Index, it takes into account changes in the pattern of demand. This correctly captures the structure of expenditures in the end period, but it can be shown that the Paasche Index overestimates the total expenditures in the base period so that it generally underestimates the rise in the general price level.

In addition to these two indexes we note a third, Fisher's ideal index. The Ideal Price Index I_P is the geometric mean of the index formulas of Laspeyres and Paasche:

$$I_P = \sqrt{L_P \cdot P_P} \tag{7}$$

Its value lies between those of the Paasche and Laspeyres indexes and therefore approximates the actual course of inflation more closely. Nevertheless, this index has not been widely used in practical economic statistics because it has no direct economic interpretation (Allen, 1975, p. 2).

2. No less a problem than the formation of a proper index is the choice of a proper method to calculate the general price level at a point in time. The most comprehensive price index is the Gross National Product (GNP) deflator, whose framework contains all the goods and services that enter into value added in the Gross National Product. The GNP deflator is a Paasche Index that shows whether and by how much the combination of goods constituting the Gross National Product valued at current prices has become more expensive relative to the prices that prevailed in the base year. The index has a weakness, however. A fictitious price index must be used for transactions that do not take place in the market (principally government services).

For the average household the GNP deflator is not an ideal index to measure the value of money, since it contains the prices of investment and export goods with which the household does not come into direct contact. In practice, therefore, the cost-of-living index or the consumer price index plays a great role. In fact, the public probably considers a rise in this index to equal inflation. However, as J.E. Triplett (1975) correctly remarked, a fundamental question about these indexes immediately arises: whose cost of living? Theoretically, one would have to construct an individual price index for each household on the basis of its own pattern of spending (or basket of goods). A judgment concerning the change in the value of money largely depends on the goods or classes of goods on which income is spent. In practice one resorts to the method of aggregation.

By means of consumer surveys, baskets of goods and services appropriate for various types of households are constructed. In the United States the Bureau of Labor Statistics calculates a representative cost-of-living index, the Consumer Price Index (CPI). The CPI, published monthly, is based on a market basket of goods and services for an average urban wage earner or clerical worker. It is composed of 250 categories of goods and services. The CPI is the most closely watched price index in the United States because it is used to escalate wage payments as well as Social Security benefits that have cost-of-living clauses. In response to criticism that the CPI reflects only the situation of wage earners, in 1978 the bureau began to publish an additional CPI for all urban consumers based on a more general expenditure pattern.

In West Germany the Federal Statistical Office calculates four cost-of-living indexes – namely, for (1) all private households, (2) four-person worker households with moderate incomes, (3) four-person white-collar and civil servant households with higher incomes, and (4) two-person pensioner and welfare recipient households.

These American and German cost-of-living indexes are constructed according to the Laspeyres Index formula and each suffers from the defects inherent in this construction. Moreover, the indexes are valid for only a representative household within each group. Statistical experiments involving further disaggregation

Table 1.2. *Summary of developments in consumer prices,
1961–1980 (rates of growth relative to previous year,
in percent)*

Year	USA	Germany	UK	Switzerland	Austria	OECD average
1961	1.1	2.3	3.5	1.9	3.5	1.7
1962	1.2	3.0	4.2	4.3	4.4	2.8
1963	1.2	3.0	2.0	3.4	2.7	3.0
1964	1.3	2.3	3.2	3.1	3.8	2.6
1965	1.6	3.4	4.8	3.5	4.9	3.2
1966	3.0	3.5	3.9	4.7	2.2	3.5
1967	2.8	1.5	2.5	4.0	4.0	3.1
1968	4.2	2.9	4.7	2.4	2.8	4.0
1969	5.4	1.9	5.4	2.4	3.1	4.7
1970	5.9	3.4	6.4	3.6	4.4	5.5
1971	4.2	5.3	9.4	6.6	4.7	5.3
1972	3.3	5.5	7.1	6.7	6.4	4.9
1973	6.2	7.0	9.2	8.7	7.5	7.7
1974	11.0	7.0	16.0	9.8	9.5	13.2
1975	9.1	5.9	24.2	6.7	8.4	11.4
1976	5.7	4.6	16.6	1.7	7.3	8.5
1977	6.5	3.9	15.9	1.3	5.5	9.1
1978	7.7	2.6	8.3	1.0	3.6	8.3
1979	11.4	4.1	13.3	3.7	3.7	9.8
1980	13.5	5.5	18.4	4.0	6.3	12.8

Source: OECD, *Main Economic Indicators, Historical Statistics* (Paris:
OECD, 1981).

suggest that the dispersion of the price indexes within each of the
four groups is very large (Triplett, 1975, p. 65). This means that
one cannot avoid redistributional effects within each group if one
uses these cost-of-living indexes to adjust incomes to inflationary
developments. Some households will be overcompensated,
whereas others will suffer real income losses despite the adjustment to the higher cost of living.

We conclude this introduction by examining the development
of inflation in some selected Organization for Economic Coopera-
tion and Development (OECD) countries for the period 1961–80,
as shown by the data in Table 1.2, which are plotted in Figure 1.1.

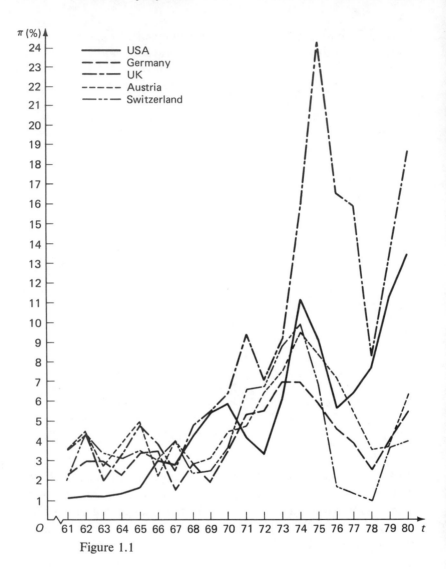

Figure 1.1

Through an inspection of the data we can reach the following purely descriptive conclusions:

1. In the first half of the 1960s one could classify the inflation that occurred in most OECD countries as "creeping."

2. At the beginning of the 1970s the rate of inflation throughout the world increased, so that moderate inflation became the rule.

3. After a further sharp acceleration in the inflation rates – namely, due to the rise in raw material and energy prices – the worldwide recession in 1974–5 led to an abrupt slowdown in the rate of inflation in most OECD countries.

4. At the beginning of the 1970s there was a tendency toward uniformity in the inflation rates in various countries. After the 1974–5 recession, however, the variation in inflation rates among countries increased.

2

Expectations and inflation

One of the major differences between the theories of inflation developed in the last fifteen years and the traditional theories (as discussed in Chapter 7) is the role of inflationary expectations. Although Keynes, Hicks, Lange, and others have discussed expectations, only recently the formation of expectations has been extensively investigated by the current models of inflation. It is no exaggeration to say that this has raised the economic theory of expectations to a new and higher level.

The traditional concept of expectations in economic theory goes back to J.R. Hicks's (1946) treatment in his major work *Value and Capital*. Hicks discussed the concept of expectations in connection with his analysis of the stability of general economic equilibrium. Whether an equilibrium point is stable depends on how expectations change as a result of a shock to the system that shifts it away from equilibrium. In this context a central problem arises – namely, how to formulate the relationship between the change in expectations and the disturbance of the equilibrium. For this purpose Hicks used the concept of the elasticity of expectations, or the relationship between the percent change in the expected value of a variable and the percent change in the actual value of the same variable. In Hicks's words: "I define the elasticity of a particular person's expectations of the price of commodity X as the ratio of the proportional rise in the expected future prices of X to the proportional rise in its current price'' (1946, p. 205).

If p^* is the price expected to prevail in the future and p is the actual price of a certain good X observed now, then we can write the Hicksian elasticity of expectations ε_p^* as follows:

$$\varepsilon_p^* = \frac{dp^*/p^*}{dp/p}$$

If $\varepsilon_p^* = 1$, then a 10 percent increase in the current price leads to a 10 percent increase in the expected future price. If $\varepsilon_p^* = 0$, a change in the current price provokes no adjustment in expectations; one expects that the price will return to its previous level. With $\varepsilon_p^* > 1$, an increase in the current price leads to the expectation that prices will rise even further in the future; economic actors expect price increases to have a positive trend.

The Hicksian concept of the elasticity of expectations is only an instrument of stability analysis. It does not explain how expectations are formed or how they change. In simple terms one can say that the equilibrium of an economic system is stable when the elasticity of expectations is less than unity. Conversely, the equilibrium is unstable if $\varepsilon_p^* > 1$, whereas $\varepsilon_p^* = 1$ represents the dividing line between stability and instability.

Before we turn to the theory of expectations as developed in the context of the new inflation theory, we shall make a few semantic remarks. All economic activity involving the future – in other words, any economic plans people may make – is affected by expectations. The fundamental difficulty in the analysis of expectations lies in their very nature. Expectations are psychological phenomena that cannot be observed directly in the way that quantities and prices can be watched. In the words of S.A. Ozga: "*Expectations proper* are attitudes, dispositions or states of mind which determine our behaviour, or at least accompany it" (1965, p. 23).

To analyze expectations one may use one of two methods: either introspection, whereby one projects one's own subjective experience onto other economic agents, or proxy formulation, whereby one establishes a relationship between the unobservable expectations and empirically observable magnitudes. The modern theory of inflation uses exclusively the second method.

Since common usage is often ambiguous, it may be useful at the outset to distinguish among (1) expectations, (2) predictions or forecasts, and (3) plans or intentions. An *expectation* is a statement about an unknown future event. An economic expectation naturally refers to economic events. It is only finely distinguishable from a prediction or a forecast. A *prediction* may be thought of as an expectation made more precise; it is the explicit and formal (mostly quantitative) form of an expectation. Predictions and expectations refer, according to H. Theil (1970, pp. 1–5), to future events that are not under the control of the economic agent who makes the forecast. In contrast, *plans* contain in addition to predictions and expectations instrumental variables that the individual can control.

Regarding the formation of expectations, one must therefore distinguish three elements:

a. The individual as the processor of certain information
b. The information or the observation itself
c. The expectation proper

The relationship among these elements is shown in Figure 2.1. As one can readily see, the individual in the scheme plays the role of an information processor. Analytically, a succession of expectations over time can be considered the result of a continuous process of receiving and processing information. The purpose of this activity is to form expectations (or predictions) concerning the future values of economic variables or to revise existing expectations. The precision of an expectation depends in turn on the information available and the model by which it is processed. As long as an agent has only rudimentary information on how the economic system functions, he must form his expectations on the basis of models that are less information-intensive. In this case the model of adaptive expectations is very suitable; the future value of a variable is related to the history of its past values. If more information is available, however, the adaptive expecta-

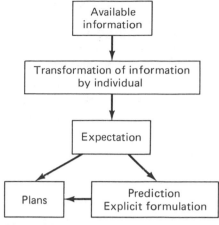

Figure 2.1

tions model is insufficient because it would "waste" the extra information (Muth, 1961). This idea is the heart of the concept of rational expectations, in which the expectation for a certain economic variable is formed within the framework of a consistent economic model. The central concept underlying the theory of rational expectations is contained in a statement by two of its chief proponents, T.J. Sargent and N. Wallace (1973): "Expectations about a variable are said to be rational if they depend, in the proper way, on the same things that economic theory says actually determine that variable."

We now turn to the two important concepts of expectations in the current literature on inflation theory.

2.1 Adaptive expectations

In discussions of the Phillips curve model and the monetarist theory of inflation, the concept of adaptive expectations is used to explain the formation of expectations. This model addresses two questions:

1. In which way do private agents correct their errors in forecasting when the expected level of the variable deviates from the actual level?

2. In which way can expectations for future inflation be related to observations of the past?

The first problem assumes the existence of expectations and concerns only their adjustment to observations of reality, but the second problem is deeper and more fundamental. It concerns the fact that expectations themselves are not directly observable and must therefore be related to observations of the past. Considering these two problems, we can develop the model of adaptive expectations in two forms:

$$\pi_t^* - \pi_{t-1}^* = \theta(\pi_{t-1} - \pi_{t-1}^*) \qquad 0 < \theta < 1 \qquad (1)$$

This equation states that the change in the expected rate of inflation (i.e., the difference $\pi_t^* - \pi_{t-1}^*$) is proportional to the forecast error, which we define as the discrepancy between the actual and expected rates of inflation in the previous period. If the present rate of inflation was anticipated exactly, then the expected rate of inflation for the next period will remain unchanged. If the present rate of inflation is greater or smaller than the expected rate, then the rate of inflation expected in the next period will be revised upward or downward by an amount equal to a percentage θ of the forecast error $(\pi_{t-1} - \pi_{t-1}^*)$. This formulation expresses the ability of economic agents to learn from their mistakes and may indeed be interpreted along the lines of psychological models of learning. According to psychological theory, one may designate as "learning" any experience-related modification of behavior (Löwe, 1970). Through a simple transformation of equation (1), we can obtain another common form of the model of adaptive expectations:

$$\pi_t^* = \theta\pi_{t-1} + (1 - \theta)\pi_{t-1}^* \qquad (2)$$

This formulation is another way of describing learning behavior: The expected rate of inflation at time t is a weighted average of the actual inflation rate and the expected inflation rate at time $t - 1$, where the adjustment parameters θ and $(1 - \theta)$ serve as weights.

The second presentation of the adaptive expectations model

attempts to explain how expectations are formed. The expectations of inflation, which are not directly observable, are linked to the observable past rates of inflation. The model of adaptive expectations implies that the expected (psychological) variable can be explained as a weighted average of past inflation rates.

Through substitution we can see that the first form of the model implies that

$$\pi_t^* = \theta\pi_{t-1} + \theta(1 - \theta)\pi_{t-2} + \theta(1 - \theta)^2\pi_{t-3} + \cdots$$
$$+ \theta(1 - \theta)^{n-1}\pi_{t-n} + (1 - \theta)^n\pi_{t-n}^* \tag{3}$$

As n approaches infinity, it follows that

$$\pi_t^* = \theta \sum_{i=1}^{\infty} (1 - \theta)^{i-1}\pi_{t-i} \tag{4}$$

In equation (4) the unobserved expected rate of inflation at time t is linked to the already known inflation rates of the past π_{t-1}, π_{t-2}, and so on, which are weighted by the parameters θ, $\theta(1 - \theta)$, $\theta(1 - \theta)^2$, and so on. This weighting scheme can be considered a "memory." If θ is close to zero, then the weights decline slowly and the economic agent (or society at large) has a "long" memory. In contrast, if θ is close to unity, then the weights decrease quickly and the economic agent has a "short" memory (Solow, 1969, p. 4).

The weighting scheme corresponds to a geometric series with elements that decrease: $1, 1 - \theta, (1 - \theta)^2, (1 - \theta)^3, \ldots$. It holds that

$$\sum_{i=1}^{\infty} (1 - \theta)^{i-1} = \frac{1}{1 - (1 - \theta)} = \frac{1}{\theta}$$

We therefore obtain the following expression:

$$\pi_t^* = \theta \sum_{i=1}^{\infty} (1 - \theta)^{i-1}\pi_{t-i} = \sum_{i=1}^{\infty} w_i\pi_{t-i}$$

where the sum of the weights equals unity:

$$\sum_{i=1}^{\infty} w_i = 1$$

Table 2.1. *Weights attached to prior rates of inflation under two different weighting schemes*

Period t	Long memory ($\theta = 0.1$)	Short memory ($\theta = 0.9$)
1	0.1	0.9
2	0.09	0.09
3	0.081	0.009
4	0.0729	0.0009
5	0.0656	0.00009
6	0.0590	0.000009
	etc.	etc.

An example may illustrate these comments. Table 2.1 shows two weighting schemes: a long memory ($\theta = 0.1$) and a short one ($\theta = 0.9$). The weights express the influence of past rates of inflation on the formation of the present expected rate of inflation. As one can see from Table 2.1, the influence of observations from the more distant past recedes only gradually in the case of a long memory. In other words, information from the more distant past influences significantly the formation of expectations for the future. In contrast, in the case of a short memory, practically only information from the recent past appears relevant, whereas observations from the more distant past have only a small weight (Klein, 1972).

2.2 **Rational expectations**

The concept of adaptive expectations, as plausible a behavioral assumption as it may seem, invites the following objections:

a. Adaptive expectations imply the possibility that the expected and actual observations deviate continuously from one another, even if the latter follows an easily discernible pattern over time. This is particularly relevant for an acceleration or deceleration of inflation.

b. If an economic agent has information in addition to a series of past observations of the variable to be forecast (e.g., observations of another economic variable), then the use of adaptive expectations would lead him to waste that information. In this case it is natural to use economic theory to process that information and to use it to form expectations.

At a very early stage, in 1961, J.F. Muth presented the concept of rational expectations (RE) as an alternative to adaptive expectations (AE). He started from the assumption that expectations, "since they are informed predictions of future events, are essentially the same as predictions of the relevant economic theory" (1961, p. 316). After Muth's original formulation it took the concept of rational expectations a decade to gain acceptance among economists. The final breakthrough occurred in connection with the criticism of the Phillips curve in three important papers by R.E. Lucas (1972a,b, 1973) followed by contributions from T.J. Sargent (1973, 1976), T.J. Sargent and N. Wallace (1975, 1976), and R.J. Barro (1976).

Some twelve years after Muth's work Sargent repeated his words almost exactly: "This (RE) amounts to supposing that the public's expectations depend, in the proper way, on the things that economic theory says they ought to" (1973, p. 431). Reduced to its core, Muth's hypothesis states: There exists a relevant economic theory and the forecasts derived from this theory are the best possible. Expectations are rational when they coincide with the forecasts derived from the relevant economic theory.

In an economic model with endogenous variables (explained by the model), exogenous variables, and predetermined variables (given from the outside), we can formulate the concept of rational expectations more precisely. Rational expectations are the unbiased estimates of endogenous variables (resulting from a model) in which all information concerning the values of the exogenous and predetermined variables is known and used for the prediction. If we designate π_t^* and π_t as the expected and actual rates of inflation and I_{t-1} as the state of information available at the end of period $t - 1$, then the existence of rational expectations implies the following two assumptions:

$$E(\pi_t/I_{t-1}) = \pi_t^* \tag{1}$$

$$\pi_t - \pi_t^* = \pi_t - E(\pi_t/I_{t-1}) = \varepsilon_t \tag{2}$$

where ε_t is a random variable with $E(\varepsilon_t) = 0$. The expression $E(\pi_t/I_{t-1})$ should be read as "E of (π_t/I_{t-1})" and not as "E times (π_t/I_{t-1})"; E is an expectations operator and not a quantity.

Assumption (1) states that the rationally expected rate of inflation depends on the amount of relevant information I_{t-1} available before the forecast at time $t - 1$. An expectation that depends on other events (in this case on a set of information about the economy) is called a *conditional* expectation. Part of the relevant information is, of course, the economic model itself.

In the language of econometrics, rational expectations are a reduced-form forecast. The endogenous variable to be forecast is a function of all exogenous and predetermined variables as well as the stochastic variable ε_t. The value of the forecast is the mathematical expectation that results from the reduced form of the equation.

Assumption (2) states that rational expectations do not imply perfect foresight. Instead, it allows for a random error ε_t, which is consistent with the assumptions underlying rational expectations. However, the estimation error $\pi_t - E(\pi_t/I_{t-1})$ cannot contain a systematic component; in statistical theory, rational expectations produce an unbiased estimate of the future values of the endogenous variable.

The model of rational expectations therefore rests on the following assumptions:

    a. All economic agents know the "true" model and its parameters; more precisely, they know the correct specification of the reduced form of the model.

    b. They know the probability distributions of the reduced forms of the equations and the principles according to which the exogenous variables change (e.g., they know the reaction functions of economic policy makers).

    c. They process all information within the framework of a consistent economic model in order to obtain a forecast.

The introduction of rational expectations to a macroeconomic model affects dramatically the ability of a government or a central bank to conduct economic policy. In the presence of rational expectations, real variables (such as relative prices and unemployment rate and the real output) are independent of changes in the anticipated monetary and fiscal policy. For example, an increase in the rate of growth of the money supply affects only the rate of inflation and has no influence on production and employment. A preannounced change in the money supply changes expectations regarding future inflation by the right order of magnitude (since the private agents know the "true" model). It therefore also changes the actual rate of inflation without affecting the real variables. With rational expectations the neoclassical dichotomy of the price system is valid.

The student who expects an example at this point will be disappointed. But there is a reason for this: One needs a closed model. The reader must wait until Chapters 3 and 4, where models are developed in which the rational expectations approach is discussed in great detail.

3

The Phillips curve

The development of contemporary inflation theory was greatly influenced by the development of the Phillips curve model, first through the formulation and acceptance of the model and later through the criticism of it. Three stages in the history of the Phillips curve can be distinguished. The first was the formulation of the concept by Phillips and Lipsey based on the assumption that there exists a stable, negatively sloped relationship between the rate of inflation and the rate of unemployment (Sections 3.1–3.3). The second stage was dominated by the "natural rate of unemployment" hypothesis (developed by M. Friedman and E. Phelps), which differentiates between a short-run and a long-run Phillips curve (Sections 3.4 and 3.5). The third stage was the discussion surrounding the rational expectations school's criticism of the Phillips curve (Section 3.6). According to the criticism, there is no systematic trade-off between inflation and unemployment.

Because the Phillips–Lipsey model, the natural rate of unemployment hypothesis, and the criticism of the rational expectations school are all important milestones on the path to contemporary macroeconomic thinking, we have to discuss the Phillips curve model chronologically. This chapter will therefore consist of, on the one hand, various theoretical models and, on the other hand, an important part of the history of economic thought, which every student of macroeconomics should know.

Section 3.1 begins with the original contribution by A.W. Phillips (1958), in which he concluded on the basis of empirical observations for Great Britain that there is a negative correlation between the rate of change in money wages and the rate of unemployment and that this relationship is stable. But this was only an empirical relationship; what was the theoretical foundation? The most influential theoretical interpretation was by R.G. Lipsey (1960), who derived the Phillips curve from a supply-and-demand system of a single labor market. The construction of a Phillips curve according to this theoretical interpretation is discussed in Section 3.2. For some time the Lipsey explanation was the authentic interpretation of the Phillips curve.

The main idea of the Phillips–Lipsey model is that wage inflation is explained by excess demand in the labor market, whereby the rate of unemployment is interpreted as an indicator of the level of excess demand. The first stage in the history of the Phillips curve was further characterized by the beliefs that a stable-relationship Phillips curve exists and that policy makers can exploit the trade-off between inflation and unemployment by choosing alternative points on the Phillips curve. (See Section 3.3 about the Samuelson–Solow interpretation of the Phillips curve.)

In the second stage the natural rate of unemployment hypothesis (the NR hypothesis), developed independently by M. Friedman (1968) and E.S. Phelps (1967), introduced the difference between the short-run and the long-run Phillips curves. The short-run Phillips curve is a negatively sloped relationship between the rate of inflation and the rate of unemployment, with inflationary expectations being constant; the long-run Phillips curve is a vertical line at some unemployment rate called the "natural" rate of unemployment.

The natural rate is consistent with any rate of inflation provided that it is fully anticipated. When policy makers attempt to drive the unemployment rate below its natural level, the rate of inflation will increase above the expected rate of inflation and there is a short-run trade-off between the unanticipated rate of inflation and the rate of unemployment. According to Friedman and Phelps, an adaptive expectations adjustment mechanism leads to a gradual revision of inflationary expectations. The increase in the expected rate of inflation leads to an upward shift of the short-run Phillips curve. If the government insists on maintaining the unemployment rate below its natural level, the rate of inflation will increase further. This in turn raises expectations and shifts the short-run Phillips curve upward again. Maintaining the rate of unemployment below its natural rate will accelerate the rate of inflation. The NR hypothesis is sometimes called the "accelerationist school." Only by managing aggregate demand in such a way as to maintain unemployment at the natural level will policy makers be able to avoid accelerating or decelerating the rate of inflation. The NR hypothesis restricts the scope of monetary and fiscal policy considerably, but a systematic exploitation of the short-run Phillips curve by economic policy remains possible.

The argument of the NR hypothesis is carefully developed with the aid of graphs in Section 3.4, "The short-run and long-run Phillips curve." A more compact and formal statement of the argument is given in the explanation of the expectations-augmented Phillips curve.

Section 3.5 discusses some of the ideas in a remarkable group of essays published as the *Microeconomic Foundations of Employment and Inflation Theory* (Phelps et al., 1971) by Alchian, Holt, Mortenson, Lucas, and Phelps. The approach of the New Microeconomics is used to analyze the concept of the natural rate of unemployment and to break it down into components. Search unemployment and wait unemployment as categories of voluntary unemployment are compared with the Keynesian definition of involuntary unemployment. The section closes with the derivation of a short-run Phillips curve in the framework of Phelps's famous "island parable" and with a criticism of the New Microeconomics.

The third stage in the history of the Phillips curve is the critique of the rational expectations school. A group of theorists (Lucas,

1972a,b, 1973; Sargent and Wallace, 1975) challenged the NR hypothesis by arguing that it is inconsistent with the concept of adaptive expectations. With adaptive expectations, economic agents usually have biased expectations (see the discussion in Chapter 2). The rational expectations school argued that inflationary expectations are formed by intelligent people who ought to take into account all the information available about the economy when they form their plans.

In Section 3.6 the Phillips curve model in its NR formulation is combined with the rational expectations approach to macroeconomics. The result is that the rate of unemployment oscillates randomly around its natural rate level. Whereas the NR hypothesis states that a short-run Phillips curve exists as long as inflation is not fully anticipated, the rational expectations school denies that the relationship between the unanticipated part of the rate of inflation and the rate of unemployment can be exploited by systematic economic policy. To simplify, one can say that with rational expectations a short-run Phillips curve does not exist.

In the last section of this chapter the Phillips curve is combined with the IS-LM model, the common framework of macroeconomic analysis. In this context the Phillips curve is interpreted as a short-run supply curve, as is common in current textbook macroeconomic models (for example, Dornbusch and Fischer, 1978). The IS-LM model amended by a (modified) Phillips curve shows the simultaneous variations in real income, the rate of interest, and the rate of inflation in situations of excess demand (supply).

3.1 The original Phillips curve

The article of A.W. Phillips (1958) that investigated the relationship between the change in money wages and the rate of unemployment was an interesting innovation in the modern theory of inflation. In Great Britain for the period 1861–1913, Phillips found a nonlinear, negative correlation between these two variables. The original Phillips curve is reproduced in Figure 3.1. On the basis of empirical evidence Phillips concluded that the relationship between the rate of change in money wages and the rate

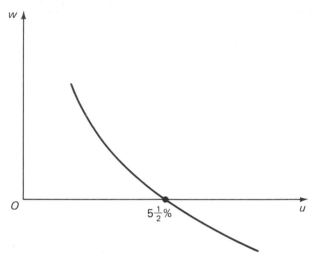

Figure 3.1. The Phillips curve. (u = Unemployment rate in %; w = rate of change of money wages in %.)

of unemployment during the period 1913–57 could be explained by the same function that had been estimated for 1861–1913. According to this function, the rate of growth in money wages decreases as the rate of unemployment rises. Two properties characterize the shape of the original Phillips curve:

1. Wages remain stationary ($w = 0$) when the rate of unemployment is 5½ percent.
2. From the dispersion of the data points, Phillips further concluded that there is a cyclical loop in a counterclockwise direction; that is, money wages rise somewhat faster as the rate of unemployment decreases and somewhat slower as the rate of unemployment increases, as one would estimate from the Phillips curve alone (Figure 3.2).

The original element in Phillips's research was not the establishment of a negative correlation between the rate of growth in money wages and the rate of unemployment, but rather his contention that the relationship between these two variables was stable.[1]

[1] For a discussion of this point, see Rothschild (1978).

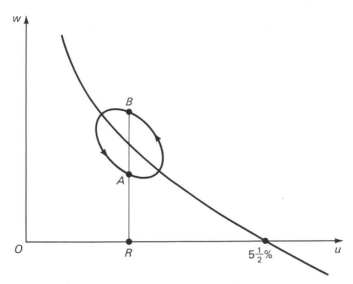

Figure 3.2

In Figure 3.2 two values of *w*, the rate of change in money wages, correspond to each value of *u*, the rate of unemployment. Corresponding to the unemployment rate *OR* are two points: the rate of wage inflation *RB*, which occurs when the unemployment rate is falling (when the demand for labor is rising), and the rate of wage inflation *RA*, which occurs when the unemployment rate is rising (when the demand for labor is falling). The rate of growth in money wages therefore depends not only on *u*, the level of excess demand, but also on the change in it, which can be approximated by du/dt. Accordingly, the Phillips curve can be expressed as $w = dW/W = h(u, du/dt)$. In this regard Phillips commented:

> There is also a clear tendency for the rate of change of money wage rates at any given level of unemployment to be above the average for that level of unemployment when unemployment is decreasing during the upswing of a trade cycle and to be below the average for that level of unemployment when unemployment is increasing during the downswing of a trade cycle.
> [Phillips, 1958, p. 247]

Once born, the Phillips curve developed a life of its own. The bulk of the discussion of inflation during the 1960s was conducted with reference to this model. The Phillips curve appeared to be a plausible, empirically verifiable explanation of continuously rising money wages, a phenomenon that the classical theory of the labor market could not immediately explain. At first the Phillips curve was an empirical relationship, "measurement without theory" in the sense of T. Koopmans, yet given its empirical validity, how can one interpret this relationship theoretically? From which model of the labor market can one derive the Phillips curve? The most influential theoretical interpretation stems from R.G. Lipsey (1960).

3.2 Lipsey's excess-demand model

Lipsey derived the Phillips curve from the supply-and-demand system of a single labor market. In contrast to the neoclassical theory of the labor market, in which the demand for and the supply of labor are functions of the real wage, Lipsey used the nominal or money wage in his model. Figure 3.3 depicts the situation in a competitive labor market. The demand for and the supply of labor (N^D and N^S, respectively) are represented as linear functions of the money wage rate. Equilibrium in the labor market is determined by the equality of N^D and N^S corresponding to point A, with (W_0, N_0). As long as $N^D - N^S = 0$, the rate of change in money wages is assumed to be zero.

A further comment concerning the interpretation of the supply and demand functions is necessary. These functions involve the *planned* demand for labor and the *planned* supply of labor for each money wage rate W. For this reason, one may not immediately conclude from a lack of excess demand in the labor market ($N^D - N^S = 0$) that nobody is unemployed. The equilibrium point A, for instance, implies only that the number of vacancies V is equal to the number seeking work U. The following identities are valid:

$$N^S = N + U \tag{1}$$

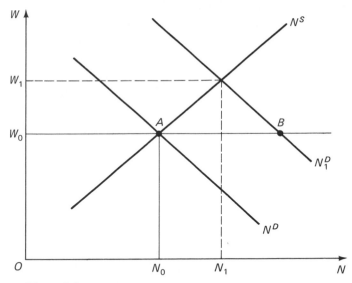

Figure 3.3

The supply of labor N^S consists of the number of employed N and the number of unemployed U.

$$N^D = N + V \qquad (2)$$

The demand for labor is composed of the number of employed N and the number of vacancies V.

The excess demand for labor X equals the difference between the number of vacancies and the number of unemployed [equation (3)]. With respect to the supply of labor, the excess demand for labor $X/N^S = x$ is the difference between the vacancy rate v and the unemployment rate u [equation (4)].

$$X = N^D - N^S = V - U \qquad (3)$$

$$x = \frac{V}{N^S} - \frac{U}{N^S} = v - u \qquad (4)$$

If the demand for labor increases from N^D to N_1^D (Figure 3.3) (for example, because of an increase in profit expectations), the excess demand for labor $\overline{AB}$ occurs at the current money wage rate W_0. During a Walrasian Tatonnement the money wage rate rises to W_1 while employment increases.

Through two functions Lipsey (1960, 1974) linked his theory of the labor market to the Phillips curve:

1. The neoclassical wage adjustment function, a positive relationship between the excess demand for labor and the change in money wages.
2. The *X-U* function, a negative relationship between the excess demand for labor and the rate of unemployment. This construction was an innovation in economic theory.

The wage adjustment function

The wage adjustment function states that the rate of change in the wage rate is determined by the difference between demand and supply – that is, by excess demand for labor. The excess demand for labor x is measured by the variable $(N^D - N^S)/N^S$, where N^D is the planned labor demand and N^S the planned labor supply. The more demand exceeds supply, the faster the wage rate increases. If the demand and supply of labor are equal, the money wage rate will be constant.

The simple, explicit formulation of the wage adjustment function is $w = dW/W = k \cdot [(N^D - N^S)/N^S]$; that is, the change in money wage rates is proportional to the excess demand for labor. In Figure 3.4 an excess demand for labor *OA* produces a relative change in money wages of *AC*. While the money wage rate and the changes in it are empirically observable, the excess demand for labor $N^D - N^S$ is the difference between two *planned* magnitudes, which escapes direct statistical observation. To approximate the excess demand for labor it is necessary to introduce an auxiliary relationship, which Lipsey established by linking the excess demand for labor and the rate of unemployment.

The X-U relationship

Lipsey established a negative correlation between the excess demand for labor $x = (N^D - N^S)/N^S$ and the rate of unemployment u on a priori grounds (Figure 3.5). Arguing that the absence of excess demand requires only that the number of unem-

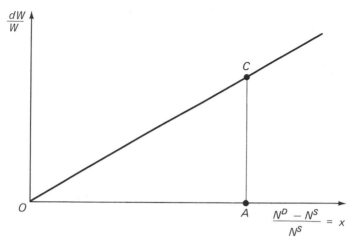

Figure 3.4

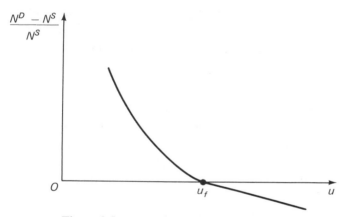

Figure 3.5

ployed equals the number of job vacancies, the *X-U* relationship
cuts the abscissa at u_f, the level of frictional unemployment that
is consistent with zero excess demand for labor. Given the level
of u_f, Lipsey argued that an increase in excess demand would
decrease u and that an increase in excess supply would increase
the rate of unemployment. (The result is the *X-U* relationship in
Figure 3.5.) The excess-supply relationship (to the right of u_f) was

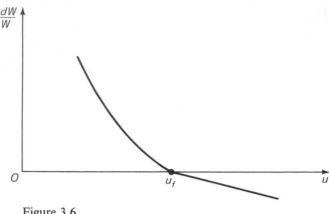

Figure 3.6

assumed to be linear. The excess-demand relationship (to the left of u_f) was assumed to be curvilinear, with the curve approaching the ordinate asymptotically because the rate of unemployment u could not become zero, not even with a high rate of excess demand.

Construction of the Phillips curve

When the wage adjustment equation and the X-U relationship are combined, a Phillips curve for an individual labor market results. Given the positive relationship between dW/W and $(N^D - N^S)/N^S$ in the wage adjustment equation and substituting dW/W for excess demand on the vertical axis in Figure 3.5, we get Figure 3.6, which shows a Phillips curve for an individual labor market. The Phillips curve for the total labor market (the macro Phillips curve) follows from the aggregation of the individual functions. The distribution of unemployment and vacancies over the individual labor markets determines the position of the macro Phillips curve.

According to the Phillips–Lipsey model, the rate of wage inflation is explained by excess demand in the labor market. The latter, which is not directly observable, is approximated by the rate of unemployment and an auxiliary construction, the X-U relationship.

3.3 The Samuelson–Solow modification of the Phillips curve

The paper by P. Samuelson and R. Solow in 1960 popularized the concept of the Phillips curve. Above all, this paper made the concept relevant to economic policy. Its success stemmed from essentially two sources.

a. The Phillips curve itself was modified so that it represented a relationship between the rate of inflation and the rate of unemployment, instead of between the rate of change in money wages and the rate of unemployment, as had been the case.

b. The Phillips curve was recommended to economic policy makers as an instrument that would allow them to formulate policy programs with alternative combinations of unemployment and inflation rates. As Samuelson and Solow (1960) expressed it, policy makers would face a "menu of choice between different degrees of unemployment and price stability."

This formulation of the Phillips curve as a relationship between the inflation rate and the unemployment rate came to dominate later discussion and research. The relationship between the Phillips–Lipsey and the Samuelson–Solow formulations of the Phillips curve is established by a markup price equation. Firms determine their product prices through a fixed markup calculated on the basis of unit labor costs. (The markup includes the usual industrywide profit margin as well as a provision for the depreciation of fixed capital.) We can follow L.R. Klein (1967) and show this relationship as:

$$P_t = (1 + a) \frac{W_t N_t}{X_t} \tag{1}$$

where P_t is the product price or the price level, W_t is the money wage rate, N_t is the number employed, and X_t is the level of real output or real GNP. The markup a represents a constant profit margin.

The expression $(W_t N_t)/X_t$ denotes unit labor costs. It can also be expressed as the ratio W_t/Λ_t of the wage rate W_t to labor productivity ($\Lambda_t = X_t/N_t$). Substituting this relationship in equation (1) and taking the natural logarithms of both sides of the equation, we get

$$\log P_t = \log (1 + a) + \log W_t - \log \Lambda_t \qquad (2)$$

If one differentiates equation (2) with respect to time [the logarithmic differentiation of equation (1)] and denotes the relative change in the variables by lowercase letters, the result is

$$\frac{dP}{P} = \frac{dW}{W} - \frac{d\Lambda}{\Lambda} \qquad \text{or} \qquad \pi = w - \lambda \qquad (3)$$

From the markup price behavior it follows that the inflation rate equals the difference between the rate of growth in money wages and the rate of growth in labor productivity.

Let us further assume that the Phillips curve has the following form:

$$w = \pi^* + bu^{-1} + \beta\lambda \qquad b > 0; 0 \le \beta \le 1 \qquad (4)$$

The rate of change in money wages (in percent) depends on the expected rate of inflation π^*, the degree of demand pressure (measured by u^{-1}), and the rate of growth in labor productivity λ.

From equations (3) and (4) we get the Phillips curve as modified by Samuelson and Solow:

$$\pi = \pi^* + bu^{-1} - (1 - \beta)\lambda \qquad (5)$$

In this formulation the rate of inflation is determined by the demand pressure on the labor market bu^{-1}, the expected rate of inflation π^*, and the term $(1 - \beta)\lambda$. This last term denotes the portion of the growth in labor productivity that is not transferred to the workers in the form of increases in money wages. The greater this component of labor productivity, the lower is the inflation rate. Correspondingly, the Phillips curve shifts downward toward the origin.

The second insight of Samuelson and Solow (1960) was to interpret the Phillips curve as a technical relationship and, hence, to suggest its use as an instrument of economic policy. Each point along the Phillips curve can be interpreted as a possible economic

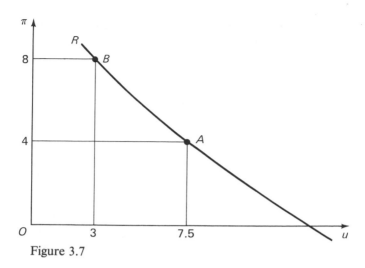

Figure 3.7

policy program. Between points *A* and *B* on the Phillips curve *R* (Figure 3.7) there is a trade-off between the rates of inflation and unemployment; in a certain sense one can "purchase" less inflation through more unemployment or less unemployment through higher inflation. For example, let us assume that for a long time prices have been rising at a rate of 4 percent per year and that the unemployment rate was consistently in the neighborhood of 7.5 percent. The government considers the rate of unemployment excessively high and attempts to reduce it through an expansive demand policy, such as increasing the budget deficit financed by an increase in the money supply. The relevant macroeconomic model here is the Keynesian employment multiplier. But one should not forget that the multiplier has a real and an inflation effect, so that the increase in (aggregate) demand not only reduces the rate of unemployment but also increases the rate of inflation. One moves along the Phillips curve from *A* to *B* by exploiting the inflation–unemployment trade-off. It therefore appears possible to reach alternative points on the Phillips curve by adjusting aggregate demand. On this point criticism of a "naive" interpretation of the Phillips curve abounds. This is extensively treated in the following section.

3.4 The short-run and long-run Phillips curve (the natural rate of unemployment hypothesis)

Is the Phillips curve a stable relationship? Does the hypothesized trade-off between unemployment and inflation also exist in the long run, or does the choice of a point along the Phillips curve influence the position of the curve itself? First posed by Friedman (1968, 1975) and Phelps (1967, 1972), these questions have guided the discussion of the Phillips curve in a new direction.[2] In contrast to the Lipsey interpretation of the Phillips curve, which does not consider the role of inflationary expectations (or works with static inflationary expectations), Friedman and Phelps criticize the Phillips curve for precisely this reason. They question the stability of the Phillips curve under changing inflationary expectations. The choice of a point along the Phillips curve produces a certain rate of inflation. After an adjustment period this produces a new expected rate of inflation and causes the Phillips curve to shift.

If the short-run Phillips curve is not stable, one can still ask whether there is a long-run trade-off between unemployment and inflation. According to Friedman and Phelps the answer is unambiguously no. Higher rates of inflation lead in the long run to higher expected rates of inflation, so that the Phillips curve keeps shifting upward, which precludes any long-run trade-off between unemployment and inflation. For example, Phelps stated,

> If expectations were for regular price increases at 4 percent per annum and aggregate demand happened to sustain an inflation at 4 percent per annum, why should the associated unemployment rate be any smaller or any larger than the unemployment rate that would prevail if expectations were generally for price stability over the future and aggregate demand behaved so as to produce stable average prices? [1972, p. 42]

To avoid any misunderstanding, it should be stressed that neither Friedman nor Phelps denies the existence of a short-run

---

[2] A summarizing discussion of this problem is given by Trevithick and Mulvey (1975, pp. 106–25) and by Santomero and Seater (1978).

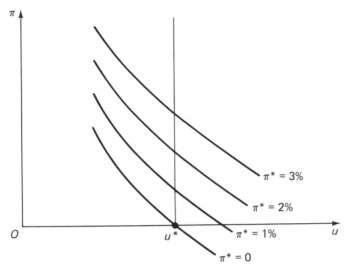

Figure 3.8

Phillips curve. They do, however, maintain that the short-run Phillips curve shifts in parametric fashion when the expected rate of inflation changes.

Figure 3.8 shows a collection of Phillips curves, each of which corresponds to a different expected rate of inflation π^*. Each curve has a shape identical with all the others; they differ only in the assumed value of the expected rate of inflation π^*. The equation for the Phillips curve therefore has to be expanded to include a parameter for the expected rate of inflation:

$$\pi = f(u) + \pi^* \tag{1}$$

We can therefore conclude:

a. Alternative expected rates of inflation correspond to alternative Phillips curves.
b. A change in the expected rate of inflation shifts the Phillips curve; an increase shifts the curve up, a decrease shifts it toward the origin.

Assume that an increase in the nominal aggregate demand (e.g., a budget deficit financed by the creation of money) leads to

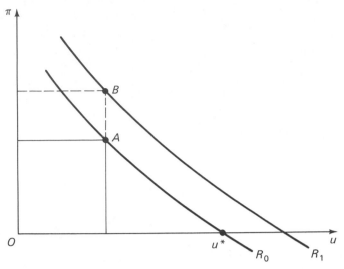

Figure 3.9

a decline in unemployment below its natural rate and to an increase in the rate of inflation (point A in Figure 3.9). In microeconomic terms this implies that money wages have risen in the labor market and prices have increased in the goods market. In general, both workers and employers experience money illusion at this stage. Friedman expressed this clearly:

> Suppose something, say, a monetary expansion, starts nominal aggregate demand growing, which in turn produces a rise in prices and wages at the rate of, say, 2 percent per year. Workers will initially interpret this as a rise in their real wage – because they still anticipate constant prices – and so will be willing to offer more labour (move up their supply curve), i.e., employment grows and unemployment falls.
>
> Employers may have the same anticipations as workers about the general price level, but they are more directly concerned about the price of the products they are producing and far better informed

about that. They will initially interpret a rise in the demand for and price of their product as a rise in its relative price and as implying a fall in the real wage rate they must pay measured in terms of their product. They will therefore be willing to hire more labour (move down their demand curve) [1975, p. 20]

Both workers and employers suffer from money illusion. Workers interpret increases in their money wages as increases in real wages. Employers think an increase in the price of their product implies an increase in its price relative to those of other goods and services. This quote from Friedman's 1975 article contains a modification of an argument provided by R.E. Lucas (1972a, 1973), which says that individual economic actors cannot in general differentiate between price increases caused by monetary factors (increase in the money supply) and price increases traceable to real factors (increase in real demand). Both firms and workers therefore at first interpret an observed increase in their product price or market wage as an increase in the relative price of their product or in their real wage. This implies that firms increase the volume of goods supplied and that workers increase the quantity of labor supplied. In the labor market an increase in money wages therefore implies a decline in frictional unemployment – more exactly, in search unemployment. The latter decreases for two reasons: First, because money wages at the present place of employment have increased, the number of quits decreases. Second, the average duration of job search becomes shorter, since job seekers find a job with a wage corresponding to their targets more quickly when the wage level is rising.

This situation represents a disequilibrium; the realized rates of change in prices and wages do not correspond to the expected values of these variables. A learning process starts, leading to the realization that prices generally have risen simultaneously with the money wage (or along with the price of the firm's product). As a result, neither the real wage nor the product's relative price has risen, since money wages and the general price level have risen at the same rate. In any case, economic agents raise their anticipated rate of inflation, so that (for a given rate of increase in money wages) the anticipated rate of increase in real wages (or in the relative product price) falls. This implies an increase in search unemployment, since additional workers who have been disappointed (by failure to achieve their expectations concerning real wages) again enter the pool of unemployed to search for wages that are increasing at an above-average rate. Those already unemployed will extend the duration of their search. Similarly, after firms have recognized that the relative price of their product has not increased at all or not as much as they had expected, they reduce the volume of goods supplied by moving back along their supply curves. The original real effect of the increase in aggregate demand on output and employment therefore tends to disappear.[3] If one wants to hold the unemployment rate consistently below the natural rate, one must resort to repeated increases in aggregate demand to produce an actual rate of inflation that continuously exceeds the anticipated rate. The inflation rate can therefore be decomposed into two elements: an anticipated and an unanticipated component, where only the latter has a positive effect on employment in the sense described by the Phillips curve. Since economic agents learn from experience (e.g., they extrapolate a weighted average of past inflation rates into the future), the actual inflation rate must constantly accelerate to prevent a reduction in the volume of output supplied or in employment. Therefore, to achieve the expansive effects on output and employment described by the Phillips curve, the inflation rate has to increase continuously. In contrast to the earlier Lipsey interpretation of the Phillips curve (according to the Friedman–Phelps analysis), a permanent reduction in the rate of unemploy-

---

[3] The adjustment of the behavior of the economic agents in the case of a discrepancy between expected and realized prices was described by Friedman in the following way: "But as time passes both employers and employees come to recognise, that prices *in general* are rising. As Abraham Lincoln said, you can fool all of the people some of the time, you can fool some of the people all of the time, but you can't fool all of the people all of the time. As a result, they raise their estimate of the anticipated rate of inflation which reduces the rate of rise of anticipated real wages, and leads you to slide down the curve back ultimately to the point E_0" (1975, p. 21).

ment below the natural rate requires an accelerating rate of inflation.

Situations in which the rate of inflation is fully anticipated, in which the unanticipated component of inflation equals zero, are steady states of the economy. The fully anticipated rate of inflation has the property that relative prices do not change. Therefore, such an inflation does not influence the real variables of the economic system. When an inflation rate of 3 percent is expected (i.e., aggregate demand grows such that a rate of 3 percent is realized), the rate of unemployment u^* is neither smaller nor larger than if inflation rates of either 5 or 10 percent had been fully anticipated and realized.

The unemployment rate existing in this steady state has been labeled by Friedman and Phelps as the "natural" rate of unemployment. The following definition results: The natural rate of unemployment has the property of remaining constant at each rate of inflation as long as that rate is fully anticipated. Another formulation of this principle is that a fully anticipated rate of inflation has no real effects.[4]

The shift in the Phillips curve

Let us return to the problem of the shift in the short-run Phillips curve. Assume that the Phillips curve R_0 in Figure 3.10 is valid and that the economic system has rested for a long time in the steady-state position A. At this point the natural rate of unemployment is $u = u^* = 5\frac{1}{2}$ percent and the actual rate of inflation equals the anticipated rate, which is zero ($\pi = \pi^* = 0$). Through a policy of expanding aggregate demand, the government reduces the unemployment rate to 4 percent, so that, according to the Phillips curve R_0, an inflation rate of 2.8 percent results (point B). Higher demand in the goods market leads to higher money wages in the labor market with which firms seek to recruit new workers.

---

[4] "In our own day this doctrine is associated with the tag 'the natural rate of unemployment.' This is the designation that Milton Friedman has given to us for the equilibrium unemployment rate in the singular case in which the equilibrium unemployment rate is independent of the expected inflation rate" (Phelps, 1972, p. 43).

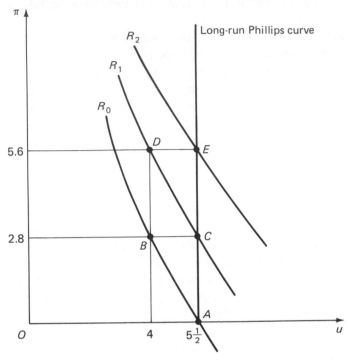

Figure 3.10

Since the expected rate of inflation at the start of this episode was zero, workers interpret the higher money wages as higher real wages and firms view the increases in product prices as increases in their relative prices. This leads to an increase in actual employment.

If prices increase at a 2.8 percent rate, then the actual real wage falls short of the expected real wage and the actual relative price received by firms is less than the expected one. Both effects are due to the occurrence of unanticipated inflation. The proponents of the natural rate of unemployment hypothesis stress the learning process that now occurs, as discussed above. Expectations of positive inflation develop among economic actors, which, for constant labor productivity, lead to an upward shift in the Phillips curve to R_1. The Philips curve R_1 is valid under the assumption that the expected rate of inflation π^* is 2.8 percent. From Figure 3.10 we can see that on R_1 an actual inflation rate of 2.8 percent again corresponds to the natural rate of unemployment of $5\frac{1}{2}$ percent (point C on R_1). A 4 percent rate of unemployment can be maintained only if a new demand impulse raises the inflation rate to 5.6 percent (point D on R_1). But this situation is only temporary, since economic actors notice a discrepancy between the anticipated rate of inflation (2.8 percent) and the actual rate of inflation (5.6 percent). Again the adjustment process begins to bring the expected rate of inflation into line with the higher actual rate of inflation. The Phillips curve shifts from R_1 to R_2; as a result, the unemployment rate again rises to $5\frac{1}{2}$ percent, but now with the fully anticipated rate of inflation at 5.6 percent. Another attempt to push u below u^* leads to a further acceleration of the inflation rate. A permanent reduction in the unemployment rate below the level of the natural rate therefore produces an accelerating inflation. However, the argument is symmetrical (Santomero and Seater, 1978, p. 517). Assume that through an attempt to reduce the unemployment rate, the inflation rate has reached the unacceptable level of 5.6 percent (point E in Figure 3.10). The economic policy makers now try to reduce the inflation rate to an acceptable level, say, about 2.8 percent. Because the Phillips curve R_2 is valid, this can occur only if the authorities adopt a deflationary policy that raises the unemployment rate above the natural rate (point B' in Figure 3.11). At point B' there again is a discrepancy between the high expected rate of inflation ($\pi^* = 5.6$ percent) and the actual rate of inflation ($\pi = 2.8$ percent). According to the model of adaptive expectations, the expected rate of inflation is revised downward. This leads to a leftward shift in the Phillips curve toward R_3 coupled with a reduction in the unemployment rate. At point C' the revision of the expected rate of inflation is complete and the unemployment rate has again receded to the level of the natural rate. A further reduction in inflation requires another implementation of a deflationary program, which again leads to a temporary rise in the rate of unem-

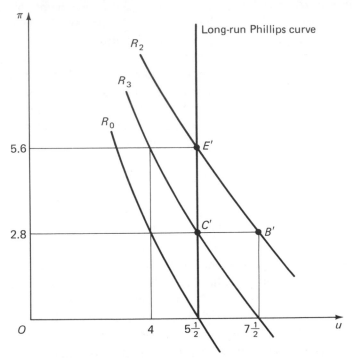

Figure 3.11

ployment above the natural rate. If the rate of unemployment is permanently held above the natural rate through a corresponding policy of deflation, this leads to a deceleration of the inflation rate until the Phillips curve R_0 is reached.[5]

The expectations-augmented Phillips curve

We can summarize the previous discussion with a simple formal model consisting of two equations. Equation $(1')$ describing the Phillips curve embodies the natural rate of unemployment

[5] The critics of the NR hypothesis indicate that prices and wages are not equally flexible in both directions. For instance, R.J. Gordon does not deny the possibility of a long-run vertical Phillips curve but doubts the validity of the NR hypothesis downward: "During the Depression the unemployment rate remained above 8.5 percent for twelve straight years in the United States without the slightest sign of accelerating deflation" (Gordon, 1977, p. 50).

hypothesis, whereas the second equation makes the adaptive expectations mechanism explicit.

The Phillips curve in the NR hypothesis formulation is given by

$$\pi_t = f(u_t) + \pi_t^* = \pi_t^* - b(u_t - u^*) \tag{1'}$$

where $f(u_t) = -b(u_t - u^*)$. The actual rate of inflation π_t is explained by the expected inflation rate π_t^* and the deviation of the actual rate of unemployment u_t from the natural rate u^*. As mentioned, the difference $u_t - u^*$ can be interpreted as an approximation of the overall excess demand in the goods and labor markets. When unemployment is below its natural level ($u - u^* < 0$), overall excess demand develops and the rate of inflation rises relative to the expected rate. Inflation falls when $u - u^* > 0$; that is, unemployment is above its natural level. Moreover, the expected rate of inflation is assumed to be generated by adaptive expectations as described in Chapter 2.

$$\pi_t^* = \theta \pi_{t-1} + (1 - \theta)\pi_{t-1}^* \tag{2}$$

From the two interpretations offered for adaptive expectations in Chapter 2, the error-learning process suits the spirit of the Friedman–Phelps modification of the Phillips curve. The Friedman–Phelps model, the expectations-augmented Phillips curve, consists of two equations and three endogenous variables, π_t, π_t^*, and u_t, so the system has one degree of freedom.

Let u_t be the variable, which can be chosen in a first step. The idea is that the authorities are able by use of their fiscal and monetary instruments to manipulate the rate of unemployment – for example, to drive unemployment to a level below u^*, say, to u_1. In the short run the pursuit of this policy increases the rate of inflation to π_1 (Figure 3.12). This in turn leads to a gradual increase in the expected rate of inflation according to equation (2). Since the Phillips curve R_0 in Figure 3.12 is drawn under the assumption that $\pi^* = 0$, the upward revision of inflationary expectations can easily be seen:

$$\pi^* = \theta \pi_1 + (1 - \theta) \cdot 0 = \theta \pi_1$$

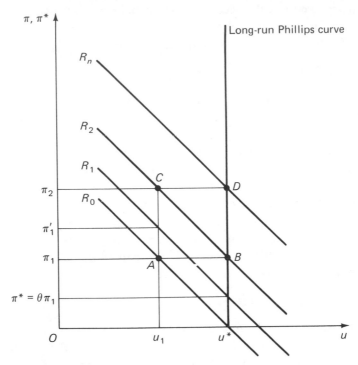

Figure 3.12

In graphic terms the process adjusting expectations implies a shift of the Phillips curve from R_0 to R_1 in Figure 3.12. The Phillips curve keeps moving upward as long as the actual rate of inflation π_t is higher than the expected rate π_t^*. Again one can easily see this by looking at equation (2) in the form

$$(\pi_t^* = \pi_{t-1}^* + \theta(\pi_{t-1} - \pi_{t-1}^*)) \tag{3}$$

Economic policy now has two options: to try to control either the rate of inflation π_t or the rate of unemployment u_t. Let us first assume that policy makers, by means of monetary policy, are able to stabilize the rate of inflation at the level π_1 in Figure 3.12. In this case, through the expectations adjustment process, the Phillips curve moves to the right toward point B, thus gradually increasing the rate of unemployment. At point B the rate of inflation

π_1 is fully anticipated, the expectations error is zero, and the situation is characterized by the following equality:

$$\pi_t = \pi_t^* = \pi_{t-1} = \pi_{t-1}^*$$

In this steady state no further upward shift occurs; the Phillips curve remains stable.

If the government chooses the second option – that is, the one discussed by Friedman – it tries to maintain the rate of unemployment at u_1 by generating excess demand through fiscal and monetary programs. Then the rate of inflation will increase to π_1' in Figure 3.12, since the expected rate π^* already equals $\theta\pi_1$. Only the unexpected part of the actual rate of inflation – namely, $\pi_1' - \theta\pi_1$ – causes u_t to deviate from u^*. By maintaining the unemployment rate u_1, the government generates an accelerating rate of inflation through a persistently shifting short-run Phillips curve.

Let us consider the long-run problem. In the long run expectations are fully adjusted; there is no deviation of the actual rate of inflation from the expected rate. The NR hypothesis states that under these circumstances the rate of unemployment is at its natural level. The natural rate can be found by setting $\pi_t - \pi_t^* = 0$ in equation (1'). It follows that $0 = -b(u_t - u^*)$, or $u_t = u^*$. This means there is no long-run trade-off between the rate of inflation and the rate of unemployment. The natural rate of unemployment u^* is compatible with different rates of inflation – for example, B and D on the long-run Phillips curve in Figure 3.12. But these inflation rates are characterized by two properties: They are fully expected and they remain constant.

We can get some additional information by solving the system (1') and (2) for π_t. Let us eliminate the expected rate of inflation in equation (1') and derive the following expression:

$$\pi_t = \theta\pi_{t-1} + (1 - \theta)\pi_{t-1}^* - b(u_t - u^*) \tag{4}$$

The problem with this equation is the unobservable π_{t-1}^*, which we eliminate by using the so-called Koyck transformation. We lag equation (1') one period and multiply by $1 - \theta$. This gives

$$(1 - \theta)\pi_{t-1} = (1 - \theta)\pi_{t-1}^* - b(1 - \theta)(u_{t-1} - u^*) \qquad (5)$$

Subtracting equation (5) from equation (4) and rearranging lead to

$$\pi_t = \pi_{t-1} + b(1 - \theta)(u_{t-1} - u^*) - b(u_t - u^*) \qquad (6)$$

This equation spells out the expectations-augmented Phillips curve in terms of observable variables. The first term $\pi_{t-1} + b(1 - \theta)(u_{t-1} - u^*)$ replaces the expectations variable π_t^*; the second term gives the slope of the Phillips curve in its NR formulation. By rearranging equation (6), we can express it in the following way:

$$\pi_t = \pi_{t-1} - b\theta(u_t - u^*) - b(1 - \theta)(u_t - u_{t-1}) \qquad (7)$$

The actual rate of inflation is now explained by the lagged rate of inflation, the level of excess demand as indicated by the deviation of u_t from u^*, and the change in the level of excess demand as expressed by a change in the rate of unemployment $\Delta u_t = u_t - u_{t-1}$.

The expectations-augmented Phillips curve, it turns out, requires that unemployment, the rate of change in unemployment, and the lagged rate of inflation all be in the relationship.

The long-run Phillips curve is a relationship between π_t and u_t in a steady-state situation in which inflation is fully anticipated and the rates of inflation and unemployment do not change. The following conditions must be met:

$$\pi_t = \pi_t^*$$

$$\pi_t = \pi_{t-1} \quad \text{and} \quad u_t = u_{t-1}$$

From these conditions together with equation (7) it follows that $u_t = u^*$. In the long run the Phillips curve is a vertical line on the abscissa at the position of the natural rate of unemployment.

Friedman's three stages of the Phillips curve

In his Nobel lecture, Friedman (1977) distinguished three stages of the Phillips curve. The first was the acceptance of a stable trade-off between inflation and unemployment, the "stable" Phillips curve. The second stage was the natural rate of unemployment hypothesis, the distinction between the short-run Phillips curve for a given inflationary expectation and the long-run expectations-adjusted Phillips curve, which is vertical at the position of the natural rate of unemployment. The second stage is now widely accepted and absorbed in the economic literature.

Friedman conjectures a third stage – namely, a positively sloped (not vertical) Phillips curve – as a "transition period" in which the monetary system is not compatible with the underlying economic development of high inflation and high unemployment. How can this be understood?

In the contemporary transition period the government's stabilization policy increases the rate of inflation on the one hand. On the other hand, the high inflation leads to frequent government interventions to control inflation, since our monetary system is still based on the notion of a normal price or price stability. The resulting stop-and-go policy causes a wide variation in the actual and anticipated rates of inflation.

The first effect of the increased variability of inflation is to shorten the optimal length of contracts. The time it takes to adjust actual contracts and existing prior arrangements introduces rigidities that lower the efficiency of the market system. This effect is clear. Less clear is the effect of these rigidities on the actual rate of unemployment. The economic answer to rigidities and uncertainties is larger average inventories. But in the labor market this can mean two opposite developments: (a) labor hoarding by firms (and so lowering unemployment) or (b) a larger number of workers between jobs and higher unemployment.

The second effect of the increased volatility of inflation is to render the market prices a less efficient system for coordinating economic activities. "The more volatile the rate of general inflation, the harder it becomes to extract the signal about relative prices from the absolute prices: the broadcast about relative prices is, as it were, being jammed by the noise coming from the inflation broadcast" (Friedman, 1977, p. 467).

Again, the difficulties of identifying the market signals decrease the efficiency of the market system. But Friedman's conclusion in this context: "it seems plausible that the average level of unemployment would be raised by the increased amount of noise in market signals" (1977, p. 67) leads to certain difficulties. More noise in the price system could mean either that frictional unemployment increases so more workers are between jobs, or that some of the unemployed shorten their search process because they confuse absolute price changes (i.e., a money wage increase) with relative price changes (a real wage increase).

Summarizing Friedman's argument, we can say that during the transition period the increased volatility of the rate of inflation and increasing government intervention render the market price system less efficient. But Friedman could not show that these factors influence the average rate of unemployment in such a way that a positively sloped Phillips curve can be established.

3.5 The New Microeconomics and the Phillips curve

The New Microeconomics combines the Walrasian theory of general equilibrium with the theory of imperfect markets. In individual markets competition prevails; there are no substantial monopoly or monopsony powers. In contrast to the Walrasian model, however, perfect information is not assumed. Market participants are not informed about all demand and supply conditions, nor do they know the full set of equilibrium prices. According to A.A. Alchian (1971), who has most carefully established the theoretical framework of the New Microeconomics, the Walrasian postulate of perfect information can be replaced by two theorems concerning the production of information:

1. The production and acquisition of information are subject to the laws of production: Faster acquisition and dissemination of information raise its costs.
2. Specialization in information activity is efficient. It follows that there are specialists who either temporarily or permanently engage in the production or use of information.

If these two theorems replace the Walrasian perfect information postulate, it follows that search processes are economically

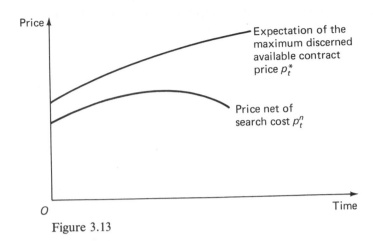

Figure 3.13

relevant. Sellers (buyers) will not accept the first offer that comes along, but they search for a better price and guide their decision according to a function of the maximum (minimum) expected contract price. The curve p_t^* in Figure 3.13 depicts this search function.

As the sample (search time) increases, the expected maximum (discoverable) price increases at a decreasing rate. When there is perfect information there is a single equilibrium or market price, and the search function follows a line parallel to the abscissa.[6]

The theory of search processes explains two important phenomena: price rigidities and search unemployment. If demand and supply were always reconciled through a movement in the market-clearing (equilibrium) price, then stochastic variations in demand would produce large unanticipated variations in that market price. Therefore, the search and information costs would rise extraordinarily for both the buyer and the seller. In most markets the search costs are reduced since, on the one hand, sellers build inventories and, on the other, buyers form queues, so that both parties can conclude transactions at predictable prices. "The stable price, accompanied by queues and inventories, will be slightly

[6] More precisely this search function is defined as the "expectation of the maximum discerned available contract price found by time t" (Alchian, 1971, p. 30).

higher than if it were not stabilized by queues and inventories – but the higher pecuniary price can save on search and disappointed, incorrect price anticipations" (Alchian, 1971, p. 36).

The variation in the market-clearing price accompanied by imperfect information also leads to price fixing in the case of excess demand in order to reduce search costs.

Applied to the labor market, the theory of search processes leads to an explanation of search unemployment as the result of the rational behavior of workers. The key passage in Alchian reads: "If looking and 'finding out' is more costly while employed, he may have reason to choose temporary unemployment as an efficient form of 'producing' or investing in information" (1971, p. 38).

A worker who enters a state of search unemployment chooses in some sense self-employment in collecting information about job opportunities and wage differentials. Therefore, the observed numbers of unemployed are too high; the number of these "self-employed" should be excluded. However, it also follows from this approach that all workers who do not employ themselves in search activity value the marginal utility of leisure more than the real wage. They are therefore voluntarily unemployed.[7] (See the section on wait unemployment.)

The natural rate of unemployment and its forms

Before we address the question of why the natural rate of unemployment is positive rather than zero,[8] we must investigate the concept of the natural rate of unemployment, which is not "natural" at all. Friedman, who introduced the term[9] in his famous essay "The Role of Monetary Policy," wrote:

> At any moment of time, there is some level of unemployment which has the property that it is consistent with equilibrium in the structure of real

---

[7] For some critical comments on this point, see Hines (1976).

[8] "Why is it realistic to suppose that any unemployment equilibrium tends to stay positive?" asked E.S. Phelps (1971a, p. 14).

[9] A critical discussion of this definition can be found in Otruba (1974).

wage rates. At that level of unemployment, real wage rates are tending on the average to rise at a "normal" secular rate, i.e., at a rate that can be indefinitely maintained so long as capital formation, technological improvements, etc., remain on their long-run trends. A lower level of unemployment is an indication that there is an excess demand for labor that will produce upward pressure on real wage rates. A higher level of unemployment is an indication that there is an excess supply of labor that will produce downward pressure on real wage rates. The "natural rate of unemployment," in other words, is the level that would be ground out by the Walrasian system of general equilibrium equations, provided there is imbedded in them the actual structural characteristics of the labor and commodity markets, including market imperfections, stochastic variability in demands and supplies, the cost of gathering information about job vacancies and labor availabilities, the costs of mobility, and so on [Friedman, 1968, p. 8].

The natural rate of unemployment is therefore an equilibrium concept. It is the unemployment rate that is consistent with equilibrium in a Walrasian system amended to account for (1) stochastic variations in demand and supply and (2) imperfect information on the part of market participants.

One may also partition the natural rate of unemployment according to motives or causes. It consists of two components: (a) search unemployment and (b) wait unemployment.

a. Search unemployment. As we have seen, search unemployment may be characterized in a certain sense as the self-employment of the worker. According to A.A. Alchian (1971), Ch.C. Holt (1971), and D.T. Mortenson (1971), the worker remains unemployed in order to search for better opportunities even though he has received a job offer at a certain wage rate. In Holt's model, which is widely accepted, an unemployed worker starts his search with a given wage aspiration level. If the wage at which a job is offered to a worker is higher than his acceptance wage (aspiration level), he will accept the job; if not, he will refuse and continue his search. The initial aspiration level depends on the worker's most recent wage and on his perception of the job opportunities available in the market. With the passage of time, for obvious reasons discussed by Holt, the aspiration level falls. In Holt's model the wage the worker is hired at will vary directly with his aspiration level and, hence, inversely with the time he has been unemployed.

More generally we can summarize that the search models state that an unemployed worker is faced with an optimization problem. He has to find the optimal duration of a job search by comparing the discounted earnings from the best wage offer found during his search with the discounted search costs.

b. Wait unemployment. Proponents of the New Microeconomics stress a second form of voluntary unemployment – namely, wait unemployment. Phelps wrote: "It is important to recognize another possibility: accepting leisure. The corresponding idleness might be called 'wait unemployment' " (1971a, p. 15). Wait unemployment results when the worker temporarily prefers leisure to employment (including self-employment) at the prevailing wage rate. In this approach a utility-maximizing household divides its fixed amount of time into working time (goods) and leisure time by comparing its subjective rate of substitution between goods and leisure and the objective rate between the two, the real wage rate. Phelps (1972, p. 3) further subdivided this type of unemployment into speculative unemployment and precautionary unemployment.

If unemployment is speculative, the household values the utility of the prevailing (depressed) real wage less than the marginal utility of leisure. The household expects to find new employment with better conditions at a later date. By waiting, the speculative unemployed attempts to avoid a reduction in the net present value of his lifetime utility (his human wealth). Precautionary unemployment fits the case of the worker who considers himself to be between jobs, but who cannot exactly anticipate the time at which he will obtain new employment because of stochastic variations in demand. An example is professional workers such as lawyers, doctors, actors, and architects who wait for their next job without reducing the "normal" price at which they offer their services.

Queue unemployment

Phelps discussed a third form of unemployment, which he calls "queue unemployment." According to his definition an unemployed worker is standing in a queue when (a) the number of vacancies demanded does not exist (in other words, there is an excess supply of labor) and (b) the individual worker is convinced that he cannot improve his position in the queue by reducing his wage demand. This type of unemployment affects, above all, the large group of less qualified workers who are laid off as a result of a decline in aggregate demand and who are waiting for an improvement in general economic conditions in the hope that they will be rehired. The difference from wait unemployment (especially the speculative type) should be apparent. Queue unemployment does not result from a voluntary choice of labor based on a comparison of the real wage with the marginal utility of leisure; it is entirely involuntary since the individual job seeker cannot choose the duration of his own wait.

Whereas the two components of the natural unemployment rate, search and wait unemployment, can be characterized as voluntary (since the rational worker can determine the duration of his unemployment), queue unemployment requires the introduction of the concept of involuntary unemployment formulated by Keynes. For a worker standing in the queue, the duration of his unemployment is exogenous and not dependent on parameters subject to his control, such as his wage demand or the intensity of his job search. We will now attempt to classify the types of unemployment discussed by the New Microeconomics into the Keynesian categories of voluntary and involuntary unemployment.

A digression on involuntary unemployment: the Keynes test

How do the concepts of unemployment developed in the New Microeconomics correspond to the Keynesian concept of involuntary unemployment? The following discussion attempts to explain these somewhat interrelated concepts. In the *General Theory,* Keynes discussed those forms of unemployment, which are compatible with the classical theory of the labor market especially as developed by Pigou (Keynes, 1936, p. 5). Keynes classifies and discusses two forms of unemployment separately: frictional unemployment and voluntary unemployment.

Keynes maintains that one may expect frictional unemployment to be always positive in a nonstationary economy, even in equilibrium, since some portion of the labor force will always find itself between jobs. As reasons for frictional unemployment, Keynes gives the following nonexhaustive list:

1. Shifts in demand among products and false calculations (of demand and supply conditions)
2. Adjustment lags in response to unanticipated changes (in demand and supply conditions)
3. Adjustment time required by a worker who is switching from one job to another

In contrast, Keynes considers a worker voluntarily unemployed if he refuses a real wage offer that corresponds to the marginal product of his labor, whether the refusal stems from legal requirements, social practices, collective wage bargaining, adjustment lags, or psychological causes.

These two forms of unemployment correspond approximately to Friedman's definition of the natural rate of unemployment. In contrast to these forms, Keynes postulated a third category: involuntary unemployment. Keynes gives a special definition, which we cite in its entirety: "Men are involuntarily unemployed, if in the event of a small rise in the price of wage-goods relatively to the money-wage, both the aggregate supply of labour willing to work for the current money-wage and the aggregate demand for it at that wage would be greater than the existing volume of employment" (1936, p. 15). As the voluminous literature concerning this passage shows, the proper exegesis of this definition is quite difficult.[10] In this context, the following observations seem important:

1. Keynes's definition depends on a test whereby one can determine only ex post (after conducting the test) whether the observed rate of unemployment represented voluntary or involuntary joblessness.
2. Firms as well as workers are tested whether they are ready to accept lower real wages. If the volume of employment rises following a decline in real wages, then the unemployment (of the previous period) was involuntary.
3. The test consists of a reduction in real wages, whereas Keynes himself prescribed an increase in consumer prices (with constant money wages) rather than a reduction in money wages as the method of the classics to reduce real wages.
4. The Keynes test is a macroeconomic process. It depends on the influence of an increase in aggregate demand on the unemployment rate and not on the behavior of individual economic actors.

The Keynesian definition of involuntary unemployment has certain empirical characteristics: If an increase in aggregate demand (consumption plus investment) leads to an increase in the volume of employment at the same time that real wages fall due to unanticipated inflation, then the unemployment observed (in the previous period) was involuntary, according to the Keynesian definition.[11]

[10] See Leijonhufvud (1968, p. 94). At this point a Keynes "connoisseur" such as R. Kahn mentioned: "I am today unable to see why it was necessary to be so complicated." He suggested the following simple definition: "There is involuntary unemployment to the extent that, at the current money wage and with the current price level, the number of men desiring to work exceeds the number of men for whose labour there is a demand" (Kahn, 1976, p. 21).

[11] It is interesting to note that Keynes did not use the distinction between voluntary and involuntary unemployment in his popular writings. Instead he spoke about "normal" and "abnormal" unemployment. In September 1930 he viewed an unemployment rate of about $6\frac{1}{2}$ percent (about 800,000 people unemployed) in the United Kingdom as "normal." According to his proposal, unemployment rates of more than 10 percent should be brought under control by adapting regional measures (Kahn, 1976, p. 27).

We now apply the Keynes test to the categories of unemployment investigated in the New Microeconomics. Assume an increase in aggregate demand raises employment as well as prices and money wages. Both search unemployment and speculative unemployment will probably fall, provided that workers are in an economic setting in which they cannot determine whether an increase in their wage rate represents a change in their real wage or only part of a general increase in the overall price level (Lucas, 1973).[12] Phelps described the circumstances in the labor market as follows:

> The general rise of money wage rates in excess of normal expectations will indeed reduce the quantity of search unemployment. The unemployed workers engaged in sampling money wage offers, not knowing that all money wage rates have tended to rise, will tend to mistake their individual observations of high money wage rates as specific to the firm or job that they have investigated rather than a general tendency of money wage rates to be higher [1971a, p. 14].

If a job seeker discovers an unexpectedly high money wage rate in the market, which he incorrectly takes to be an increase in real wage, he will end his search sooner than planned. Similarly, the average duration of speculative unemployment will shorten because of the increased level of money wage rates. Finally, the queue of unemployment will also become shorter as a direct result of the increase in aggregate demand. Of course, it is assumed that the unemployed in the queue do not increase their wage demands as a result of the increased demand in the labor market.

Queue unemployment is the form that most closely approximates the Keynesian concept of involuntary unemployment. It

[12] The Lucas illusion is emphasized by most representatives of the New Microeconomics. For instance, A.A. Alchian stated: "Changes in aggregate demand confuse the public. Each seller notices a changed demand for his current product, but he cannot tell if that is a change also in aggregate demand which affects options elsewhere. Whether he should shift to another option, as he should not if the demand change is general, or stay where he is and change price, is the question to be answered" (1971, p. 42).

	Voluntary		Involuntary
Frictional	Search unemployment		Adjustment unemployment
Nonfrictional	Wait unemployment (speculative and precautionary)		Queue unemployment

Figure 3.14. Forms of unemployment.

follows that both search and wait unemployment are not independent of the changes in aggregate demand. This also holds for queue unemployment. Therefore, some search and speculative unemployment is "involuntary," according to Keynes's special definition.

One difference between the Keynesian theory of unemployment and the New Microeconomics concerns the influence of the level of aggregate demand on frictional and speculative unemployment. Whereas Keynes considered these forms of unemployment to be independent of the level of aggregate demand and to depend solely on market imperfections or preferences, the New Microeconomics starts with the assumption that these forms of unemployment also depend on the level of and the change in aggregate demand, even though this dependence may be only indirect.[13]

The New Microeconomics is further differentiated from the Keynesian view through its abandonment of the Keynesian concept of involuntary unemployment and its suggestion that all forms of unemployment are voluntary; that is, they may be classified as search or speculative unemployment.

Figure 3.14 summarizes the foregoing discussion. The forms of unemployment are categorized by means of a 2×2 matrix with columns for voluntary and involuntary unemployment and rows

[13] Phelps stated: "What is most significantly different about the modern theories herein from the concepts of the Keynesians is the former's treatment of 'unemployment' as frictional and greatly subject to the influence of aggregate demand *because* of frictions; Keynesians had treated frictional unemployment as irreducible whatever the pressure of demand" (1972, p. 31).

for frictional and nonfrictional unemployment. For the purpose of this presentation we can use the following definition: If the duration of unemployment depends on parameters subject to the individual job seeker's control, then one may speak of voluntary unemployment; if not, then one must classify unemployment as involuntary. The shaded areas in Figure 3.14 show that under the Keynesian definition of "voluntary," part of the unemployment classified as voluntary by the New Microeconomics would be placed in the category of involuntary unemployment.

Now let us examine the matrix row by row. Frictional unemployment consists of search unemployment as well as joblessness due to adjustment lags. The former is voluntary as defined by the New Microeconomics. Together these two categories constitute frictional unemployment as defined by Keynes. However, in terms of his definition of "voluntary," one cannot make a sharp distinction between search unemployment and adjustment unemployment.

If the job seeker cannot influence the duration of his unemployment by a reduction in his money wages or the acquisition of information (a more intensive job search), and if, in addition, aggregate demand has remained constant overall but its distribution among products has shifted, then any resulting unemployment can be classified as involuntary frictional unemployment. This type of unemployment results from a worker's lack of qualifications, which he cannot overcome in the short run by either adjusting his wage demand or gaining a better knowledge of the labor market. The shaded area divides the first row according to the Keynesian definition of involuntary unemployment. If the level of aggregate demand increases, and if workers mistake money wage increases as real wage increases, then the average duration of unemployment will shorten.

Nonfrictional unemployment consists of two forms of voluntary unemployment – namely, speculative and precautionary unemployment – as well as involuntary queue unemployment. As long as job seekers continue to misinterpret price changes in the sense of the New Microeconomics, speculative unemployment will not be independent of the level of aggregate demand. Search unemployment as well as speculative unemployment must therefore be at least partly involuntary according to the Keynesian definition.

If one uses the definition that a job seeker is voluntarily unemployed if he can affect the duration of his unemployment through a change in either his wage demand or the intensity of his job search (information acquisition), and if one subsumes all other forms of unemployment under the complementary heading "involuntary," then the shaded areas vanish and the unemployment rate can be divided into two distinct components.

Derivation of the short-run Phillips curve according to the New Microeconomics

The New Microeconomics differentiates between the short-run and the long-run Phillips curves. The short-run Phillips curve or, as Phelps called it, the momentary Phillips curve, is valid for only a given expected rate of inflation. The long-run Phillips curve degenerates into a line perpendicular to the abscissa as shown in Section 3.5. In the long run the rate of unemployment is therefore independent of the rate of inflation to the extent that the latter is fully anticipated. Friedman and Phelps designated this rate of unemployment as the natural rate.

How do the theorists of the New Microeconomics derive the short-run Phillips curve? The island parable of Phelps (1971a, p. 6) expresses their approach particularly clearly. As an aid to understanding, it should be noted that the island parable depends on two fundamental assumptions:

1. The rational worker prefers self-employment in search unemployment to a position that pays less than his reservation wage.[14]
2. Job seekers cannot distinguish aggregate from local demand shocks.

[14] In his criticism of the New Microeconomics, Hines stressed that "In a disequilibrium situation, the theory of search unemployment implies that individuals *voluntarily* choose to work for an employer or to search for better options (which constitutes self-employment in the gathering of information about job opportunities and wages) in any given situation. This self-employment, so to speak, is not measured by the recorded employment figures, so that actual data overstate unemployment" (1976, p. 68).

The island parable. Let us assume that the economy consists of a number of islands among which it is costly to exchange
information. A worker can obtain information about wage rates
on other islands only by visiting them and taking a sample. This
implies that a worker who wishes to know about wage rates elsewhere must sacrifice a day at work on his own island to search
and collect information. In other words, he must spend most of
the day in his rowboat visiting other islands rather than at his job.
On each island the labor market is competitive and jobs are homogeneous. Each morning an auction occurs on each island in which
the market-clearing wage rate and the level of employment are
determined. This world of islands is in a state of quasi-Walrasian
equilibrium, in which wage rates on other islands are not actually
known (as they are in the pure Walrasian model) but are estimated in a consistent way.

Assume that a reduction in aggregate demand disturbs this
equilibrium and the requirements of a quasi-Walrasian equilibrium are no longer fulfilled. The course the economy will take
now depends on how economic agents interpret this decline in
aggregate demand and the consequent reduction in the demand
for factors of production. If they assume that the reduction in
demand is general and affects all islands, then wages and prices
on all islands will fall and employment (on each island) will remain constant. However, if economic agents misinterpret this
aggregate shock – in other words, if workers regard the decline in
money wages as specific to their own island – then, according to
Phelps, the following will occur: "Some workers will refuse employment at the new (lower) market-clearing money wage rates,
preferring to spend the time searching for a better relative money
wage elsewhere. Effective labor supply thus shifts leftward at
every real wage rate; real wage rates rise, and profit-maximizing
output and employment fall" (1971a, p. 7). Finally, the extent of
search unemployment will be greater, the greater is the difference
between the actual (lower) rate of money wages and the expected
wage rate.

We can summarize the island parable as follows: A reduction in demand on the auction market for labor leads to an unexpected decline in money wages. The resulting discrepancy between the expected and actual money wages causes an increase in voluntary quits and leads to an increase in search unemployment. The parable is symmetrical and is also valid for changes in demand in the opposite direction. An increase in aggregate demand leads to an unanticipated increase in money wages in the world of islands described by the New Microeconomics. Job seekers will search for shorter periods of time, since they receive unexpectedly high wage offers; the tendency of employed workers to quit will decline, since they consider at least part of the increase in money wages to be specific to their own island. Therefore, a decline in aggregate demand induces a decrease in money wages and an increase in search unemployment, whereas an increase in aggregate demand implies a rise in money wages and a drop in search unemployment. In other words, periods of unanticipated wage inflation generally correlate with below-average search unemployment. Consequently, there is a short-run Phillips curve that shows a negative correlation between the rate of change in money wages and the rate of unemployment.

Criticism of the New Microeconomics

Above all, the critics of the New Microeconomics doubt that search unemployment is empirically relevant. The search for suitable or better jobs need not require the worker to leave his present job, since the employed job seeker can still use various forms of communication such as the telephone, newspaper advertisements, and conversations with colleagues.[15] For example, H. König stated with respect to West Germany: "The major component of job search occurs while the worker retains his current position and in general he quits only after he has successfully concluded his search, so that he may complete the transfer from one position to another without an intervening period of unemployment" (1979, p. 39). K.W. Rothschild (1978) described an

[15] This point was stressed by J. Tobin (1972), J.P. Mattila (1974), and A.G. Hines (1976).

analysis of the Austrian microcensus according to which more than four-fifths of the workers who changed their jobs in the past were not unemployed during their job search.

A further objection to the New Microeconomics is the lack of consistency of its implications with empirical observations. This concerns the question of whether voluntary quits exhibit a pro- or anticyclical pattern. From Phelps's island parable, we can derive that voluntary quits should follow an anticyclical course. According to the New Microeconomics the number of voluntary quits should increase in a recession (a worker quits when his expected real wage falls and he employs himself in search activity) and decrease in a boom, since workers overestimate the real wage as money wage rates rise. R.J. Gordon (1977) and K.W. Rothschild (1978) provided empirical evidence against this implication of the New Microeconomics. They show that voluntary quits behave procyclically; that is, they decline in recessions and increase in periods of economic expansion.

The main criticism of the New Microeconomics, however, is directed against its tendency to view all unemployment as voluntary search unemployment. The New Microeconomics concerns itself with only quits and not at all with involuntary layoffs. In an empirical study R.E. Brinner (1977) differentiated between two cycles:

1. The quit–new hire cycle, which contains an intervening period of voluntary search unemployment
2. The layoff–rehire cycle, which leads to an intervening period of involuntary unemployment

The New Microeconomics deals exclusively with the first cycle and mostly ignores the second.[16] Brinner found that business cycle movements are reflected in the rate of layoffs and that the latter largely explains the changes in the total rate of unemployment.

[16] "This model correctly identifies labour force turnover as a source of unemployment but mistakenly focuses on the quit and new-hire turnover rates rather than the layoff–rehire cycle, a cycle that is essentially involuntary and certainly unrelated to the difference between actual inflation and employee expectations" (Brinner, 1977, pp. 389–418).

Table 3.1. *Unemployment in tight and slack markets (percent of the labor force)*

Reason for unemployment	Tight market 1974	Slack market 1975
On layoff	0.8	1.8
Lost job	1.6	2.9
Left job	0.8	0.9
Wanted temporary work	0.9	1.1
Left school	0.4	0.5
Other	1.1	1.3
Total	5.6	8.5

Source: Hall, 1980.

R.E. Hall (1980) broke down the total rate of unemployment into six categories according to the reason for unemployment: (1) on layoff, (2) lost job, (3) left job, (4) wanted temporary work, (5) left school, and (6) other. He compared these categories for a tight labor market in 1974 and for a slack labor market in 1975 (Table 3.1).

The table shows the significance of the different components of the rate of unemployment. Workers on layoff and those who lost jobs can be considered as involuntary unemployment, since their employers unexpectedly told them to stop work. These two components amounted to 43 percent of the total rate in 1974 and 55 percent in 1975. The category of unemployed quitters (left job) can be interpreted as voluntary unemployment. They made up 14 percent in 1974 and only 10.5 percent in the recession year 1975. The other categories cannot clearly be categorized as voluntary or involuntary unemployment.

More instructive is the change in the composition of the unemployment rate brought about by the recession in 1975. Of the increase in total unemployment of 2.9 percentage points, 1.0 occurred for workers on layoff and 1.3 percentage points for those who lost jobs. In other words, four-fifths of the rate of increase in total unemployment can be attributed to a corresponding increase in involuntary layoffs and lost jobs.

These results seem to imply that variations in economic activity are reflected in the categories of layoffs and lost jobs and that these categories explain the changes in the total rate of unemployment. Even this small sample shows that the involuntary component of layoffs and lost jobs, which is ignored by the New Microeconomics, plays a significant role in explaining the level and composition of the total rate of unemployment.

3.6 Rational expectations and the Phillips curve

The difference between the long-run and the short-run Phillips curves in the Friedman–Phelps analysis is a logical consequence of the adaptive expectations mechanism. The concept of adaptive expectations is, however, open to two objections:

1. It might lead to systematically biased expectations (Lucas, 1972b).
2. It leads to information being wasted whenever economic agents possess additional information.

Theorists of rational expectations such as R. Lucas (1972b) and T.J. Sargent (1973) argue that inflationary expectations are formed by intelligent people who ought to take advantage of all information available about the economy when they form their plans. We can therefore apply the concept of rational expectations to the Phillips curve model in its NR formulation. The following discussion is a bit technical, but unfortunately this model cannot be explained without such details. For this purpose we have to close the Phillips curve model by introducing a macroeconomic excess-demand equation that determines u_t. The model now consists of three equations and three endogenous variables.

a. The Phillips curve in its NR formulation:

$$\pi_t = \pi_t^* - b(u_t - u^*) + \varepsilon_t \tag{1}$$

b. An excess-demand equation:

$$u_t = u^* - \psi(m_t - \pi_t) + \eta_t \tag{2}$$

c. Rational expectations:

$$\pi_t^* = E(\pi_t/I_{t-1}) \tag{3}$$

Equation (1) is the Phillips curve in its NR formulation, well known from the previous section. The difference here is the random variable ε_t, which is serially independent with variance σ_ε^2 and mean zero ($E\varepsilon_t = 0$). The excess-demand equation can be considered as derived from an IS-LM system and an Okun curve. It determines u_t, or more precisely $u_t - u^*$, the deviation of u_t from its natural rate as a function of the rate of growth of the real money supply, $m_t - \pi_t$. If m_t, the rate of monetary expansion, exceeds the rate of inflation, the positive real balance effect generates overall excess demand (not seen in this model) and reduces u_t. The excess-demand equation depends also on the random variable η_t with constant variance σ_η^2 and $E\eta_t = 0$.

What is the rational expectation of the rate of inflation in this model? Substituting equation (2) into equation (1) and solving for π_t leads to

$$\pi_t = \frac{\pi_t^* + b\psi m_t + \varepsilon_t - b\eta_t}{1 + b\psi} \tag{4}$$

Equation (4) is a so-called semireduced-form equation in which π_t is explained by the expected rate of inflation π_t^*, the rate of growth of the money supply m_t, and the two random variables ε_t and η_t. The rational expectation of the rate of inflation π_t is the mathematical expectation of equation (4). By the rational expectations equation (3),

$$\pi_t^* = E(\pi_t/I_{t-1})$$

If we apply the expectation operation E on equation (4), we get

$$E(\pi_t/I_{t-1}) = \frac{E(\pi_t/I_{t-1}) + b\psi E(m_t/I_{t-1})}{1 + b\psi} \tag{5}$$

since $E(\varepsilon_t) = 0$ and $bE(\eta_t) = 0$, or

$$(1 + b\psi)E(\pi_t/I_{t-1}) = E(\pi_t/I_{t-1}) + b\psi E(m_t/I_{t-1}) \tag{6}$$

It then follows that

$$\pi_t^* = E(\pi_t/I_{t-1}) = E(m_t/I_{t-1}) \tag{7}$$

In words, the rational expected rate of inflation is equal to the expected rate of growth of the money supply $E(m_t/I_{t-1})$. By substituting equation (7) into equation (4), we get the actual rate of inflation:

$$\pi_t = \frac{E(m_t/I_{t-1}) + b\psi m_t + \varepsilon_t - b\eta_t}{1 + b\psi} \tag{8}$$

Let us assume that the monetary authority is able to control the rate of growth of the money supply completely and that this rate is announced one period in advance. Therefore the public anticipates correctly the rate of growth of the money supply.

$$E(m_t/I_{t-1}) = m_t \tag{9}$$

In that case we get

$$\pi_t = E(m_t/I_{t-1}) + \frac{\varepsilon_t - b\eta_t}{1 + b\psi} \tag{10}$$

The rate of inflation is equal to the expected rate of growth of the money supply plus a linear combination of the random variables of the system.

Substituting equation (10) into equation (2) and again assuming that $E(m_t/I_{t-1}) = m_t$, we derive the following for the rate of unemployment:

$$u_t = u^* - \psi m_t + \psi \left[E(m_t/I_{t-1}) + \frac{\varepsilon_t}{1 + b\psi} - \frac{b\eta_t}{1 + b\psi} \right] + \eta_t \tag{11}$$

$$= u^* + \frac{\psi\varepsilon_t + \eta_t}{1 + b\psi} \tag{12}$$

The rate of unemployment u_t equals the natural rate u^* plus a stochastic component. The implication of the rational expectations assumption is that the actual rate of unemployment oscillates randomly around the natural rate u^*.

The NR hypothesis, the Friedman–Phelps model, states that

the short-run trade-off between the unanticipated part of the rate of inflation and the deviation of u_t from its natural rate u^*, can be exploited by a systematic economic policy.

In the case of rational expectations there is also a Phillips relationship [see equation (1)] but with a crucial difference. Systematic deviations of the rate of inflation from the expected rate cannot be generated by monetary policy to influence u_t. An increase in the rate of growth of the money supply that is known to the economic agents will raise inflationary expectations and simultaneously shift the Phillips curve. In other words, as soon as the trade-off is exploited by a systematic economic policy, this trade-off disappears. In the case of rational expectations, even the short-run Phillips curve is unstable (with regard to fully anticipated variations of monetary policy).

The rational expectations model can explain the existence of unemployment in any particular year, but it is not adequate to explain persistent movements in the unemployment rate as observed in real-world business cycles. The deviation of u_t from its natural rate is explained only by the stochastic term $(\psi \varepsilon_t + \eta_t)/(1 + b\psi)$ in equation (12). The random variables ε_t and η_t are not correlated with any variable whose value is known at the time expectations are formed, including its own past values. A straightforward implication of this is that the time path of the rate of unemployment should not show any serial correlation. Yet it is well known that the time series of GNP and unemployment data have a high degree of serial correlation (Maddock and Carter, 1982, p. 44). Periods in which unemployment is below its natural rate alternate with periods in which it is above the natural rate. The failure of the rational expectations hypothesis (in its strongest form) to explain the systematic movements of the rate of unemployment during a business cycle expansion or contraction was dubbed by R. Gordon "the persistence dilemma" of the rational expectations hypothesis (1981, p. 509f).

On this point the contemporary theoretical discussion has not reached a consensus. We will return to some problems of the rational expectations hypothesis in Chapter 4.

3.7 The place of the Phillips curve in macroeconomic models

The preceding discussion raises an important question: Does the Phillips curve have a general significance in macroeconomic model building or is it only a special case of inflation theory?

In this section we combine the Phillips curve with the IS-LM model, the common framework of macroeconomic analysis (Lipsey, 1978). The IS-LM model is based on the notion that the economy can be divided into two markets: a market for final goods (summarized by the IS curve) and a money market (represented by the LM curve). But this is not sufficient. We must add a third market, the labor market, to determine the rate of unemployment and the rate of inflation. The combination of the IS-LM system and the Phillips curve offers the advantage that situations of disequilibrium can be analyzed. Disequilibrium in this context means that aggregated real demand X as a result of the IS-LM system is not equal to the full-employment output X^*. (The rate of unemployment at X^* is equal to the natural rate.) For an output level above the full-employment output, $X - X^* > 0$, the implied overemployment causes money wages to rise and is thus reflected in inflation. On the other hand, for an output level below the full-employment output, $X - X^* < 0$ (which implies unemployment above the natural rate), money wages and therefore prices fall, a deflationary development.

The modified Phillips curve and the IS-LM system jointly provide: (a) a link between the goods, the labor, and the money markets and (b) an explanation of simultaneous variations in the real output and the price level (or the rate of inflation) where $X \neq X^*$.

The elements of an amended IS-LM model

Although most macroeconomic textbooks present the IS-LM model,[17] for the convenience of the reader the model is briefly

---

[17] See, for instance, Laidler (1977, chap. 1), Dornbusch and Fischer (1978), Branson (1979), and Gordon (1978).

summarized here. The amended IS-LM system consists of three building blocks:

   a. The goods sector (summarized by the IS curve)
   b. The monetary sector (summarized by the LM curve)
   c. The short-run supply curve (summarized by the Phillips–Okun curve)

   a. The goods market. This sector is modeled by four linear equations for the sake of simplicity.

$$C = A + bX \qquad b > 0 \qquad \text{(consumption function)} \qquad (1)$$
$$I = B + dr \qquad d < 0 \qquad \text{(investment function)} \qquad (2)$$
$$G = \bar{G} \qquad\qquad\quad \text{(government expenditures)} \qquad (3)$$
$$X = C + I + G \qquad\quad \text{(equilibrium condition)} \qquad (4)$$

These four equations are formulated in real terms. The consumption function [equation (1)] explains real consumption (nominal consumption expenditure deflated by the price level) with an autonomous component A and the real income X. The marginal propensity to consume b is assumed to be less than one. Real investment [equation (2)] has an autonomous component B and is inversely related to the market rate of interest r. A fall in the rate of interest raises the present value of expected earnings of real capital and encourages investment, and vice versa. Equation (3) states that government expenditure is determined from outside. According to equation (4), equilibrium in the goods market is achieved when the sum of consumption, investment, and government expenditures is just sufficient to buy the produced level of output.

   Substituting equations (1), (2), and (3) into the equilibrium condition (4), we get

$$X = (A + B + \bar{G}) + bX + dr \qquad (5)$$

Solving this equation for r, we get the well-known IS curve:

$$r = \frac{1 - b}{d} X - \frac{A + B + \bar{G}}{d} \qquad (6)$$

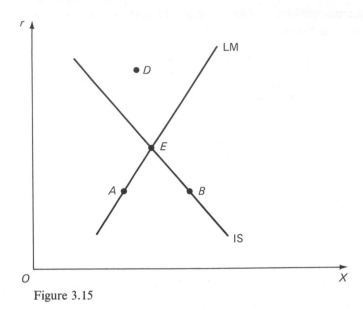

Figure 3.15

The IS curve is a schedule of combinations of the interest rate r and real income X such that the goods market is in equilibrium. For a graphic representation of the IS curve, see Figure 3.15.

    b. The monetary sector. The monetary sector is modeled by three equations:

$$\frac{M^D}{P} = kX + lr \qquad k > 0; l < 0 \qquad \text{(demand for money)} \qquad (7)$$

$$M^S = \bar{M}^S \qquad \text{(supply of money)} \qquad (8)$$

$$M^D = M^S \qquad \text{(equilibrium condition)} \qquad (9)$$

The real demand for money M^D/P is explained by two terms. The positive term kX is called the transaction demand for money and the negative term lr, the speculative demand for money (k is the transaction coefficient and l reflects the interest sensitivity of the money demand). The supply of money according to equation (8) is exogenous. Equilibrium is reached when the transaction demand and the speculative demand for money are just sufficient to absorb the existing money supply [equation (9)].

By substituting equations (7) and (8) into equation (9) and rearranging, we get the LM curve:

$$r = \frac{\bar{M}^S}{P} \cdot \frac{1}{l} - \frac{k}{l} X \qquad l < 0 \qquad (10)$$

The LM curve is a schedule of combinations of the interest rate r and real income X such that the money market is in equilibrium. The relationship is plotted in Figure 3.15.

The intersection of the IS curve and the LM curve determines jointly the levels of r and X so that they are compatible with equilibrium in both markets; that is, the equilibrium values of r and X have to lie on both the IS curve and the LM curve as point E indicates. Any other combination of points (X, r) would mean that the goods market (point A) or the money market (point B) or both markets are in disequilibrium (for example, point D).

c. The short-run supply curve. The intersection of the IS and LM curves denotes the intended demand of households and firms at a given price level and a given rate of interest, but the level of production that is implied by this intersection may require the use of more or less labor than is willing to work at the existing price and wage levels. In Figure 3.16 the vertical line X^* is the full-employment position. It is the level of income that would be produced if unemployment were at the natural rate level u^*.

Since the IS-LM intersection is to the right of X^*, the aggregated intended demand (X_1 in Figure 3.16) exceeds the equilibrium level of production X^*. Therefore, excess demand in the goods and labor markets results.

By contrast, if $X - X^* < 0$, a demand deficit arises in the goods market; that is, the actual output X falls short of the potential output X^* (not depicted in Figure 3.16). The difference $X - X^*$ is called the GNP gap. To analyze this situation one has to bring a new concept into the model: the short-run supply function, which

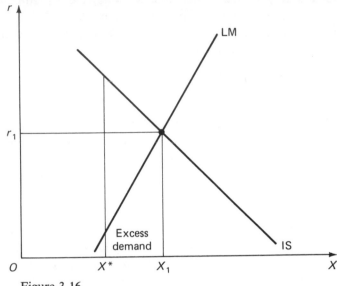

Figure 3.16

is composed of two well-known relationships: the Phillips curve and Okun's law (Dornbusch and Fischer, 1978, pp. 404–7).

The Phillips curve proposes, as we know, a negative correlation between the rate of inflation and the rate of unemployment. Okun's law is an empirical law that states a negative correlation between the rate of unemployment u and excess demand in the goods market (approximated by the GNP gap). Accordingly it asserts a link between excess demand in the goods market and excess demand in the labor market. Okun's law is used in the following formulation:[18]

$$u - u^* = -a(X - X^*)$$

where u is the actual rate of unemployment, u^* is the natural rate of unemployment, X is the actual output, and X^* is the potential output (at this output level $u = u^*$).

[18] Okun's original formulation was $u = u^* - a[(X - X^*)/X^*]$, where X^* is the potential output. Okun's estimation of the coefficient a for the period 1947–60 in the United States was approximately 0.3. This says that if real output exceeds the long-run potential output by 1 percent, the actual rate of unemployment will be 0.3 percentage points below the natural rate.

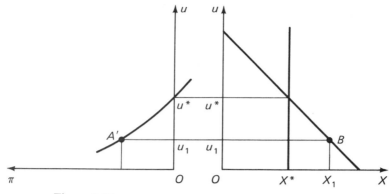

Figure 3.17

Figure 3.17 is a graphic of the supply side of the amended IS-LM model. On the left side is the Phillips curve (turned by 90 degrees); the right side represents Okun's law. On the abscissa the level of real income is depicted; on the ordinate, the rate of unemployment u. Full equilibrium in this model means that the output X, as a result of the intersection of the IS and LM curves, is equal to X^*. In this case $u = u^*$ and the rate of inflation is zero. When X, the actual output demanded, exceeds X^* (distance $\overline{X^*X_1}$ in Figure 3.17), the actual unemployment rate falls to u_1, below the natural rate u^*.

Algebraically we have three equations:

$$u - u^* = -a(X - X^*) \qquad \text{(Okun's law)} \qquad (11)$$
$$w = \pi^* - b(u - u^*) + \lambda \qquad \text{(Phillips curve)} \qquad (12)$$
$$\pi = w - \lambda \qquad \text{(markup pricing)} \qquad (13)$$

Equation (12) denotes a Phillips curve as introduced in Section 3.3 with $\beta = 1$. Combining these three equations, we obtain a Phillips–Okun curve [equation (14)], which we want to interpret as the short-run aggregate supply function of the amended IS-LM model (Dornbusch and Fischer, 1978, p. 406).

$$\pi = \pi^* + ab(X - X^*) \qquad (14)$$

Figure 3.18 gives a graphical representation of this new relationship.

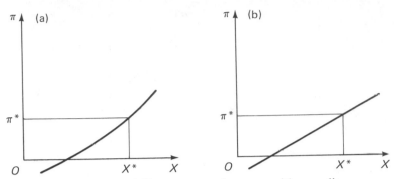

Figure 3.18. (a) Short-run supply curve with a nonlinear Phillips curve. (b) Short-run supply curve with a linear Phillips curve.

The aggregate supply function [equation (14)] is made up of two terms. First, the actual rate of inflation is explained by the expected rate of inflation. The higher the expected rate of inflation, the higher is the actual rate of inflation. Second, the conditions of the labor market are reflected in the actual rate of inflation. For an output level above the potential output, $X - X^* > 0$, wages and prices will rise and the actual inflation rate will be greater than π^*. Conversely, if $X - X^* < 0$, the implied increase in unemployment will reduce the wage and price rise and the current rate of inflation will be below the expected inflation rate π^* or even turned into a rate of deflation (i.e., a fall in the price level). The influence of the GNP gap $(X - X^*)$ on the rate of inflation is measured by the slope of the supply curve – that is, by the term ab in equation (14). The parameter a shows the influence of the GNP gap on the rate of unemployment; b reflects the influence of the rate of unemployment on nominal wages. The higher either of these parameters is, the higher is the rate of inflation caused by a given GNP gap and the less favorable is the inflation–output trade-off.

The working of the amended IS-LM model
The amended IS-LM model is composed of three equations: the IS curve represented by equation (6), the LM curve represented by equation (10), and the short-run supply curve in

equation (14). The latter is simplified by the assumption $\pi^* = 0$; that is, the supply curve cuts the abscissa at the position $X = X^*$. Let us summarize the three equations.

$$r = \frac{1-b}{d} X - \frac{A + B + \bar{G}}{d} \qquad \text{(IS curve)}$$

$$r = \frac{\bar{M}^S}{P} \cdot \frac{1}{l} - \frac{k}{l} X \qquad l < 0 \qquad \text{(LM curve)}$$

$$\pi = ab(X - X^*) \qquad \text{(supply curve)}$$

In the context of this model we consider two experiments:

1. A one-shot increase in the money supply
2. An expansionary fiscal and monetary policy

1. A one-shot increase in the money supply. We start with full-employment equilibrium E in Figure 3.19, with $X = X^*$ and $\pi = 0$. When the money supply is increased from M_0 to M_1 (the central bank is buying bonds in the bond market), the LM curve shifts to the right to position LM_1 (broken line in Figure 3.19). The new position of the LM curve (at point A') is determined by a level of the real money supply M_1/P_0, where P_0 is the initial price level prior to the increase in M. However, the output demanded at point A' cannot be produced at the initial price level P_0. The increase in real output X requires an increase in employment that can take place only when money wages increase in the labor market, which in turn leads to an increase in the price level to P_1. The rise in the price level [measured by the rate of inflation $\pi_1 = (P_1 - P_0)/P_0$ in Figure 3.19b] causes a decrease in the level of the real money supply to M_1/P_1 and therefore a shift of the LM curve to LM_2 in Figure 3.19. At the new intersection A of LM_2 and IS_0 the price level has risen enough to induce firms to produce the real output level X_1. In the following period excess demand persists, $X - X^* > 0$. This causes nominal wages and prices to rise again. The further rise in the price level reduces the real money supply again (the stock of money was raised only once!), which in turn moves the LM curve farther to the left (see the

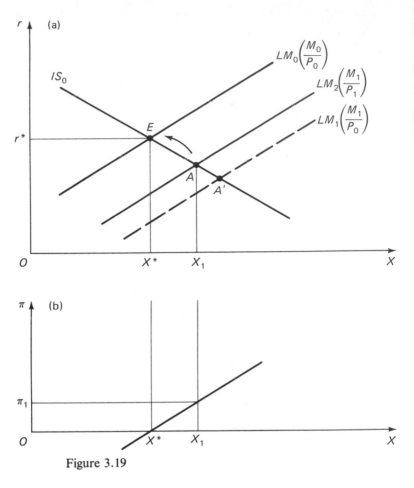

Figure 3.19

arrow). The upward shift of the LM curve occurs because the higher price level increases the nominal demand for money, thus pushing the rate of interest up again. The increase in the interest rate discourages investment and reduces excess demand, which in turn causes a decrease in output and employment (move from point A to E). The LM curve continues to shift to the left as long as excess demand in the goods and labor markets and a positive rate of inflation persist.

The initial outward shift of the LM curve to LM_2 along a stable IS curve (expansive phase) is followed by a contracting phase in which LM moves back to LM_0. The increase in the real output to X_1 as a consequence of the increase in the money supply was only temporary.

The macroeconomic standard IS-LM curve closed by the Phillips–Okun curve not only provides a solution of X, r, and P, but it also shows the simultaneous variations in the real income, the rate of interest, and the rate of inflation in situations of excess demand.

2. An expansionary fiscal and monetary policy. Let us consider a second experiment. As before, we start with a full-employment equilibrium at point E, where $X = X^*$ and the rate of inflation is zero. The government increases autonomous expenditures $\bar{G}$, which shifts the IS curve to the right to IS_1 (Figure 3.20). Now we assume that the expansionary fiscal policy is accommodated by monetary policy; that is, the nominal money supply is increased just sufficiently to hold the LM curve stationary at the initial position LM_0. This can be accomplished by setting $dM^S/M^S = \pi$, that is, expanding the money supply at a rate equal to the rate of inflation. In this case, the level of real money balances $[M_{-1}(1 + \pi)]/[P_{-1}(1 + \pi)]$ remains fixed and also the position of the LM curve. The model then predicts that the rate of inflation and the level of income will remain stable at the new solution of the amended IS-LM system (X_1, π_1). By implementing an expansive expenditure program that shifts the IS curve to the right (by increasing $\bar{G}$) and stabilizing the LM curve at the original position (by a continuously increasing money supply), the government can maintain any combination of the rate of inflation and the level of real income and consequently the rate of unemployment. In this way we have shown the macroeconomic conditions necessary for a stable point to appear on the Phillips curve. Point A' in Figure 3.20b is equivalent to point A' in Figure 3.17.

This analysis is valid for only given inflationary expectations (in Figures 3.19 and 3.20 above the inflationary expectation of

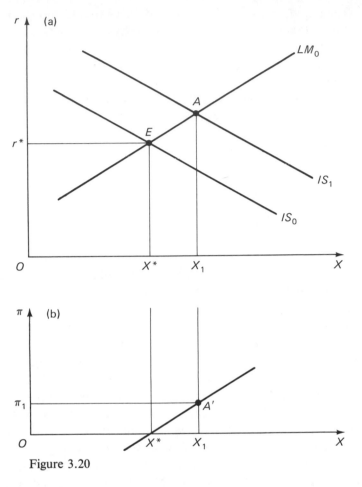

Figure 3.20

zero). The problem of the stability of the Phillips curve can be reconsidered in the context of the amended IS-LM system. The positive rate of inflation, as a consequence of the expansionary demand management, creates a positive expected rate of inflation π^*. The inflationary expectations adjustment process sets in motion an upward shift in the short-run supply curve (Figure 3.20b), which decreases the expansionary effect of the demand management through a higher rate of inflation and enforces an upward shift of the LM curve (Figure 3.20a), as long as the rate of growth of the money supply is fixed at π_1 in Figure 3.20b. However, the addition of an expectations adjustment mechanism makes the model significantly more complex and we can no longer use the simple graphic method.

The point of this section was to show that the Phillips curve not only was an episode in the history of inflation analysis but also has a place in the standard macroeconomic model as the short-run supply equation.

4

Monetarist inflation theory

The so-called monetarist debate has provided a critical analysis of the foundations of macroeconomics. The discussion reached a peak at the beginning of the 1970s in Milton Friedman's two articles "A Theoretical Framework for Monetary Analysis" (1970a) and "A Monetary Theory of Nominal Income" (1971) as well as in the theoretical debate surrounding them. In addition, the writings of K. Brunner (1970), K. Brunner and A.H. Meltzer (1976), A. Meltzer (1977), H.G. Johnson (1972a), D.E.W. Laidler (1975a, 1976, 1981), and M.J. Parkin (1975) have significantly contributed to the formulation and popularization of monetarism as a macroeconomic theory. In these monetarist works the explanation of inflation has played a central role. Although these authors applied different theoretical approaches, three hypotheses continually reappear in their works:

    a. Inflation is in essence a monetary phenomenon.[1]
    b. Keynesian theory, which monetarists equate with a simple Phil-

---

[1] Laidler and Parkin stated in their well-known article, "Inflation – A Survey" (1975, p. 741): "Inflation is then, fundamentally a monetary phenomenon." However, many authors, for example, Friedman, go somewhat further and propose a stronger form of monetarism – namely, a direct causal relationship between the money supply and the rate of inflation: "Inflation is always and everywhere a monetary phenomenon . . . and can be produced only by a more rapid increase in the quantity of money than in output" (Friedman, 1970b, p. 24).

lips curve without adjustment for expectations, cannot explain the problem of inflation, especially the acceleration of inflation.
c. The rate of growth and the acceleration of the money supply explain the rate of inflation and its acceleration, respectively.

"Monetarism" (an expression Karl Brunner coined) contends to be more than just a theory of inflation, however. It can be conceived as an attempt to establish an alternative theoretical macroeconomic paradigm to the Keynesian view. Since monetarist authors are not a homogeneous group and since they differ sharply in methodology as well as in the specification of models, it is difficult to characterize monetarism as a school of thought on macroeconomics through a list of generally accepted theorems. Nevertheless, several authors have made such attempts: J.L. Stein in his introduction to the volume *Monetarism* (1976), H. Frisch (1977b), D.E.W. Laidler (1981), and, above all, Th. Mayer et al. (1978), who tried to characterize monetarism through twelve propositions.

Adherence to the following four propositions seems to constitute membership in the monetarist school:

1. The private sector of the economy is inherently stable. The economic system returns automatically to a full-employment equilibrium after a disturbance; the unemployment rate returns to the "natural" rate.
2. Any rate of growth of the money supply is compatible with a full-employment equilibrium, although different rates of inflation result.
3. A change in the rate of growth of the money supply first alters the rate of real economic growth (and hence the unemployment rate). In the long run this real effect vanishes and there remains only a permanent increase in the *trend* rate of inflation (acceleration theorem).[2]

---

[2] Laidler (1976, p. 77) especially emphasized these points. They also correspond approximately to the presentation of Brunner and Meltzer: "A theory is not a monetarist theory unless three conditions are met. One, the long-run position to which the system moves is determined by stocks, particularly the stock of money, and not by flows. . . . Two, the adjustment to a change in money involves substitutions between money, other assets and new production. . . . Three, the economic system is stable. Cumulative movements of prices or output result mainly from the decisions or actions of governments not individuals or private institutions" (1976, p. 97).

4. There is dislike of activist demand management policy, either monetary or fiscal, and preference for long-run monetary policy "rules" or prestated "targets."

The stability postulate is not at the head of the list by chance. Actually, the assumption of an inherently stable economic system is a presupposition of monetarist theory, as A. Leijonhufvud (1976) noted. The stability of the market as an economic system is assumed, not proven; in particular, it is asserted that the labor market is always approaching equilibrium; that is, the rate of unemployment is equal to the natural rate, which represents only frictional unemployment. On the basis of the stability postulate, monetarism excludes the possibility of a Keynesian underemployment equilibrium characterized by an excess supply of goods and labor, such as E. Malinvaud recently investigated in detail (1977). Here monetarism steps across the boundaries of pure economic theory and assumes ideological aspects. H.G. Johnson expressed this clearly with reference to the stability postulate:

> The Keynesian position is that the real economy is highly unstable and that monetary management has both little relevance to it and little control over it; the monetarist position on the contrary is that the real economy is inherently fairly stable, but can be destabilized by monetary developments, which therefore need to be controlled as far as possible by intelligent monetary policy [Johnson, 1972a, p. 6].

For the purposes of inflation theory we shall end the discussion of stability at this point. It should be mentioned that, in addition to the question of the existence of an equilibrium, the speed of convergence to that equilibrium is important. Is equilibrium quickly or slowly restored after a disturbance to the economic system? Is the adjustment path asymptotic or oscillating?

Recently G. Tintner et al. (1977) proposed introducing the concept of "half-life" as used in physics as a practical measure in investigating the stability of economic systems. For example, if it takes ten years for half the disturbance to be eliminated, then the system can be regarded as economically unstable; the system is stable if it takes only ten months.

The second theorem of monetarism simply formulates the long-run quantity theory. In the steady state, when all variables are correctly anticipated, the rate of growth of the money supply completely determines the rate of inflation. In other words, a full-employment equilibrium is independent of a fully anticipated rate of inflation.

Whereas the long-run quantity theory is relatively trivial, the third theorem of monetarism has greater importance. One can designate this as the short-run quantity theory, which maintains that an acceleration in the rate of growth of the money supply (i.e., a faster rate of nominal spending on final goods) temporarily raises the rate of real economic growth and, hence, reduces the rate of unemployment. The subsequent inflation leads to an adjustment in the economic system. During this adjustment process, the rate of real economic growth again returns to the original rate. Thus, the acceleration in real growth achieved through a faster rate of money growth is only temporary. Brunner (1970) labeled this principle the "acceleration theorem." Most monetarist authors, such as Friedman (1970a), Brunner (1970), and Laidler (1975a), use this principle, though with different model specifications. Nevertheless, in all these models, the acceleration theorem plays a central role in the analysis of the short-run adjustment process. In that respect, it figures prominently in the "standard" monetarist model.

The main aspect of proposition 4 is the rejection of discretionary fiscal and monetary policy. Activist demand management and compensatory countercyclical policy are considered as a source of instability. The monetarist model implies that output and employment can be influenced by economic policy only to the extent that they cause price changes that are not foreseen by agents in the private sector. In the long-run the effect on the real variables will peter out but the higher price level (or rate of inflation) remains. Monetarists also doubt that policy makers have the ability to forecast future changes in the relevant economic variables and especially to forecast the future effect of current changes in policy instruments. The main policy issue, therefore, is to replace activist economic policy by rules like the constant growth rate rule for the money supply or constant rules for fiscal policy.

Some authors such as J. Tobin (1980) and F.H. Hahn (1980) distinguish two schools of monetarism – namely, monetarism Mark I and monetarism Mark II. Monetarism I is the theory of the authors mentioned at the beginning of this chapter; monetarism II is another label for the rational expectations school (RE school), comprising the works of R. Lucas (1972a,b, 1973), T.J. Sargent (1973, 1976), T.J. Sargent and N. Wallace (1975, 1976), and their collaborators. Of the four propositions that characterize monetarism I, Lucas and Sargent would agree with propositions 1, 2, and 4 but would not underwrite the essential proposition 3.

Monetarism I rests on the distinction between the short-run and the long-run Phillips curves; for monetarism II not even a short-run Phillips curve exists. The main difference between the two schools is that monetarism I allows for short-run adjustment processes in which the commodity and labor markets may not be in equilibrium, whereas monetarism II assumes that there is not just a tendency toward long-run equilibrium but a continuous sequence of equilibria. A change in the rate of growth of the money supply can be divided into a systematic part (correctly anticipated by the agents) and an unexpected "surprise" part. A change in the systematic part increases the expected rate of inflation and simultaneously the actual rate of inflation. It does not affect real variables such as the rate of unemployment or output. Systematic monetary policy does not matter.

According to the rational expectations approach, proposition 3 of the monetarist program has to be changed as follows. Monetary policy has real effects but they are caused by the unpredictable component of the money supply and therefore cannot be used by a systematic economic policy. With this modification of proposition 3, the authors of the rational expectations school might be considered as espousing monetarism II.

According to monetarism I, changes in the rate of growth of the money supply are not neutral in the short run, even if they are fully anticipated. As long as the expectations adjustment process is not terminated, the rate of unemployment and output deviate from their "natural" levels. According to monetarism II, changes in the rate of growth of the money supply that are correctly anticipated are neutral even in the short run.

The first part of the following presentation of monetarist inflation theory concerns a question posed by Friedman: How in the short run is a monetary impulse divided into an impact on inflation and an impact on real economic activity or output? Then follows an analysis of Friedman's variant of monetarist inflation theory, as formulated in 1970 and 1971 in the two papers mentioned at the beginning of the chapter. The core of the entire chapter, however, is the formulation and specification of the standard model of monetarism Mark I.

The transition from monetarism I to monetarism II is accomplished easily. As will be shown in Section 4.5 the well-known results of the rational expectations approach can be derived by changing the monetarist standard model in two respects:

1. By introducing rational expectations instead of adaptive expectations
2. By modifying the Okun curve

The last part of this chapter concerns the monetarist theory of the open economy. The monetary approach to the balance-of-payments theory, which principally R. Mundell (1971) and H.G. Johnson (1972b) developed, focuses on the model of a small, open economy that is linked to the world economy through the balance of payments. In contrast to the monetarist theory of the closed economy, this model stresses that an increase in the domestic money supply does not raise the domestic rate of inflation but leads to a deterioration in the balance of payments (current account balance). However, the monetary approach supersedes the model of the single economy and sketches a theory of world inflation, according to which changes in the world price level depend on changes in the world money supply. In contrast to Friedman's version, this "worldwide quantity theory" is only an elementary theoretical formulation.

4.1 The division of a monetary impulse into an inflation and an output effect

The question of how a change in nominal income is apportioned between an inflation effect and an output effect is a central problem of short-run macroeconomic analysis. In this context Friedman wrote:

> The key need is for a theory to explain
> a. The short-run division of a change in nominal income between prices and output
> b. The short-run adjustment of nominal income to a change in autonomous variables
> c. The transition between this short-run situation and a long-run equilibrium described essentially by the quantity-theory model [1970a, p. 223].

Although Friedman certainly stressed the problem anew, Keynes had already concerned himself with it. Keynes considered the division of a change in nominal income into ΔP and ΔX as the central problem. He stated: "The sum of elasticities of price and output in response to changes in effective demand . . . is equal to unity. Effective demand spends itself, partly in affecting output and partly in affecting price, according to this law" (Keynes, 1936, p. 285).

For the analysis of the short run, Friedman suggested the following linearized hypothesis:

$$\pi = \pi^* + \alpha(y - y^*) + \gamma(\log X - \log X^*) \tag{1}$$

$$x = x^* + (1 - \alpha)(y - y^*) - \gamma(\log X - \log X^*) \tag{2}$$

Lowercase letters represent the relative changes in the respective variables; capital letters, the levels. The two equations are a linearized approach to a portrayal of the effect of a monetary impulse (deviation of the rate of growth of nominal GNP from the expected rate) on the rate of inflation and on the rate of real growth. According to these equations, the deviation of the nominal rate of growth from the expected rate $(y - y^*)$ raises both the rate of inflation (through the coefficient α) and the rate of growth in real GNP (through the coefficient $1 - \alpha$). Either relationship X/X^* or $\log X - \log X^*$ can be interpreted as a "capacity index." If X/X^* exceeds unity ($\log X - \log X^* > 0$), the index expresses overutilization of the available capacity (overtime or depreciation of the stock of fixed capital), which reduces real growth [equation (2)] and accelerates inflation [equation (1)]. In contrast, an index value less than unity denotes excess capacity, which slows the inflation rate and accelerates real growth, given a positive nominal growth impulse $(y - y^* > 0)$.

In the following discussion we define X^*, the level of real GNP at which capacity is fully utilized, as the full-employment level of real GNP. Viewed from the demand side, $X/X^* > 1$ implies excess demand in the system.

Equations (1) and (2) may also be used to portray the quantity theory and the simple Keynesian model. The latter may be reduced to the assumption that every change in nominal income raises real income exclusively as long as real income lies *below* its full-employment level $(X < X^*)$. This corresponds to the following specification of the parameters: $\alpha = 0$ and $\gamma = 0$. Finally, one can let the expectation of inflation be constant under Keynes's own assumption that the price level remains constant in underemployment or that the expected rate of inflation π^* is zero. If the full-employment boundary is reached or exceeded $(X \geq X^*)$, then the parameters α and γ assume the values specified by the quantity theory ($\alpha = 1$ and $\gamma = \infty$).

In his comment on Friedman's work, J. Tobin pointed out that equation (1) may also be interpreted as a Phillips curve. With the aid of the identities $y = x + \pi$ and $y^* = x^* + \pi^*$, equation (1) can be written as the Phillips relationship:

$$\pi = \pi^* + \frac{\alpha}{1 - \alpha} (x - x^*) + \frac{\gamma}{1 - \alpha} (\log X - \log X^*) \tag{3}$$

With respect to this specification, Tobin remarked: "The variable $x - x^*$ is related to the change in unemployment and the variable

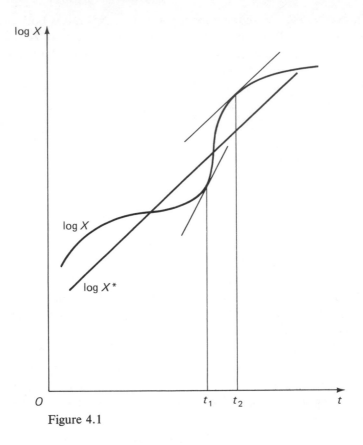

Figure 4.1

log X/X^* to its level. That the long-run Phillips curve is vertical is ensured by entering the expected price change π^* with the coefficient 1, X^* corresponds to the natural rate of unemployment'' (1974, p. 84).

In the context of Friedman's specification of the Phillips curve, both an overutilization of capacity [the extent of excess demand $(\log X - \log X^*)$] and an unanticipated acceleration of the rate of real growth $(x - x^*)$ raise the rate of inflation. Figure 4.1 illustrates this relationship in two situations. For example, at t_2 there is excess demand, while the actual rate of real growth corresponds to the anticipated rate. In contrast, at t_1 a recession prevails; the actual level of real GNP lies below the full-employment level ($X > X^*$). The actual rate of real growth exceeds the anticipated rate (slope of the X curve), however, so that the acceleration effect produces inflationary pressure.

4.2 Okun's law and the Phillips curve

Okun's law links Friedman's specification of the Phillips curve with the original Phillips curve. It describes the short-run relationship between the GNP gap and the unemployment rate. Okun's law maintains the existence of a negative relationship between the deviation of the unemployment rate from the natural rate and the deviation of actual real income from potential real income (the GNP gap). This empirical relationship developed by A.M. Okun (1970, 1974) was stated as follows:

$$u = u^* - a\left(\frac{X - X^*}{X^*}\right)$$

where $a > 0$ is a constant term, u and u^* are the actual and natural rates of unemployment, X is the actual real income, and X^* is the potential real income.

Okun's estimate of parameter a for the United States was approximately 0.3. Okun's law states that if the actual real output is greater than the potential real output by 1 percent, then the rate of unemployment falls 0.3 percentage points below the natural rate u^*.

Okun's original formula is used in this model in a modified form. We rewrite Okun's law as a relationship between the rate of unemployment and the rate of growth of real income. This is not exactly identical with the original formulation but it captures the essence of the law.

Figure 4.2 is a graph of Okun's law. The Okun equation is

$$u - u_{-1} = -a(x - x^*)$$

On the abcissa is the expected rate of real growth x^*. If the actual rate of growth exceeds the expected rate (distance AB in Figure 4.2), then the actual unemployment rate u_0 falls below the rate

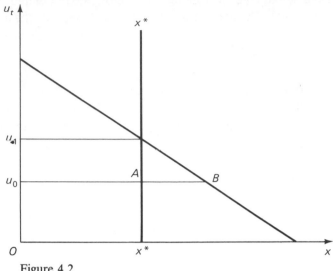

Figure 4.2

u_{-1}, which prevails when real growth is perfectly anticipated ($x = x^*$).

Finally, we can combine Okun's law with the Phillips curve to derive a characterization suited to the approach of Friedman. To do so, we use the Phillips curve in its natural rate form:

$$\pi = \pi^* - b(u - u^*)$$ (Phillips curve, natural rate of unemployment hypothesis) (1)

$$u - u_{-1} = -a(x - x^*)$$ (Okun's law) (2)

Substituting Okun's law into the Phillips curve, the following expression results, the Phillips–Okun curve:

$$\pi = \pi^* + ab(x - x^*) - b(u_{-1} - u^*)$$ (3)

The Phillips–Okun curve has the characteristics demanded by Friedman. The inflation rate is explained by the expectations of inflation π^*, the unexpected acceleration of real growth ($x - x^*$), and the level of excess demand, expressed here by the deviation

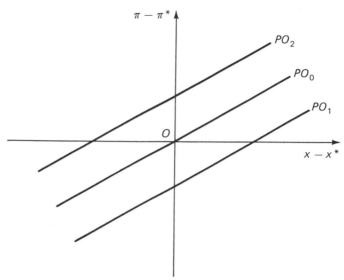

Figure 4.3

of the unemployment rate from its natural rate lagged one period
$(u_{-1} - u^*)$.

Figure 4.3 graphs the Phillips–Okun curve. It is easy to see that
the slope of the PO curve is greater, the greater are coefficients a
and b. If we assume that excess demand at time $t - 1 = 0$, and
therefore that the unemployment rate $u_{-1} = u^*$, then the deviation of the inflation rate from the anticipated rate is proportional
to the deviation of the rate of real growth from the trend rate of
growth (PO_0 in Figure 4.3). PO_1 represents the Phillips–Okun
curve for a given excess supply $(u_{-1} - u^* > 0)$; PO_2, for a given
excess demand $(u_{-1} - u^* < 0)$.

The long-run equilibrium condition or the steady-state condition is characterized by two properties:

    i. $x = x^*$
    ii. $u = u_{-1} = u^*$

that is, the real economy is growing at the expected rate x^* and
the unemployment rate has reached its natural level u^*. Assump-

tions i and ii further imply that $\pi = \pi^*$. One can say, therefore, that in a long-run equilibrium, the unemployment rate has reached its natural level and remains constant, while all actual variables correspond to their expected values.

The short-run equilibrium is characterized by property i alone or by $x = x^*$. This implies that Okun's law is suspended so that the unemployment rate does not change. Property ii is not required for a short-run equilibrium. In the short run, therefore, u can be greater, less than, or equal to u^*, because π is greater, less than, or equal to π^*.

4.3 From the quantity theory to the monetary theory of nominal income

Friedman has devoted a major part of his scientific work to a revitalization of the quantity theory. He introduced a new conception of the quantity theory in his "Restatement" (1956) by interpreting it as a macroeconomic demand for money function. Fifteen years later, under the pressure of his critics, he developed in his two articles "A Theoretical Framework for Monetary Analysis" (1970a) and "A Monetary Theory of Nominal Income" (1971) a more general formulation of his monetarist model. In these articles Friedman attempted to develop a new approach to macroeconomics, which he called a "third way" between the "classical" quantity theory and the Keynesian model.

In the discussion of the difference between his third path and the other two conceptions of macroeconomics, Friedman used a simple model, which we reproduce here in a linear form. The Friedman model consists of a real and a monetary sector.

Real sector:

$$\frac{C}{P} = c \cdot \frac{Y}{P} \qquad \text{(consumption function)} \qquad (1)$$

$$\frac{I}{P} = A - ar \qquad \text{(investment function)} \qquad (2)$$

$$\frac{Y}{P} = \frac{C}{P} + \frac{I}{P} \qquad \text{(equilibrium condition in the goods market)} \qquad (3)$$

Monetary sector:

$$M^D = P \cdot [k\frac{Y}{P} - lr] \qquad \text{(demand for money)} \qquad (4)$$

$$M^S = \bar{M} \qquad \text{(money supply)} \qquad (5)$$

$$M^S = M^D \qquad \text{(equilibrium condition in} \\ \text{the money market)} \qquad (6)$$

The model is self-explanatory. The real sector consists of a simplified consumption function [equation (1)], in which real consumption C/P is proportional to real income Y/P. Real investment has an autonomous part A (equal to private and state investment independent of the interest rate) and a component lr that is dependent on the rate of interest. Equation (3) expresses the equilibrium condition in the goods market. The "planned" real expenditures for consumption and investment equal the real national income. One can also express this condition in the usual form, $S/P = I/P$, or planned saving equals planned investment, insofar as one recalls that $(Y - C)/P = S/P$ [equation (3)]. The variables C, I, and Y are nominal; if deflated by the price level P, they express real magnitudes.

The monetary sector comprises the demand for money, which itself consists of two components: the demand for transactions balances, expressed by $k(Y/P)$, and the demand for speculative balances lr.

Transactions balances expand in proportion to real national income; speculative balances are the interest-sensitive part of the demand for money. With rising market interest rates, the opportunity costs of holding money balances increase and the demand for money falls. According to equation (5), the supply of money is exogenous; in other words, it is determined by the central bank. Finally, equation (6) conveys the equilibrium condition in the money market.

Note that this model has six equations and seven unknowns (C, I, Y, P, M^D, M^S, r) and is therefore underdetermined. To Friedman this presents the problem of a missing equation. The difference among the quantity theory, the Keynesian model, and the "third way" reduces to the specification of an additional relationship through which one of the variables is determined outside the model.

We combine equations (1), (2), and (3) of the real sector and obtain the expression

$$\frac{Y}{P} = A + c\frac{Y}{P} - ar \tag{7}$$

Equation (7) denotes all combinations of Y/P and r at which the goods market is in equilibrium. This is the well-known IS curve.

If we combine equations (4), (5), and (6) of the monetary sector, the so-called LM curve results:

$$\frac{\bar{M}}{P} = k\frac{Y}{P} - lr \tag{8}$$

The LM curve consists of all combinations of real income Y/P and the rate of interest r at which the supply of money is equal to the demand for money.[3]

Friedman's "simple" system can therefore be reduced to the IS and LM curves with the unknowns Y, P, and r. Usually the IS and LM curves are presented in the following forms:[4]

$$r = \frac{A}{a} - \frac{1-c}{a} \cdot \frac{Y}{P} \quad \text{(IS curve)}$$

$$r = \frac{k}{l} \cdot \frac{Y}{P} - \frac{1}{l} \cdot \frac{\bar{M}}{P} \quad \text{(LM curve)}$$

By means of these two equations we can now discuss the macroeconomic concepts cited at the start of the chapter.

[3] For a more elaborated discussion of the IS-LM model, see such standard textbooks as Dornbusch and Fischer (1978) and Gordon (1978).
[4] The reader can compare the following discussion of the Friedman model and the debate surrounding it with Teigen (1972) and Laidler (1971).

The quantity theory

The classical quantity theory provides as the missing equation the determination of real income:

$$\frac{Y}{P} = X_0 \qquad X_0 \text{ is exogenous} \tag{9}$$

According to Friedman, in the quantity-theory approach real national income is determined outside the system presented in equations (1) through (6) – namely, through the Walrasian system of supply and demand equations as well as market equilibrium conditions. In simpler terms, we can say that with perfectly flexible prices and wages, the assumption behind equation (9) is that the labor market is always in equilibrium. X_0 is therefore the full-employment or equilibrium level of real income.

If the level of real income is predetermined, then the model based on the quantity theory can be solved recursively. We derive the equilibrium rate of interest r_0 from the IS curve [equation (10)] and the price level P_0 from the LM curve [equation (11)].

$$r_0 = \frac{A}{a} - \frac{1-c}{a} X_0 \tag{10}$$

$$P_0 = \frac{\bar{M}}{kX_0 - lr_0} = \frac{\text{nominal money supply}}{\text{demand for real cash balances}} \tag{11}$$

While the market rate of interest is determined in the goods sector of the economy – namely, through the IS curve – the supply and demand for money determine the price level, as shown by equation (11). The quantity-theory approach therefore expresses the classical dichotomy of the price system. Relative prices, including the rate of interest, are determined in the real sector of the system; the price level, in contrast, is set by the relationship of money supply to money demand. The classical quantity equation is obtained by a simple transformation of equation (11) and the use of the definition of the velocity of money:

$$V = \frac{X_0}{kX_0 - lr_0}$$

$$\bar{M} = P(kX_0 - lr_0)\frac{X_0}{X_0} = PX_0\frac{1}{V} \tag{12}$$

$$P = \frac{\bar{M}V}{X_0} \tag{13}$$

In the quantity-theory model (or classical system), therefore, the price level is determined by the quantity of money, with the velocity V constant.

The Keynesian approach

According to Friedman the Keynesian approach may be characterized by the assumption that the price level is determined outside the system. It is either historically given or determined by the institutional structure of the economic system (Friedman, 1974, p. 32). The Keynesian variant of the solution to the problem of the missing equation is therefore

$$P = P_0 \tag{14}$$

The number of equations again corresponds to the number of unknowns. This system exhibits no dichotomy; instead, all variables are determined simultaneously. In this model, both real income and the interest rate are affected by changes in the money supply and/or autonomous expenditures.

If we substitute equation (14) for price-level determination into equations (7) and (8) and solve for r, we obtain the equations for the IS and LM curves as originally developed by Hicks (1937, pp. 147–59).

$$r = \frac{A}{a} - \frac{1-c}{a}\left(\frac{Y}{P_0}\right) \qquad \text{(IS curve)} \tag{15}$$

$$r = \frac{k}{l}\left(\frac{Y}{P_0}\right) - \frac{1}{l}\left(\frac{\bar{M}}{P_0}\right) \qquad \text{(LM curve)} \tag{16}$$

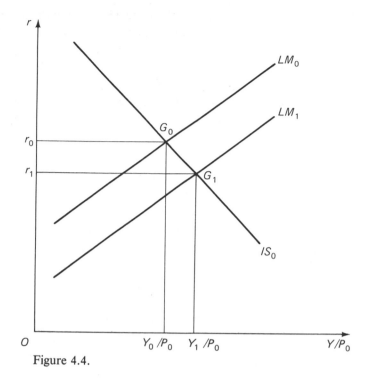

Figure 4.4.

Together the two equations determine the rate of interest r and the level of real income Y/P_0.

Figure 4.4 depicts the solution graphically. One can see the IS and LM curves as well as the equilibrium point $G_0(r_0, Y_0/P_0)$.

An increase in the money supply M and/or a decline in the price level P_0 (in other words, an increase in the real money supply M/P_0) shifts the LM curve to the right to LM_1. This leads to a decline in the market rate of interest r and an increase in real income (equilibrium point G_1). The Keynesian transmission mechanism proceeds as follows: The increase in real cash balances M/P lowers the rate of interest, thus inducing, via the investment function, an increase in investment, which in turn leads to an increase in real income.

If autonomous expenditures A (autonomous investment or government expenditures) increase, then the IS curve shifts to the right, while the LM curve retains its original position. The new equilibrium point (not shown in the figure) is characterized by a higher level of real income and a higher rate of interest. Since the supply of money remains constant during the increase in A, the rate of interest must increase, so that speculative balances will be reduced and transactions balances can rise.

Friedman's "third way"

Friedman's solution to the problem of the missing equation is to introduce an interest rate equation by which the rate of interest is predetermined. From elements of the Keynesian theory of interest as well as the theory of Irving Fisher, Friedman developed the following interest rate equation (Friedman, 1971, pp. 323–37):

$$r = \rho^* + \pi^* \tag{17}$$

The nominal rate of interest r is explained through the anticipated real rate of interest ρ^* and the anticipated rate of inflation π^*. If we consider the identity

$$y^* = \pi^* + x^* \tag{18}$$

We can also write the interest rate equation in another way:

$$r = \rho^* + (y^* - x^*) \tag{19}$$

or

$$r = (\rho^* - x^*) + y^* \tag{19'}$$

Friedman specifically assumed

$$\rho^* - x^* = k_0 \tag{20}$$

The difference between the anticipated real rate of interest and the anticipated rate of real growth is constant. In the following discussion Friedman's interest rate equation therefore takes the form:

$$r = k_0 + y^* \tag{21}$$

The interest rate is presented as the sum of a constant and the expected rate of growth of nominal income, a variable not explained in the model. This interest rate equation plays the same role in Friedman's third way as does the price-determination equation in the Keynesian model or the determination of real income in the quantity-theory approach.

It is Friedman's explicit intention to formulate solely a monetary theory of nominal income and not to explain further its price and real income components. In this regard he said: "This third way involves bypassing the breakdown of nominal income between real income and prices and using the quantity theory to derive a theory of nominal income rather than a theory of either prices or real income" (Friedman, 1971, p. 323).

Friedman's monetary theory of nominal income considers only the monetary sector of the basic model, which is further modified in the following ways:

$$M^D = Y \cdot l(r) \qquad l'(r) < 0 \qquad \text{(money demand)} \qquad (22)$$

$$M^S = M(t) \qquad \text{(money supply)} \qquad (23)$$

$$M^D = M^S \qquad \text{(equilibrium condition)} \qquad (24)$$

$$r = k_0 + y^* \qquad \text{(interest rate equation)} \qquad (21)$$

where M^D is the nominal demand for money, M^S is the nominal supply of money, and Y is the nominal income.

$$y^* = \left(\frac{dY}{dt} \cdot \frac{1}{Y}\right)^* \qquad \text{(expected rate of growth of nominal income)}$$

$$y = \frac{dY}{dt} \cdot \frac{1}{Y} \qquad \text{(rate of growth of nominal income)}$$

$$m = \frac{dM}{dt} \cdot \frac{1}{M} \qquad \text{(rate of growth of the money stock)}$$

Equation (22), the money demand function, implies an income elasticity of unity.[5] The desired coefficient of nominal money

---

[5] The income elasticity of the demand for money can be written as $\eta_{M,Y} = (dM/dY)(Y/M)$. From equation (22) it follows that $dM/dY = l(r)$, so that $\eta_{M,Y} = l(r) \cdot (Y/M) = [l(r)]/[l(r)] = 1$.

balances with respect to nominal income, $l(r)$, varies inversely with the rate of interest r.

According to equation (23) the supply of money is exogenous. All endogenous and exogenous variables are functions of time.

Equations (22), (23), and (24) may be combined to produce the following representation of nominal income:

$$Y(t) = \frac{M(t)}{l(r)} \tag{25}$$

or

$$Y(t) = M(t) \cdot V(r) \tag{25'}$$

where $V(r) = 1/l(r)$; that is, the income velocity of money equals the reciprocal of the cash balance coefficient. Together with the interest rate equation (21), equation (25) or (25′) determines at each time t the value of nominal income.

Friedman hesitates to apply his interest rate equation (21) to the real sector because it implies a constant real rate of interest (more exactly, a constant difference between the real rate of interest and the real rate of growth).

Since the demand for money is principally determined by the rate of inflation and by real income, the hypothesis of a constant real rate of interest hardly harms the working of the monetary sector. In the goods sector, however, such an assumption excludes a central economic determinant of saving and investment behavior. Friedman therefore limited his analysis to the formulation of a monetary theory of nominal income and considers the "saving-investment sector as unfinished business" (1974, p. 40). In this way he partially retracts his assertion to develop a theory that shows how a monetary impulse can be apportioned into an inflation effect and a real growth effect.

Friedman's third way has not escaped criticism. In his comment on Friedman's solution, Tobin pointed to unexpected properties of the model. If one increases government expenditures (parameter A on the IS curve), real income rises by the full amount of the multiplier effect, since the interest rate in the IS curve equation is fixed by means of the interest rate equation. In contrast, if one increases the supply of money M, the IS curve remains unchanged, as does the LM curve (since the rate of interest and real income are fixed). The price level therefore increases pari passu with M, so that real cash balances are unaffected. An increase in the money supply therefore produces only inflation and no real effects. Thus Friedman's model, according to Tobin, is paradoxically "ultra-Keynesian" in the sense that fiscal policy alone (a change in government expenditures) affects output and employment, whereas monetary policy is 100 percent ineffective in this respect (Tobin, 1974, pp. 77–89).

The monetary theory of nominal income: some dynamic implications

Friedman converted equations (21) and (25) into a dynamic system into which he also introduced an expectations adjustment process. Through the total differentiation of equation (25) and the division of both sides of the equation by Y, we obtain the following expression for the rate of growth of nominal income:

$$\frac{dY}{Y} = \frac{1}{V} \frac{dV}{dr} \frac{dr}{dt} + \frac{dM}{M} \tag{26}$$

From the interest rate equation (21) we can get an expression for the change in the rate of interest as a function of time:

$$\frac{dr_t}{dt} = \frac{dy_t^*}{dt} \tag{27}$$

where y_t^* is the expected rate of change of nominal income.

If the relative change of velocity $(dV/dr)(1/V) = \mu$, then

$$\frac{dY}{Y} = \mu \frac{d}{dt} y_t^* + \frac{dM}{M} \tag{28}$$

The above-mentioned expectations adjustment process is specified so that the change in the expected rate of growth of nominal income is proportional to the deviation of the observed from the anticipated rate of growth.

$$\frac{d}{dt} y_t^* = \beta(y_t - y_t^*) \tag{29}$$

In this fashion one obtains the following "dynamic" formulation of the monetary theory of nominal income:

$$\frac{dY}{Y} = \left(\frac{dY}{Y}\right)^* + \frac{1}{1 - \beta\mu}\left[\frac{dM}{M} - \left(\frac{dY}{Y}\right)^*\right] \tag{30}$$

As Claassen (1972) emphasized, equation (30) can be called the basic equation for the short-run monetarist theory of nominal income.

Under the assumption of stability ($0 < \beta\mu < 1$), the following interpretations result:

a. If the economic system is in a long-run equilibrium, the quantity of money grows at the same rate as expected nominal income, which in turn equals the rate of growth of actual nominal income. In the steady state all three rates of growth are therefore equal:

$$y_t^* = y_t = m_t$$

b. If the exogenously determined rate of growth of the money supply exceeds the anticipated rate of growth of nominal income, then the actual rate of growth of nominal income will exceed the anticipated rate:

$$y_t - y_t^* > 0$$

c. In contrast, if the rate of growth of the money supply falls short of that of anticipated nominal income, then the rate of growth of actual nominal income will be less than that of anticipated nominal income:

$$y_t - y_t^* < 0$$

In each case an unanticipated change in the rate of growth of the money supply produces a discrepancy between the actual and the anticipated rates of growth of nominal income according to the multiplier $1/(1 - \mu\beta)$.

If we subtract the rate of growth of the money supply from both sides of equation (30) and substitute the relative change in velocity dV/V for $(dY/Y) - (dM/M)$, we get

$$\frac{dV}{V} = \frac{\mu\beta}{1 - \mu\beta} \left(\frac{dM}{M} - y_i^* \right) \tag{31}$$

In the long-run equilibrium characterized by $dM/M = y^*$, the income velocity of money remains constant. As $dM/M > y^*$ in the boom phase of the business cycle, the velocity increases. In the recession phase $(dM/M < y^*)$ the velocity declines. Friedman's model therefore brings out the procyclical behavior of the velocity of money.

One can conclude that Friedman has succeeded in providing a simple and elegant formulation of his monetary theory of nominal income. The content of his fundamental equation (30) may be summarized by two statements:

  a. In a long-run equilibrium, $y_t = y_i^* = m_t$; that is, the actual rate of growth of nominal income is equal to the anticipated rate and these are equal to the rate of growth of the money supply.
  b. The deviation of the actual rate of growth of nominal income from the anticipated rate $(y - y^*)$ is proportional to the difference between the rate of growth of the money supply and the rate of growth of anticipated nominal income.

Why does an unanticipated change in the rate of growth of the money supply produce a deviation in the rate of growth of nominal income from its anticipated trend rate of growth? The answer stems from the monetarist transmission mechanism whose macroeconomic foundations support the model. This mechanism sharply distinguishes between real and nominal cash balances (Friedman, 1969; Fand, 1970). In an equilibrium economic agents hold an optimal level of real cash balances $(M/P)^*$. If, through an unexpected change in the money supply (e.g., an increase), the actual level of real cash balances M/P deviates from the optimal or desired level $(M/P)^*$, economic agents will alter their expenditure behavior (Morgan, 1978, p. 83).

The excess supply of money appears as an excess demand for a broad spectrum of real assets, securities, investment goods, and consumer durables. This leads to an increase in the prices of goods and securities. The latter, of course, is equivalent to a decline in the effective yield of securities. In his theory of nominal income, Friedman does not further investigate the extent to which this excess demand produces inflation and output effects. The consequence of this expenditure process is that nominal income increases to the point where a new equilibrium at a higher level of nominal income is established at which the supply of money is again equal to the demand for money.

In contrast, the typical Keynesian transmission mechanism depends on effects unleashed by a change in the rate of interest in this model. An increase in the money supply (e.g., through open-market purchases of the central bank) leads to an increase in the price and a decrease in the effective yield of securities; in other words, it leads to a fall in the rate of interest. The higher prices of fixed-interest bonds and equities induce firms to expand their stock of real capital by issuing new securities (Tobin, 1961). Through the multiplier mechanism these additional investments raise aggregate demand and therefore national income. The major difference between the monetarist and the Keynesian transmission mechanisms concerns the effect of an increase in the supply of money on consumption expenditures. In the monetarist model an excess supply of money ($M/P > M^*/P$) leads directly to an increase in expenditures for both consumption and investment, whereas in the Keynesian mechanism an excess supply of money affects consumption expenditure only indirectly through the interest rate–investment multiplier mechanism (Morgan, 1978, p. 85).

In summary we can say that Friedman's monetarist theory of nominal income may be interpreted as a theory of long-run inflation. The long-run real rate of growth, "the secular or trend rate of growth" (Friedman, 1974, p. 36), is determined outside the system. An increase in the supply of money, therefore, raises only the rate of inflation in the long run, since the rate of real growth is predetermined. When the higher rate of inflation is finally anticipated, the system reaches a new steady state with a higher rate of monetary expansion but an unchanged rate of real growth. Friedman's model does not exclude that a change in the rate of growth of the money supply can have a *short-run* effect on the real variables of the system such as output and employment (acceleration theorem). However, this point of view is not developed further in the monetarist theory of nominal income. Although Friedman, in his article "A Theoretical Framework for Monetary Analysis" (1970a), designated the division of a monetary impulse into inflation and real growth effects as the central question of monetary theory, in his subsequent article "A Monetary Theory of Nominal Income" (1971) he reduced appreciably his objectives and confined himself to a theory of nominal income.

In the following section we will turn our attention to Friedman's original question concerning the division of a monetary impulse into inflation and real growth effects. We do this in the context of a standard monetarist model.

4.4 A monetarist model with a Phillips–Okun curve (monetarism Mark I)

We begin with the structure of a simple monetarist model, which we extend following the approach of J. Vanderkamp (1975).[6] The model consists of three components: the quantity equation, the Phillips curve, and Okun's law. The model belongs to the Friedman school of thought on the monetarist theory of inflation and, despite its simplicity, it contains all the essential properties and conclusions of the monetarist theory of inflation. Without exaggeration one may consider it the standard monetarist model of inflation. The model is monetarist because the rate of growth of the money supply determines the rate of inflation, while the Phillips curve connects the monetary sector with the real sector: "Ultimately the rate of monetary expansion determines the rate of inflation in this model, but the Phillips curve plays a very important role in the adjustment process" (Vanderkamp, 1975, p. 120).

[6] A similar approach is used by R. Dornbusch (1975) and H. König (1978). A modified version can be found in Dornbusch and Fischer (1978, pp. 390–434).

The monetarist theory of inflation differs from the classical quantity theory through the introduction of the Phillips curve and Okun's law. A monetary impulse (i.e., an unexpected increase in the rate of growth of the money supply[7]) raises the actual rate of real growth above the anticipated rate, leading to a reduction in the unemployment rate (Okun's law). The reduced rate of unemployment in turn leads to an increase in the rate of inflation via the Phillips curve. That increase corresponds exactly to the difference between the rate of expansion of the money supply and the rate of real growth (weighted by the income elasticity of money demand). The quantity theory and the monetarist theory of inflation have only this last principle in common. In contrast, the monetary theory of inflation is characterized by the linkage of the quantity equation with the real sector of the economy through the Phillips curve and Okun's law.

In the discussion of the model, Vanderkamp's instructive graphic exhibition is largely used, but it is extended and made more precise. The model consists of three linear equations and three unknowns: the rate of real growth x_t, the rate of inflation π_t, and the rate of unemployment u_t.

$$m_t = x_t + \pi_t \qquad \text{(quantity equation)} \qquad (1)$$

$$\pi_t = \pi_t^* - b(u_t - u^*) \qquad \begin{array}{l}\text{(linearized version of the}\\ \text{Phillips curve with the}\\ \text{natural rate hypothesis)}\end{array} \qquad (2)$$

$$u_t - u_{t-1} = -a(x_t - x^*) \qquad \text{(Okun's law)} \qquad (3)$$

The endogenous variables are: x_t, the rate of growth of real income; π_t, the rate of inflation; and u_t, the rate of unemployment (in percent). The exogenous variables are: m_t, the rate of growth of the nominal money supply; π_t^*, the anticipated rate of inflation; x_t^*, the trend (anticipated) rate of real growth; u^*, the natural rate of unemployment; and u_{t-1}, the rate of unemployment lagged one period.

[7] More exactly, a positive monetary impulse occurs when the rate of growth of the money supply exceeds the sum of the anticipated rate of inflation and the anticipated rate of real economic growth $[m - (x^* + \pi^*) > 0]$.

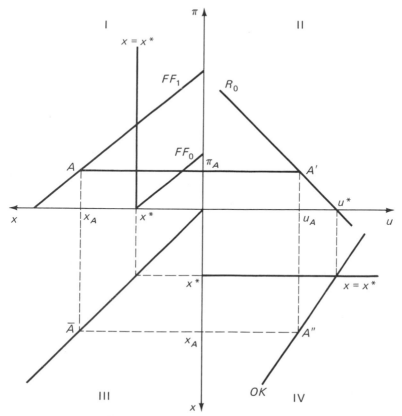

Figure 4.5

The model has three equations and three unknowns – namely, x_t, π_t, and u_t. Vanderkamp provided a geometric solution of the model, which is reproduced in Figures 4.5 and 4.6. In each figure the two upper quadrants show Vanderkamp's presentation; the lower half is added to show Okun's law and its role in the adjustment process.

We begin with the upper right-hand quadrant of the system. In the (π, u) space the function R_0 graphs a linear Phillips curve given fixed inflationary expectations ($\pi^* = 0$) [equation (2)]. The intersection of the Phillips curve with the abscissa denotes the

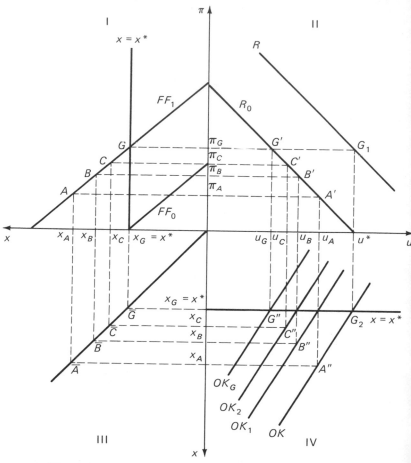

Figure 4.6

natural rate of unemployment u^*. In the upper left-hand quadrant the rate of real growth x is on the abscissa and the rate of inflation π is on the ordinate. Note that the variable x increases as one moves to the left along the abscissa. In this quadrant we find a graphic representation of equation (1), namely, the quantity equation expressed in terms of rates of growth. Lines FF_0 and FF_1 show equation (1) for two different values of the rate of growth of the money supply m_0 and m_1. Each point along the FF line shows a possible combination of π and x for a given rate of growth of nominal expenditures. Finally, the vertical line $x = x^*$ denotes the constant equilibrium rate of real GNP, which results from the rate of growth of employment and labor productivity.

The lower right-hand quadrant contains a graphic presentation of Okun's law. It is the same as Figure 4.2 with the coordinates rotated by 90 degrees. The line OK shows the Okun curve in the initial situation. It denotes the rates of unemployment that correspond to the alternative rates of real growth. Since the Okun curve brings out a first-order difference equation, it shifts (to the left in the graph) when the rate of unemployment declines because of an unanticipated increase in the rate of real growth (e.g., the distance $\overline{x_A x^*}$ in Figure 4.5). The lower left-hand quadrant transfers the x values through a mirror mapping from the first to the fourth quadrant.

The short-run adjustment process

In this monetarist system we discuss the effects of an increase in the money supply or, more precisely, the effects of an increase in the rate of growth of the money supply. The starting point is a steady state with the following properties:

$$x_t = x_{t-1} = x^*$$
$$\pi_t = \pi_t^* = 0$$
$$u_t = u_{t-1} = u^*$$

In both Figures 4.5 and 4.6 this corresponds to the points x^* on the x coordinate and u^* on the u coordinate. The constant rate of growth of the money supply m_0 (represented by the FF_0 line) is fully used to finance the real growth of the economy x^*. The rate of unemployment corresponds to the natural rate u^*, the intersection of R_0 with the abscissa. The Phillips curve R_0 is valid under the special assumption that the expected rate of inflation π^* is zero.

What happens then when money accelerates, that is, when the

rate of growth of the money supply increases from m_0 to m_1? The following analysis describes the short-run adjustments that occur in this system through an interaction of the change in the money supply, the Phillips curve, and Okun's law. "Short-run" means that during the adjustment processes, *no* change in inflationary expectations takes place.

We begin with the upper left-hand quadrant of Figure 4.5, the monetary system. The *FF* line shifts from FF_0 to FF_1 as a result of the increase in the rate of monetary expansion. The first-round effect is an increase in the rate of real growth to x_A (above the steady-state rate x^*), a reduction in the rate of unemployment to u_A, and an increase in the rate of inflation to π_A. In Figure 4.5 points A on the FF_1 line, A' on the Phillips curve, and A'' on the Okun curve *OK* correspond to this situation.

Let us consider the first round in more detail: The monetary acceleration, the shift of the FF_0 line to FF_1, has produced an unanticipated acceleration in the rate of real growth (real expenditure) to the extent $x_A - x^*$. The latter is reflected onto the abscissa of the fourth quadrant and results in point A'' along the Okun curve *OK* corresponding to an unemployment rate u_A. In the second quadrant the reduced rate of unemployment leads through the Phillips curve to a positive rate of inflation – namely, π_A. In the first quadrant point A on the FF_1 line shows the division of the rate of growth of nominal expenditures into a real component x_A and an inflation component π_A. This concludes the first-round effect.

Let us repeat this analysis algebraically. We begin with the structural form of the model.

$$m_t = x_t + \pi_t \qquad \text{(quantity equation)} \qquad (1)$$

$$\pi_t = \pi^* - b(u_t - u^*) \qquad \text{(Phillips curve)} \qquad (2)$$

$$u_t - u_{t-1} = -a(x_t - x^*) \qquad \text{(Okun's law)} \qquad (3)$$

In this model the variables π_t, x_t, and u_t are endogenous (explained by the model) and m_t, x^*, π^*, u^*, and u_{t-1} are exogenous.

With the following operation the model is transformed into its reduced-form version, in which each endogenous variable is expressed as a function of the exogenous variables of the system. We rewrite equations (1), (2), and (3) in the following way:

$$(x_t - x^*) + \pi_t = m - x^* \tag{4}$$

$$\pi_t + bu_t = \pi^* + bu^* \tag{5}$$

$$a(x_t - x^*) + u_t = u_{t-1} \tag{6}$$

This system may be written in matrix form as

$$\begin{bmatrix} 1 & 1 & 0 \\ 0 & 1 & b \\ a & 0 & 1 \end{bmatrix} \begin{bmatrix} x_t - x^* \\ \pi_t \\ u_t \end{bmatrix} = \begin{bmatrix} 1 & 0 & 0 & 0 \\ 0 & 1 & b & 0 \\ 0 & 0 & 0 & 1 \end{bmatrix} \begin{bmatrix} m - x^* \\ \pi^* \\ u^* \\ u_{t-1} \end{bmatrix}$$

$$\begin{bmatrix} x_t - x^* \\ \pi_t \\ u_t \end{bmatrix}$$

$$= \frac{1}{1 + ab} \begin{bmatrix} 1 & -1 & b \\ ab & 1 & -b \\ -a & a & 1 \end{bmatrix} \begin{bmatrix} 1 & 0 & 0 & 0 \\ 0 & 1 & b & 0 \\ 0 & 0 & 0 & 1 \end{bmatrix} \begin{bmatrix} m - x^* \\ \pi^* \\ u^* \\ u_{t-1} \end{bmatrix}$$

This gives the reduced-form version of the monetarist model:

$$x_t = x^* + \frac{1}{1 + ab}(m - x^* - \pi^*) + \frac{b}{1 + ab}(u_{t-1} - u^*) \tag{7}$$

$$\pi_t = \pi^* + \frac{ab}{1 + ab}(m - x^* - \pi^*) - \frac{b}{1 + ab}(u_{t-1} - u^*) \tag{8}$$

$$u_t = u^* - \frac{a}{1 + ab}(m - x^* - \pi^*) + \frac{1}{1 + ab}(u_{t-1} - u^*) \tag{9}$$

In the first round we start with $u_{t-1} = u^*$, so the last term in equations (7), (8), and (9) is zero. The monetary acceleration (i.e., the increase in the rate of growth of the money supply above the rate $x^* + \pi^*$) leads simultaneously to an increase in x_t and π_t and to a reduction in u_t. In the numerical example in Table 4.1 (p. 125), $a = 0.4$ and $b = 2$, so that the reduced-form parameters have the following values:

$$\frac{1}{1 + ab} = 0.56 \qquad \frac{ab}{1 + ab} = 0.44 \qquad \frac{a}{1 + ab} = 0.22$$

The monetary acceleration of 5 percent ($m - x^* = 5\%$) therefore alters the real rate of growth, the rate of inflation, as well as the rate of unemployment as follows:

$$\Delta(x - x^*) = 0.56 \times 5 = 2.8$$

$$\Delta\pi = 0.44 \times 5 = 2.2$$

$$\Delta u = -0.22 \times 5 = -1.1$$

In the first round the increase in the money supply increases the real rate of growth by 2.8 percent and the rate of inflation by 2.2 percent. At the same time the rate of unemployment falls by 1.1 percent. In Figure 4.5 points A on the FF_1 line, A' on the Phillips curve, and A'' on the Okun curve OK correspond to this situation.

The salient point now is that the situation is not stable. In the fourth quadrant the position of the Okun curve changes in the following period. The new unemployment rate is $u_{t-1} = u_A$, so that the new equation for Okun's law OK_1 is $u_t = u_A - a(x - x^*)$ and thus the curve shifts to the left in Figure 4.6, corresponding to the new distance along the ordinate $u = u_A$. Given the position of the Okun curve OK_1, the new representation of the monetarist system in Figure 4.6 is the rectangle $(B, B', B'', \bar{B})$.

The second round is characterized by a reduction of the growth differential to $x_B - x^*$ and an increased rate of inflation π_B (point B' in the second quadrant). Because the growth of the money supply remains constant, the increased inflation rate leads to a reduction in the rate of growth of the real economy to x_B (point B in the first quadrant) and, consequently, to the lower unemployment rate u_B. A further representation of the monetarist system is given by the rectangle $(C, C', C'', \bar{C})$ with the corresponding

Okun curve OK_2, where the constant term of the Okun curve is determined by the unemployment rate u_B. The movement from A' to G' proceeds along the Phillips curve with an increasing rate of inflation and a falling rate of unemployment. The corresponding movement from A to G on the FF_1 line shows the change in the components of the nominal rate of growth in favor of the rate of inflation. The dynamics of this adjustment process are determined by the shift of the Okun curve. As long as the Okun curve is shifting to the left, no equilibrium is possible, since both the rate of inflation and the rate of unemployment are changing. The Okun curve will keep shifting as long as there is a positive difference $x - x^*$ (e.g., the distances $\overline{x_A x^*}, \ldots, \overline{x_C x^*}$) in Figure 4.6 or, in other words, as long as the rate of real growth continues to exhibit an unexpected acceleration.

We now examine points G, G', G'', and $\bar{G}$ in Figure 4.6. From the first quadrant we can determine the components of nominal income growth (x_G, π_G). The graph shows that $x_G - x^* = 0$, so there is no unexpected acceleration in the rate of growth. In the fourth quadrant G'' lies at the intersection of the Okun curve OK_G and the line $x = x^*$, so that at this point Okun's law is no longer in effect and thus the line OK_G remains stable. Point G'' represents an equilibrium point in the labor market and the corresponding rate of unemployment u_G does not change further.

The short-run equilibrium is characterized by the following three properties:

$$m_t = x^* + \pi_G$$

$$\pi_G = b(u^* - u_t)$$

$$u_t = u_G$$

If inflationary expectations are not revised, the Phillips curve remains stable and a short-run equilibrium prevails.

In the new equilibrium there is a higher rate of inflation π, a lower rate of unemployment u, but the same steady-state rate of real growth x^* as existed before the monetary impulse. The increase in the rate of growth of the money supply (growth in nomi-

nal expenditures) therefore leads to a temporary growth acceleration, which induces an increase in the inflation rate and a
decrease in real wages. In the new equilibrium, a higher rate of
inflation and the same rate of real growth prevail along with a
higher level of employment and a higher real GNP. This short-run
equilibrium can persist only until the expectations of inflation
(especially those reflected in money wages) adjust to the actual
rate of inflation.

The short-run adjustment process in the monetarist model can
be summarized as follows: A monetary impulse (i.e., a shift of the
FF line) leads simultaneously to an unexpected acceleration of
real growth, to an increase in the inflation rate, and to a decline in
the unemployment rate. In other words, a monetary impulse
leads to a real and an inflationary effect.

In the subsequent period the Okun curve shifts to intersect the
$x = x^*$ line at the unemployment rate of the previous period. As
long as there is a positive difference $x - x^*$ in the first quadrant,
the short-run adjustment process continues. As the adjustment
progresses, the growth differential $x - x^*$ disappears, the rate of
unemployment declines, and the rate of inflation rises. [Compare
the two representations of the system $(B, B', B'', \bar{B})$ and $(C, C',
C'', \bar{C})$ in Figure 4.6.]

For each rate of monetary expansion (m_0, m_1, etc.) one obtains
a different parallel *FF* line in the upper left-hand quadrant. The
intersection of the *FF* line with the $x = x^*$ line (e.g., point *G*) is
always an equilibrium point, which shows the actual rate of inflation – namely, $\pi = m - x^*$. In the upper right-hand quadrant one
obtains the corresponding point on the Phillips curve and thus the
corresponding rate of unemployment. "Thus, looking at one side
of the picture we obtain a perfect Phillips curve explanation of
inflation, while the other side gives us a fine quantity theory explanation of inflation" (Vanderkamp, 1975, p. 119).

The short-run adjustment process (a numerical example)

A numerical example will illustrate the short-run adjustment process. Assume the following parameter values for the

Table 4.1 (*in percent*)

t	$x_t - x^*$	π_t	π_t^*	u_t
0	0.0	0.0	0.0	3.5
1	2.8	2.2	0.0	2.4
2	1.5	3.5	0.0	1.8
3	0.9	4.1	0.0	1.4
4	0.5	4.5	0.0	1.2
5	0.3	4.7	0.0	1.1
6	0.1	4.9	0.0	1.1
7	0.0	5.0	0.0	1.0

three equations of the monetarist standard model:

Phillips curve: $b = 2$

Okun equation: $a = 0.4$

The starting point is a steady state with the following properties:

$$m = x^* = 3\% \quad \pi = \pi^* = 0 \quad u^* = 3.5\%$$

Now introduce the acceleration of the money supply discussed earlier. The rate of growth of the money supply increases from 3 to 8 percent per year, so that a monetary impulse of $m - x^* = 5$ percent results. Table 4.1 shows the short-run adjustments of the variables $x_t - x^*$, π_t, and u_t for the monetarist standard model.

The table reveals very clearly the developments of the monetarist model in the first round ($t = 1$). The subsequent adjustment is characterized by a continuous fall in the unanticipated growth differential ($x - x^*$) and a continuous rise in the inflation rate or, more precisely, in the unanticipated rate of inflation. In terms of the graph of the system in Figure 4.6, we move upward along the Phillips curve so that the unemployment rate falls step by step until $u = 1$ percent (last column of Table 4.1).

With the parameters chosen, the system converges relatively quickly to a short-run equilibrium with two properties: The operation of Okun's law is suspended, and no adjustment in the expected rate of inflation has taken place. The parameters of the short-run equilibrium are

$$x = x^* = 3\% \quad m - x^* = \pi_G = 5\% \quad u_G = 1\%$$

The long-run equilibrium

Naturally expectations of inflation do not remain constant in the long run; they change according to the experience of economic agents regarding inflation. Let us assume that the process of expectation adjustment can be described by the model of adaptive expectations as in equation (10).

$$\pi_t^* - \pi_{t-1}^* = \theta(\pi_{t-1} - \pi_{t-1}^*) \qquad 0 < \theta < 1 \tag{10}$$

According to this equation the expected rate of inflation changes in proportion to the forecast error $\pi_{t-1} - \pi_{t-1}^*$.

In the long run the two propositions $\pi = \pi_G > 0$ and $\pi^* = 0$ cannot be valid simultaneously; in other words, the expected rate of inflation cannot remain zero if the actual rate of inflation π_G exceeds zero. This would imply inconsistent behavior by economic agents. According to the adaptive adjustment process described in equation (10), the expected rate of inflation π_t^* therefore starts to increase and keeps rising until $\pi^* = \pi_G$. In graphic terms this process of expectation adjustment implies a shift in the Phillips curve from R_0 to R, as we can see in Figure 4.6. In the new steady state there are no surprises and the actual values of the variables in the system correspond exactly with their anticipated values. Therefore, the following relationships are valid: From the first quadrant of Figure 4.6 we discern: (1) $x = x^*$ and (2) $\pi_G = m_1 - x^*$. In the upper right-hand quadrant we find the relationships (3) $\pi_G = \pi^*$ and (4) $u = u^*$ (point G_1 on the Phillips curve R). Finally, point G_2 on the original Okun curve OK is an equilibrium point that repeats the steady-state relationships (1) $x = x^*$ and (4) $u = u^*$.

The difference between the long-run equilibrium (G, G_1, G_2, $\bar{G}$) and the short-run equilibrium (G, G', G'', $\bar{G}$) arises from the fact that in the former both the unanticipated growth differential ($x - x^*$) and the real effect on the labor market have disappeared. As a result of the shift of the Phillips curve upward and to the right caused by the higher expected rate of inflation, the unemployment rate again increases until, at point G_2, the natural rate u^* again prevails. The shift in the Phillips curve also causes a shift in the Okun curve, a topic we will discuss in greater detail. In the long-run equilibrium the rate of inflation is fully anticipated and, as in the short-run equilibrium, is equal to the difference between the rate of expansion of the money supply and the rate of real growth x^*. This analysis shows that a monetary impulse (defined as a shift from FF_0 to FF_1) unleashes an unexpected growth acceleration that vanishes during a short-run adjustment process via the Okun equation. In the long-run adjustment process, which leads to a shift in the Phillips and Okun curves, the unemployment rate increases again to the natural rate.

The long-run adjustment process

So far we have compared two equilibrium positions, but now we turn to the analysis of the long-run adjustment process. In contrast to the short-run adjustment process, which is determined by a shift in the Okun curve, the long-run process involves a shift in the Phillips curve because of a change in the expected rate of inflation. Due to the complexity of the long-run adjustment process, an analysis by means of the graphs used in the previous section is not instructive. The essential features of this process can be described by three properties:

a. The Phillips curve for each "round" is determined by the lagged rate of expected inflation π^*_{-1} and the "forecast error" $(\pi_{-1} - \pi^*_{-1})$. In the case of an unanticipated acceleration of the rate of inflation $(\pi_{-1} - \pi^*_{-1} > 0)$, the Phillips curve shifts upward; in the case of $\pi_{-1} - \pi^*_{-1} < 0$, downward.

b. The position of the corresponding Okun curve is determined by the lagged rate of unemployment u_{-1}. If the rate of unemployment increases $(u_{-1} > u_{-2})$, the Okun curve moves to the right; if the rate of unemployment decreases $(u_{-1} < u_{-2})$, it moves to the left.

c. If the Phillips curve and the Okun curve for a certain period are determined from the values of the preceding period, the rate of real growth x (more precisely $g = x - x^*$) and the Okun curve determine the corresponding rate of unemployment. Inserting the unemployment rate into the Phillips curve gives us the actual rate of inflation.

In this model the adjustment of inflationary expectations leads to oscillations of the endogenous variables π_t, π_t^*, u_t, and g_t.

The long-run adjustment process can be presented in a system of linear difference equations. The conditions for the appearance of an oscillatory time path of the variables (complex roots) is $ab < 4\theta/(1 - \theta)^2$. The fluctuations are stable if $1/(1 + ab) < 1$; that is, the time path of the endogenous variables is characterized by damped oscillations.

For the long-run adjustment process we proceed with the numerical example used to demonstrate the short-run adjustment process. The long-run adjustment process is triggered from the shift in the Phillips curve that results from a revision in the expectations of inflation. The example was calculated on the basis of the following parameters:

$$m_t = x_t + \pi_t \tag{11}$$

$$\pi_t = \pi_t^* - 2(u_t - u^*) \tag{12}$$

$$u_t - u_{t-1} = -0.4(x_t - x^*) \tag{13}$$

$$\pi_t^* = 0.8\pi_{t-1} + 0.2\pi_{t-1}^* \tag{14}$$

$$u^* = 3.5\% \tag{15}$$

$$x^* = 3.0\% \tag{16}$$

Equation (14) implies a relatively quick adjustment of the expected rate of inflation to errors in the forecasted rate, as we can see from the known transformation $\pi_t^* - \pi_{t-1}^* = 0.8(\pi_{t-1} - \pi_{t-1}^*)$. Equations (15) and (16) describe the long-run steady-state values for the unemployment rate and the rate of real economic growth.

The starting point is the short-run equilibrium calculated earlier, to which the following numerical values correspond:

$$\pi_G = 5\%$$

$$x_G = x^* = 3\%$$

$$u_G = 1\%$$

Table 4.2 *(in percent)*

t	$x_t - x^*$	π_t	π_t^*	u_t
0	0.0	5.0	0.0	1.0
1	−2.2	7.2	4.0	1.9
2	−2.7	7.7	6.6	3.0
3	−2.0	7.0	7.4	3.7
4	−0.9	5.9	7.1	4.1
5	0.0	5.0	6.1	4.1
6	0.5	4.5	5.2	3.9
7	0.6	4.4	4.6	3.6
8	0.4	4.6	4.4	3.4
9	0.2	4.8	4.5	3.4
10	0.0	5.0	4.8	3.4
11	−0.1	5.1	5.0	3.4
12	−0.1	5.1	5.1	3.5
13	−0.1	5.1	5.1	3.5
14	0.0	5.0	5.1	3.5
15	0.0	5.0	4.9	3.5
16	0.0	5.0	5.0	3.5

The numerical values are listed in Table 4.2 and graphed in Figure 4.7.

At a constant rate of monetary expansion, the higher expected rate of inflation leads to a reduction in the rate of real growth below x^* and induces a simultaneous increase in the rate of unemployment because of the simultaneous operation of Okun's law. The inflation rate does not increase to the full extent of the inflationary expectations, since the increase in the unemployment rate slows the rise in the inflation rate because of the Phillips curve (see $t = 1$ in Table 4.2).

One may discern, however, that the rate of inflation converges to an equilibrium value of $m - x^* = 5$ percent with oscillations of decreasing amplitude. The same path is followed with a lag by the expected rate of inflation π_t^*. Because of equation (11), $m = x_t + \pi_t$, fluctuations in the rate of inflation lead to movements of equal magnitude but of opposite sign in the rate of real growth about the trend rate $x^* = 3$ percent when the rate of growth of the money supply remains constant. If, therefore, the rate of inflation rises

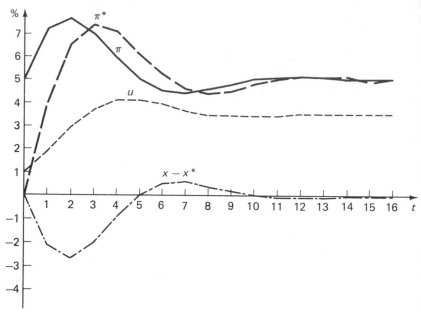

Figure 4.7

about 5 percent, the rate of real growth must correspondingly sink below 3 percent, since at a constant rate of growth of the money supply ($m = 8$ percent), the equation $m = \pi + (g + x^*)$ must always remain valid.

In Figure 4.7 we can observe this relationship directly. During the adjustment process when π is less than 5 percent, $g = x - x^*$ is positive; in other words, the rate of real growth is above its trend value x^*. The growth differential g is at first negative, then changes signs repeatedly and converges to an equilibrium value of zero. Two factors influence the rate of unemployment: First, Okun's law leads to an increase in the unemployment rate when g is negative and to a decrease when g is positive. Second, the difference between the actual and the expected rates of inflation increases the unemployment rate (relative to the natural rate) in periods when inflation is overestimated ($\pi^* - \pi > 0$) and decreases the unemployment rate in periods when inflation is under-estimated ($\pi^* - \pi < 0$).

In summary, we can say that adjustment proceeds monotonically until a short-run equilibrium is achieved, but the problem of overshooting arises during the long-run adjustment. As a result of the revision in inflationary expectations, the Phillips curve shifts and, consequently, the actual rate of inflation increases. Since nominal expenditures are growing at a constant rate, the increase in the actual rate of inflation depresses the rate of real growth below its long-run trend rate x^*. By reason of Okun's law this leads to an increase in the unemployment rate, so that it also exceeds the natural rate. Because this system oscillates (with a declining amplitude), periods of overshooting alternate with periods of undershooting.

4.5 A monetarist model with rational expectations (monetarism Mark II)

We now combine a modified version of the monetarist standard model with rational expectations. This new model, which can serve as the standard model of monetarism II, consists of the following three equations:

$$m_t = \pi_t + x^* + g_t + \varepsilon_t^1 \qquad \text{(monetary system)} \qquad (1)$$

$$\pi_t = \pi_t^* - b(u_t - u^*) + \varepsilon_t^2 \qquad \text{(Phillips curve)} \qquad (2)$$

$$u_t = u^* - ag_t + \varepsilon_t^3 \qquad \text{(Okun's law)} \qquad (3)$$

The model differs from the standard monetarist model in two points:

a. In the formulation of Okun's law, the term u_{-1} is replaced by u^*. It is assumed that an acceleration of real growth pushes the unemployment rate below the natural rate u^*, whereas in the standard model the unemployment rate falls below its level in the previous period.

b. In the extension of the model the stochastic variables ε_t^1, ε_t^2, and ε_t^3 are included in the respective equations as disturbance terms. We assume that they are independent of one another and of the exogenous variables of the model and that each has an expected value of zero [$E(\varepsilon_t^i) = 0$, $i = 1, 2, 3$].

In the model the endogenous variables are π_t, the actual rate of inflation; g_t, the deviation of the real rate of growth from its trend value ($g_t = x_t - x^*$); and u_t, the unemployment rate. The exogenous variables are m_t, the rate of growth of the money supply; π_t^*, the expected rate of inflation; u^*, the natural rate of unemployment; ε_τ^i ($i = 1, 2, 3$), stochastic terms; and x^*, the long-run rate of real growth in equilibrium.

The system of equations (1)–(3) shows the model of inflation in its structural form; exogenous and endogenous variables appear in each equation. Through the following matrix operation we bring this system of equations to its so-called reduced form [equations (4), (5), and (6)]. The reduced forms are characterized by the property that on the left-hand side of each equation there is only one endogenous variable (g_t, π_t, and u_t), which is presented as a function of all the exogenous variables and the stochastic components of the system of structural equations.

$$g_t + \pi_t = (m_t - x^*) - \varepsilon_t^1$$

$$\pi_t + bu_t = \pi_t^* + bu^* + \varepsilon_t^2$$

$$ag_t + u_t = u^* + \varepsilon_t^3$$

In matrix form this is:

$$\begin{bmatrix} 1 & 1 & 0 \\ 0 & 1 & b \\ a & 0 & 1 \end{bmatrix} * \begin{bmatrix} g_t \\ \pi_t \\ u_t \end{bmatrix} = \begin{bmatrix} (m_t - x^*) - \varepsilon_t^1 \\ \pi_t^* + bu^* + \varepsilon_t^2 \\ u^* + \varepsilon_t^3 \end{bmatrix}$$

$$\begin{bmatrix} g_t \\ \pi_t \\ u_t \end{bmatrix} = \frac{1}{1 + ab} \begin{bmatrix} 1 & -1 & b \\ ab & 1 & -b \\ -a & a & 1 \end{bmatrix} * \begin{bmatrix} (m_t - x^*) - \varepsilon_t^1 \\ \pi_t^* + bu^* + \varepsilon_t^2 \\ u^* + \varepsilon_t^3 \end{bmatrix}$$

$$g_t = \frac{1}{1 + ab} (m_t - x^* - \pi_t^*) + \frac{1}{1 + ab} (b\varepsilon_t^3 - \varepsilon_t^1 - \varepsilon_t^2) \tag{4}$$

$$\pi_t = \pi_t^* + \frac{ab}{1 + ab} (m_t - x^* - \pi_t^*) + \frac{1}{1 + ab} (\varepsilon_t^2 - ab\varepsilon_t^1 - b\varepsilon_t^3) \tag{5}$$

$$u_t = u^* - \frac{a}{1 + ab} (m_t - x^* - \pi_t^*) + \frac{1}{1 + ab} (a\varepsilon_t^1 + a\varepsilon_t^2 + \varepsilon_t^3)$$

$$(6)$$

The stochastic disturbance terms in the three reduced-form equations may be expressed compactly as follows:

$$ST_t^1 = \frac{1}{1 + ab} (b\varepsilon_t^3 - \varepsilon_t^1 - \varepsilon_t^2)$$

$$ST_t^2 = \frac{1}{1 + ab} (\varepsilon_t^2 - ab\varepsilon_t^1 - b\varepsilon_t^3)$$

$$ST_t^3 = \frac{1}{1 + ab} (a\varepsilon_t^1 + a\varepsilon_t^2 + \varepsilon_t^3)$$

Note that the endogenous variables g_t, π_t, and u_t are determined by the difference $(m_t - x^* - \pi_t^*)$ as well as by the stochastic components ST_1, ST_2, and ST_3.

The formation of rational expectations

The basic model in equations (1), (2), and (3) must be closed by an assumption about the generation of the rate of growth of the money supply m_t. In rational expectations models the generation of m_t is described by a monetary policy rule (Sargent and Wallace, 1975, 1976), and it is common practice to specify the policy rule as a linear feedback equation (McCallum, 1980). In this context the following rule is an example:

$$m_t = \mu_0 + \mu_1 g_{t-1} + \mu_2 \pi_{t-1} + e_t \qquad (7)$$

The rate of growth of the money supply depends on an autonomous component μ_0, the deviation of the rate of real growth from its natural rate g_t, and the rate of inflation π_t (both lagged by one period). Friedman would set μ_1 and μ_2 at zero, being satisfied with a passive money rule $m_t = \mu_0$. Other authors who recommend a more active policy rule would set μ_1 and μ_2 less than zero, based on the concept of a countercyclical monetary policy. The first three terms of equation (7) form the systematic part of the policy rule. The stochastic disturbance term e_t (with mean zero and constant variance) refers to the unsystematic aspect of monetary policy. A crucial assumption of rational expectations models at this point is that all economic agents (the "public") know the systematic component of the rate of growth of the money supply and take it into account. The public's expectations of m_t at time $t - 1$, expressed by the variable $E(m_t/I_{t-1})$, is therefore the systematic part of equation (7).

$$E(m_t/I_{t-1}) = \mu_0 + \mu_1 g_{t-1} + \mu_2 \pi_{t-1} \qquad (8)$$

Equation (7) can be rewritten as:

$$m_t = E(m_t/I_{t-1}) + e_t \qquad (9)$$

The actual value of the rate of growth of the money supply has a systematic component, predicted rationally by the public, and a random component, which cannot be predicted.

Let us begin with the formation of rational expectations regarding inflation by means of equation (5). After substituting equation (9) into the reduced-form equation (5), all relevant information for period t is in the right-hand side of the equation. As mentioned in Chapter 2, the formation of rational inflationary expectations π_t^* is defined as the conditional expectation $E(\pi_t/I_{t-1})$. Only the conditions $E(ST_t^2/I_{t-1}) = E(ST_t^2) = 0$ and $E(e_t/I_{t-1}) = E(e_t) = 0$ need to be considered. Thus,

$$\pi_t^* = E(\pi_t/I_{t-1}) = \pi_t^* + \frac{ab}{1 + ab} [E(m_t/I_{t-1}) - x^* - \pi_t^*] \qquad (10)$$

From this it follows that

$$\pi_t^* = E(m_t/I_{t-1}) - x^* \qquad (11)$$

Equation (11) expresses the rationally expected rate of inflation considering all exogenous and endogenous variables and their interrelationships in the model of equations (1), (2), (3), and (7). The rationally expected rate of inflation is therefore the difference between the systematic component of the rate of growth of the money supply $E(m_t/I_{t-1})$ and the trend rate of real economic growth x^*. An increase in the expected rate of expansion of the money supply leads immediately to an increase in the expected rate of inflation.

By substituting equation (11) into equation (5) and taking account of equation (9), we get

$$\pi_t = [E(m_t/I_{t-1}) - x^*] + \frac{ab}{1 + ab} [m_t - E(m_t/I_{t-1})] + ST_t^2 \quad (12)$$

The actual rate of inflation π_t is explained by two components: the rationally expected rate of inflation (first term) and the unsystematic part of the money supply, the difference between the actual rate of growth of the money supply and the expected rate $E(m_t/I_{t-1})$. From equation (12) the following results immediately:

$$\pi_t - \pi_t^* = \frac{ab}{1 + ab} [m_t - E(m_t/I_{t-1})] + ST_t^2 \quad (13)$$

This equation indicates that the difference between the actual rate of inflation π_t and the anticipated rate π_t^* is determined by the expectational error of the money supply. Equation (13) is, of course, also influenced by the stochastic component ST_t^2.

We now turn to the real sector of the model. If we substitute equation (11), the rationally expected rate of inflation, into equations (4) and (6), the result is

$$u_t - u^* = - \frac{a}{1 + ab} [m_t - E(m_t/I_{t-1})] + ST_t^3 \quad (14)$$

$$g_t = \frac{1}{1 + ab} [m_t - E(m_t/I_{t-1})] + ST_t^1 \quad (15)$$

Equations (14) and (15) describe the solution of the real variables of the system. From both equations it is apparent that the rate of unemployment u_t and the rate of growth of real output g_t are influenced by the expectational error of the money supply $m_t - E(m_t/I_{t-1})$. For example, a positive difference $m_t - E(m_t/I_{t-1})$ will, via a deviation $\pi_t - \pi_t^* > 0$, decrease u_t below u^* in equation (14) and increase g_t in equation (15). But these real effects are caused by e_t, the unpredictable component of the rate of growth of the money supply m_t, and therefore cannot be used by a systematic economic policy. To quote Bert, one of the very clever students in R. Maddock's and M. Carter's parable (1982, p. 43):

> Any government that relies upon a policy rule – one that has a fixed growth of money supply, or one systematically related to income or unemployment – will never cause any deviation from the natural rate . . . one designed with stabilization in mind, will be perfectly anticipated, and therefore have no effect on output or employment.

In summary we can say that under rational expectations the real sector of the model is completely independent of anticipated monetary policy. In the model at hand, the expected rate of inflation fully reflects any change in the systematic component of the growth of the money supply [equation (11)] and this directly raises the actual rate of inflation without any repercussions in the real sector. This result of the RE school is known as the "policy ineffectiveness" proposition and has been the subject of heated dispute (McCallum, 1980, p. 724).

After a slow start the concept of rational expectations became widely accepted, primarily because it seems to be the "natural" hypothesis in the neoclassical model (McCallum, 1980, p. 717). But many economists disagree with some conclusions of the RE school. The controversial issue is the policy ineffectiveness postulate, according to which anticipated demand management policy will be ineffective in influencing unemployment and real output when expectations are formed rationally. However, it was soon pointed out that the policy ineffectiveness is based on not one but two assumptions (Tobin, 1980; Buiter, 1980; Frydman, 1981; Gordon, 1981): rational expectations and market-clearing prices.

St. Fischer (1977) constructed a model in the spirit of Sargent and Wallace and assumed that expectations are rational, but he replaced the market-clearing hypothesis in the labor market by the assumption of multiperiod contracts negotiated in nominal terms. These contracts inject an element of short-run wage stickiness into the model. In this context the policy ineffectiveness proposition is not valid. Monetary policy can affect output and employment if the length of the period of the labor contracts is larger than the time it takes the monetary authority to react to changing economic circumstances. For instance, if the monetary authority increases the money supply (reacting to some recent economic disturbance) during the negotiated time period, this will affect the price level and therefore the real wage (for the contract period) and in turn employment and real output. In this model public and private agents have the same information set at any time, but the public agent has the larger opportunity set.

This approach was further developed by an elegant model of J.B. Taylor (1979) in which he combined rational expectations with staggered wage setting. All wage contracts in the economy are not made at the same time but are staggered throughout the year. This unsynchronized wage setting explains the persistence or stickiness of aggregate wages. Taylor argues that this model is capable of explaining not only the serial correlation of unemployment but also the hump-shape property of this persistence.

A similar result was produced by E. Phelps and J.B. Taylor (1977). In their model prices and wages are sticky because firms set their prices one period in advance of the period in which they will apply. Again, in this model monetary and fiscal policy is effective despite the fact that price expectations are formed rationally. W. Buiter (1980), in surveying the rational expectations debate, distinguished two types of models: the Walrasian model with frictionless markets and market-clearing prices and non-Walrasian models with sluggish wage and price adjustments. If the Walras type is combined with rational expectations, the policy ineffectiveness proposition will result; if a non-Walrasian model is combined with rational expectations, demand management policy will have real consequences – that is, will influence employment and the output rate.

Summarizing, we can say that rational expectations are a necessary but not a sufficient condition to derive the policy ineffectiveness result.

4.6 Monetarism in the open economy

The monetarist models of inflation discussed so far concern a closed economy. A group of authors, such as H.G. Johnson (1972b), R.A. Mundell (1971), J.A. Frenkel (1976), A.K. Swoboda (1976), M. Mussa (1974), and E.-M. Claassen (1978), who can be considered in a broad sense to be adherents of the monetarist theory of inflation, substitute the concept of an open economy. Without a doubt Johnson's article "The Monetary Approach to Balance-of-Payments Theory" is the most influential contribution to this approach. Johnson first developed a monetarist model of a small, open economy that is linked to the world economy through its balance of payments. The point of the model is the conclusion that changes in the supply of domestic money do not influence the domestic inflation rate but the overall balance of payments. In addition Johnson sketched a monetarist theory of world inflation in which a change in the world price level depends on a change in the world money supply. In the following discussion, therefore, the monetarist theory of an open economy is treated in two parts: (1) the monetarist model of a small, open economy (the monetary approach in a narrow sense) and (2) a monetarist theory of world inflation, which one may interpret as a "worldwide quantity theory."

We begin with a few preliminary definitions. The consolidated balance sheet of the banking system, including the central bank, may be presented as follows:

Assets	Liabilities
D	M
R	

where M represents the supply of money, D denotes the assets of the banking system minus nondeposit liabilities, and R is the country's reserves of gold and foreign exchange.

The balance-sheet identity $R = M - D$ holds, as does

$$\frac{dR}{dt} = \frac{dM}{dt} - \frac{dD}{dt}$$

Or, to cite Swoboda, one can use the following description of changes in the consolidated balance sheet of the banking system: Since dR/dt is nothing else but the balance of payments and is identically equal to the difference between the rate of change of the money stock and the rate of domestic credit creation, it is obvious that the balance of payments is a monetary phenomenon [Swoboda, 1976, p. 5].

It is undoubtedly correct that the change in foreign exchange reserves (including gold) equals the difference between the change in the existing supply of money and the change in the volume of domestic credit, and that this difference also corresponds exactly to the overall balance B of the balance of payments.

$$B(t) = \frac{dR}{dt} = \frac{dM}{dt} - \frac{dD}{dt}$$

However, the conclusion that the balance of payments is therefore a monetary phenomenon seems too hasty and is not logically permissible.

At present there are three separate models to explain the balance of payments, each of which depends on identical assumptions. These are (1) the elasticity approach, (2) the absorption approach, and (3) the monetary approach to the balance of payments. For simplicity assume there are no international capital movements, so that the current account (sum of trade balance, net services, and transfers) equals the overall balance. The three approaches can then be characterized as follows:

1. The *elasticity approach* defines the balance of payments B as the difference between nominal exports EX and nominal imports IM, $B = EX - IM$, where exports and imports are broadly defined to include services and transfers.
2. The *absorption approach* stems from the Keynesian income-expenditure model and defines the balance of payments as the difference between nominal income Y and absorption A, $B = Y - A$, where A equals domestic and foreign output consumed by domestic residents.

3. The *monetary approach* defines the balance of payments as the difference between the change in the domestic money supply ΔM and the change in the volume of domestic credit ΔD, $B = \Delta M - \Delta D$.

R.A. Mundell (1968, p. 149) pointed out that none of these approaches is more "correct" than any other, since all three, under proper definitions, can be derived from balance-sheet identities.[8] The following relationships hold:

$$Y = A + B \qquad \text{(national income accounts)}$$

$$\Delta M = \Delta R + \Delta D \qquad \text{(consolidated balance sheet of the banking system)}$$

$$B = \Delta R \qquad \text{(overall balance of payments)}$$

The following identities therefore hold:

$$\Delta R \equiv B \equiv Y - A \equiv \Delta M - \Delta D$$

The three approaches are thus logically equivalent, a fact recognized by Frenkel and Johnson, two pioneers of the monetary approach. They commented: "The monetary approach should in principle give an answer no different from that provided by a correct analysis in terms of the other accounts" (Frenkel and Johnson, 1976, p. 22).

The difference among the three approaches is their explanation of the balance-of-payments accounts. The elasticity approach is explicitly directed toward the balance of goods and services and explains exports and imports as functions of relative prices and real income. The monetary approach substitutes the analysis of the money market for the analysis of the current account and is therefore directed toward the relationship between the balance of payments and the supply of money. Since the presentation of the balance of payments usually begins with the balance of trade and services and shows the change of foreign exchange reserves "be-

[8] If one introduces the balance of international capital movements and designates the country's net capital exports as T, then the identities change as follows: $\Delta R = B - T = Y - A - T = \Delta M - \Delta D$ (Mundell, 1968, pp. 149–51).

low the line" as the result of all partial balances, one may agree with M. von N.-Whitman (1975) that the elasticity approach analyzes the balance of payments from the "top down," whereas the monetary approach analyzes it from the "bottom up."

The monetary approach is therefore a general method that concerns itself with the change in foreign exchange reserves and ignores the components of the balance of payments above the line. The absorption approach, which S. Alexander (1952) formulated as an extension of the Keynesian model of the open economy, in contrast to the elasticity approach, has been shifted toward the monetarist approach by monetarist authors who have depicted absorption as a function of real cash balances.[9]

We now turn to the monetary approach to the balance of payments in the narrow sense – namely, the model of an open economy that has a direct connection with the international price level.

The monetary approach to balance-of-payments theory

The model, which was developed mainly by Johnson (1976), starts with a small, open economy that produces one internationally traded good. Analogous to the model of perfect competition, it assumes that a small, open economy cannot influence the world price of internationally traded goods through the volume of its exports or imports. A small, open economy is therefore a pure price taker or quantity adjuster. In addition, fixed exchange rates are assumed, from which it follows that the domestic price of goods is proportional to their price on the world market (the constant of proportionality is the exchange rate) and that the rate of domestic inflation equals the world inflation rate. If P is the price of goods in domestic currency and $\bar{P}$ is the price in foreign

---

[9] N.-Whitman goes so far as to interpret the monetary approach as a form of the absorption approach. She commented: "As already noted, the monetary approach can be characterized as a kind of absorption approach in which the relation between desired and actual money stock determines absorption relative to income" (1975, p. 509).

currency, then the relationship $P = e\bar{P}$ holds, where e is the exchange rate. With a fixed exchange rate, the domestic rate of inflation equals the international rate, $\pi = \bar{\pi}$.

Essential to the monetary approach is the assumption that the equilibrium in the money market can always be restored in a relatively short time. Johnson wrote: "In addition, it is assumed that the supply of money is instantaneously adjusted to the demand for it, because the residents of the country can get rid of or acquire money either through the international market for commodities or through the international securities market" (1976, p. 156).

This idea expresses implicitly the monetarist assumption that domestic economic agents wish to hold an optimal level of real cash balances. They use real cash balances in excess (of the optimal level) to import goods and securities, and they try to offset a shortfall in real cash balances below their optimal level by exporting additional goods and securities. In detail, the monetarist model of a small, open economy consists of the following equations:

$$M^D = P \cdot f(X,i) \qquad f_x > 0; f_i < 0 \qquad \text{(the money demand function)} \quad (1)$$

The variables have their usual interpretations: M^D is the nominal demand for money, X is the real national product, i is the market rate of interest, and $\bar{P} \equiv P$ is the domestic and international price level. The rate of exchange e is therefore equal to unity.

$$M^r = \frac{M^D}{P} = f(X,i) \qquad \text{(real demand for money)}$$

Multiplication of the real demand for money $f(X,i)$ by the price level P expresses the well-known homogeneity postulate of money demand.

$$M^S = R + D \qquad \text{(money supply equation)} \qquad (2)$$

The money supply consists of two components: foreign exchange reserves R, which are determined in the model, and the volume of domestic credit D, which is introduced as a policy variable.

$$M^D = M^S \qquad \text{(equilibrium condition)} \tag{3}$$

$$B(t) = \frac{dR}{dt} \qquad \text{(balance-of-payments equation)} \tag{4}$$

The overall balance of the balance of payments is defined as the change in foreign exchange reserves. From equations (2) and (3), the expression

$$R = M^D - D \tag{4.1}$$

holds whenever the system is in equilibrium.

Given equation (4) the logarithmic differentiation of equation (4.1) leads to the following result:

$$g_R = \frac{dR}{R} = \frac{B(t)}{R} = \frac{M^D}{R} m^D - \frac{D}{R} d \tag{4.2}$$

where $m^D = dM^D/M^D$ and $d = dD/D$. Equation (4.2) explains the rate of change in the country's foreign exchange reserves as a function of the difference between the rate of growth of money demand m^D and the rate of growth of domestic credit d. From this relationship it becomes clear that the central bank cannot control the supply of money. If, for example, the volume of domestic credit (the domestic component of the money supply) increases while the demand for money remains constant, then foreign exchange reserves will decline, as will the overall balance of payments. Any surplus in the overall balance will be reduced, and in fact may turn into a deficit. In other words, the central bank does not control the supply of money, but for a given money demand it controls merely the composition of the money supply – namely, the relationship between its two components: domestic credit and foreign exchange reserves.

According to a well-known theorem concerning the representation of functions by means of elasticities, we can write the demand for money [equation (1)] in the form of rates of growth and elasticities (see Johnson, 1976, p. 155):

$$m^D = \pi + \eta_x x + \eta_i g_i \tag{5}$$

where $\pi = dP/P$ and $x = dX/X$; g_i denotes the percent change in the rate of interest $g_i = di/i$; $\eta_x = dM^r/dX \cdot X/M^r > 0$ is the income elasticity of demand for real cash balances; and $\eta_i = dM^r/di \cdot i/M^r < 0$ expresses the elasticity of demand for real cash balances with respect to the nominal rate of interest. Equation (5) contains no more information than equation (1); it presents the demand for money in the form of rates of growth. According to equation (5) the rate of growth of money demand equals the sum of the inflation rate π, the rate of growth of real output (weighted by the income elasticity of the demand for real cash balances) $\eta_x x$, and the rate of change in the market rate of interest (again weighted by the interest elasticity of the demand for real cash balances) $\eta_i g_i$.

The money supply equation can also be presented in rate-of-growth form:

$$m^S = \frac{R}{R+D} g_R + \frac{D}{R+D} d = \frac{dM^S}{M^S} \tag{6}$$

For $R/(R+D)$ we write A and for $D/(R+D)$ we write $1 - A$, so that equation (6) reads: $m^S = Ag_R + (1 - A)d$.

The equilibrium condition for the money market, when expressed in rate-of-growth form, is

$$m^S = m^D \tag{7}$$

By substituting from equations (5) and (6), we get

$$Ag_R + (1 - A)d = \pi + \eta_x x + \eta_i g_i \tag{8}$$

and from equation (8) we can derive the equation for the relative rate of change of the (country's) foreign exchange reserves:

$$g_R = \frac{1}{A}(\pi + \eta_x x + \eta_i g_i) - \frac{1-A}{A} d \tag{9}$$

Under the additional assumption of a constant rate of interest, equation (9) is simplified to

$$g_R = \frac{1}{A}(\pi + \eta_x x) - \frac{1-A}{A} d \tag{10}$$

This well-known result of the monetary approach implies that the increase in the country's foreign exchange reserves (or the overall balance of payments) is positively correlated with the rate of growth of domestic real income (multiplied by the income elasticity of the demand for real cash balances) and with the international rate of inflation. In contrast, an increase in the volume of domestic credit [weighted by $(1 - A)/A = D/R$, the ratio of domestic credit to foreign exchange reserves] operates to reduce the level of foreign exchange reserves. The immediate conclusion for economic policy is therefore: For a given rate of world inflation and under the condition of rapid domestic real growth, a small, open economy accumulates foreign exchange reserves or runs a balance-of-payments surplus when it pursues a fairly restrictive monetary policy.

This conclusion of the monetary approach contradicts sharply the result one may derive from the Keynesian model. According to the latter, a strong rate of real economic growth in a small country would weaken its balance-of-payments position because its imports depend on the level of real income, whereas its exports can be viewed as given (Kyle, 1976, p. 32). K. Rose described this point of view of the Keynesian model:

> For example, if one implements additional investments in the context of an expansive employment policy, then national income and employment will increase, but the current account will simultaneously deteriorate, so that the objective of a higher level of employment can be purchased only at the price of an external disequilibrium [1976, p. 112].

For the theory of inflation one must stress the fundamental difference between the monetarist model of a closed economy and the monetary approach to the balance of payments. In the closed-economy model the central bank controls the supply of money (or its rate of growth) and therefore it also controls in the long run the price level (or the rate of inflation). In the monetarist model of a small, open economy (with fixed exchange rates) the rate of inflation equals the world rate and is therefore exogenous. An increase in the domestic component of the money supply does *not* increase the domestic rate of inflation; instead, it produces a deficit in the balance of payments. The excess supply of domestic credit manifests itself in an excess demand for foreign goods and securities – in other words, in a balance-of-payments disequilibrium. According to the monetary approach the central bank controls the rate of inflation not by varying the rate of growth of the volume of domestic credit, but rather, for a given demand for money, by controlling the balance of payments or the development of the country's foreign exchange reserves.

The adjustment process according to the monetary approach

In his model Johnson indicated how one should picture the adjustment process according to the monetary approach when he referred to the real balance effect and the absorption approach of Alexander. This concerns the following fundamental principle: In the absorption approach one must distinguish between real income and absorption (domestic and foreign output consumed by domestic residents). As a starting point for the analysis, choose the level of real cash balances that economic agents wish to hold in equilibrium. If actual cash balances deviate from their desired (optimal) level through changes in the supply of nominal money or changes in the price level, economic agents alter their expenditure plans (absorption). If actual real cash balances are too high, expenditures (absorption) will exceed income, thus producing a deficit in the balance of payments. In the opposite case domestic absorption falls short of the level of domestic income and a balance-of-payments surplus results. These balance-of-payments disequilibria caused by absorption effects lead to a change in the nominal money supply through declines or increases in the country's foreign exchange reserves, so that the country can adjust real cash balances to their desired level. In the case of a fixed price level, of course, changes in the nominal supply of money are equivalent to changes in the country's real money supply.

The model of a small, open economy as formulated by Johnson assumes that the adjustment takes place immediately. However, one can also imagine that a certain time is necessary to complete

the adjustment process, as discussed by Swoboda (1976, 1977).
This model consists of three equations:

$$B = \bar{X} - A \tag{11}$$

$$A = \bar{X} + \alpha \left(\frac{M}{P} - k\bar{X} \right) \tag{12}$$

$$B = \frac{1}{P} \frac{dR}{dt} = \frac{dM}{dt} \frac{1}{P} \tag{13}$$

Equation (11) defines the balance of payments according to the
absorption approach as the difference between real national income $\bar{X}$ and real expenditures (absorption) A. Equation (12) formulates real absorption as a direct function of real income and a
second factor that is proportional to the excess supply of real
cash balances – namely, $\alpha(M/P - k\bar{X})$. This implies that the desired level of real cash balances (M^*/P) is proportional to real
national income $(M^*/P = k\bar{X})$. Finally equation (13) defines the
overall balance of the balance of payments in a well-known fashion as the change in the country's foreign exchange reserves or in
the supply of money. In this model the price level P as well as real
national income $\bar{X}$ are given exogenously. Equilibrium prevails at
the quantity of real money for which absorption equals real income (in other words, where $A = \bar{X}$). Therefore at this point (E in
Figure 4.8)

$$B = \frac{dM}{dt} \frac{1}{P} = \frac{dR}{dt} \frac{1}{P} = 0$$

Figure 4.8 presents this system in a graph. On the abscissa is
the economy's real cash balances; on the ordinate, real absorption and real output.

If real cash balances increase because of an expansion of domestic credit at a given price level, then absorption increases
relative to output and this induces a deficit in the balance of
payments in the amount of the difference between absorption and
output (*FH* in Figure 4.8). This deficit reduces the country's foreign exchange reserves (and the supply of money) and therefore
subsequently reduces real absorption.

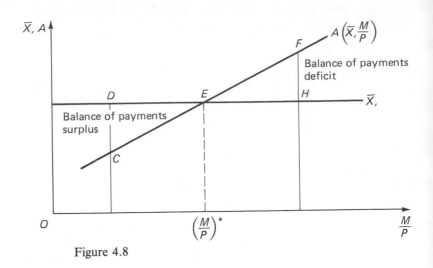

Figure 4.8

In contrast, if real cash balances decrease (e.g., by reason of an exogenous increase in the international price level), a balance-of-payments surplus of magnitude DC occurs because absorption falls below real output. One can easily show that the stability of this process depends on two conditions: (1) a positive relationship between absorption and real cash balances and (2) a positive relationship between the overall balance of payments and a change in the nominal supply of money.

The monetarist theory of world inflation

In his influential article Johnson also formulated a monetarist model of world inflation. This model has been further developed and popularized by Johnson's students and colleagues, such as A.K. Swoboda (1977) and E.-M. Claassen (1976, 1978).

In its conception the mathematical model of world inflation is nearly trivial. It attempts to apply the "classical" form rather than the modern Friedman version of the quantity theory to the world economy. The most important results of this approach as they concern the theory of inflation can be summarized in three theorems:

a. The world price level is an endogenous variable and is determined by the world money supply. According to this approach the entire world is viewed as a closed economy.
b. The distribution of the world money supply among individual economies is also endogenous and proportional to the magnitude $k_i X_i$ – that is, the individual country's real income weighted by its cash balance coefficient k_i (the reciprocal of the country's velocity of money).
c. The effect of an increase in the world money supply on the world price level is independent of its national origin.

These conclusions are valid for only the simplest type of monetarist world model in which there is only one world money and different national credit does not exist.

We now describe the three theorems for a simple two-country case by means of a graph. The following five equations are valid:

$$M^D = kXP \qquad \text{(domestic demand for money)} \qquad (14)$$

$$\bar{M}^D = \bar{k}\bar{X}\bar{P} \qquad \text{(foreign demand for money)} \qquad (15)$$

The variables have their usual meanings and a bar over a variable refers to the foreign country.

$$P = e\bar{P} \qquad (16)$$

$$M_w = M + \bar{M} = (kX + \bar{k}\bar{X})P_w \qquad \text{(equilibrium condition for the world money market)} \qquad (17)$$

or, equivalently,

$$P_w = \frac{M_w}{kX + \bar{k}\bar{X}} \qquad \text{(quantity equation for the world price level)} \qquad (18)$$

The world price level P_w (for simplicity it is assumed that $e = 1$) is determined by the relationship between the world money supply M_w and world demand for money $kX + \bar{k}\bar{X}$ in real terms. Following Swoboda (1977, p. 18) we present the two-country case of the monetarist world inflation model in a simple geometric fashion. The existing world money supply is measured by the distance $O\bar{O}$ on the abscissa of Figure 4.9. The rays OM and $\bar{O}M$ express the domestic and foreign demand for money according to

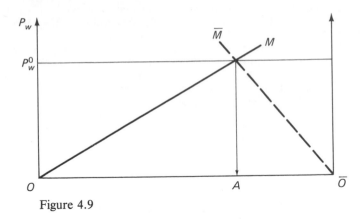

Figure 4.9

equations (14) and (15). The slope of the money demand function $1/kX$ is determined by the magnitudes of the country's real income and its cash balance coefficient. In Figure 4.9 country 1 possesses the greater share of the world money supply, since the slope of its money demand function OM is smaller than the slope of the foreign country's $\bar{O}\bar{M}$. The intersection of the two lines determines the world price level and the distribution of the world money supply between the two countries. The equilibrium distribution at point A can also be expressed algebraically as

$$\frac{M}{M_w} = \frac{kX}{kX + \bar{k}\bar{X}}$$

We now turn to the third theorem of the monetarist theory of world inflation, according to which the effect of a change in the world money supply is independent of its national origin. We assume that the foreign country increases the money supply by the amount AC in Figure 4.10. In the figure the abscissa must be extended by $AC = \bar{O}\bar{\bar{O}}$; that is, the new origin for the money demand function of the foreign country is $\bar{\bar{O}}$. The foreign money demand function therefore shifts to the right parallel to the new origin. At the old world price level P_w^0 the result is an excess supply of money amounting to AC. If we make the usual assump-

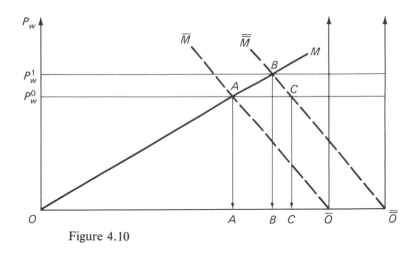

Figure 4.10

tion of the classical quantity theory – namely, full employment in both countries as well as flexible prices – then the excess supply of money can be absorbed only through a higher world price level P_w^1. This also implies a new distribution of the world money supply. In the new equilibrium, country 1 holds a quantity of money equal to OB; country 2, a quantity equal to $B\bar{O}$. The reader can easily see that the result would be the same if the original increase AC in the supply of money had been induced by country 1.

In a concluding observation on the monetarist model of world inflation, it is difficult to suppress several questions concerning the model's assumptions (see Tobin, 1977). Is the price level the only variable that adjusts when the world money supply changes? A necessary condition for this result is the existence of full employment in all countries of the world economy, so that output and employment are limited by supply conditions. The model does not allow a monetary impulse to unleash short-run output effects or variations in capacity. The world inflation model, therefore, clearly remains a step behind Friedman's formulation of monetarism for a closed economy. The short-run problem of a division of a monetary impulse into output and inflation effects (the problem posed by Friedman) has again been stricken from the agenda. The model further implies that prices and wages are fully flexible in all countries, which in turn guarantees full employment. Finally, even at this level of abstraction, the additivity of national money supplies to a world money supply is extremely problematical. Because the change in the world money supply is independent of its national origin, according to the theory money produced by the German Bundesbank must influence the world money supply in the same way as money produced by the central bank of Uganda.

5

The hypothesis of structural inflation

Whereas the Phillips curve model and the monetarist theory of inflation are concerned with the problem of inflation in the narrow sense of the word, the structural hypothesis attempts to explain the long-run trend in Western economies of rising price levels. The idea of linking the long-run tendency toward inflation to structural factors dates back to the work of P. Streeten (1962) and W. Baumol (1967). More recently G. Maynard and W. v. Ryckeghem (1976) carefully formulated this hypothesis and empirically tested it for a series of OECD countries. The long-run inflationary tendency is traced to the interaction of four factors, which are partly technological and partly behavioral. They constrict the operation of the market mechanism. The factors are

1. Differences in productivity in the industrial and service sectors.
2. A uniform rate of growth of money wages in both sectors.
3. Different price and income elasticities for the output of the industrial and service sectors.
4. Limited flexibility of prices and wages; that is, wages and prices are rigid in a downward direction.

"Structural" models are characterized by the assumption that economic activity can be aggregated into two sectors; a "progressive" (industrial) sector and a "conservative" (service) sector. Given different rates of productivity growth in the industrial and

153

service sectors, a uniform rate of growth of money wages throughout the economy must lead to permanent cost pressures in the service sector, which is assumed to have the lower productivity growth. Because firms in this sector use the markup pricing rule (a fixed profit margin imposed on rising unit labor costs), this cost pressure creates cost-push inflation for the economy as a whole. Structural inflation, therefore, implies a change in the relative supply prices of the two sectors. The supply price of the service sector rises relative to the supply price of the industrial sector. Finally, in simple terms, this type of inflation assumes a small price elasticity but a large income elasticity of demand for the output of the service sector.

We will first examine Baumol's (1967) model of unbalanced growth, which may be considered the prototype of a structural model. Baumol divides the economy's activity into two sectors: a progressive industrial sector characterized by an increase in labor productivity and a conservative service sector characterized by constant labor productivity. The model is the simplest imaginable; it has a single factor of production, labor, and both sectors have linear production functions. Baumol makes a central assumption: Money wages increase at the same rate in both sectors – namely, at the same rate g as labor productivity increases in the productive sector:

$$W_t = W_0 \cdot e^{gt} \tag{1}$$

where W_t is the money wage rate at time t. The production functions for the two sectors may be written as follows:

a. Conservative (static) sector (sector 1):

$$X_{1t} = aN_{1t} \tag{2}$$

b. Progressive sector (sector 2):

$$X_{2t} = bN_{2t} \cdot e^{gt} \tag{3}$$

where X_{1t} and X_{2t} denote real outputs and the factors a and $b \cdot e^{gt}$ represent the productivity of labor in the two sectors. It should be noted that labor productivity increases in the progressive (indus-

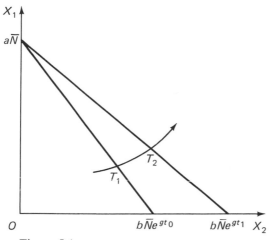

Figure 5.1

trial) sector at a constant rate g. Under the assumption that the total "physical" supply of labor $\bar{N}$ remains constant, we can write

$$\bar{N} = N_{1t} + N_{2t} \tag{4}$$

From these equations we can derive the transformation curve by substituting $N_{1t} = \bar{N} - N_{2t}$ into equation (2) and solving equation (3) for N_{2t}.

$$X_{1t} = a\bar{N} - \frac{a}{be^{gt}} X_{2t} \tag{5}$$

The transformation curve describes the possible combinations of X_1 and X_2 that can be produced at each time t given a constant supply of labor. Figure 5.1 depicts the transformation curve that prevails at two different times t_0 and t_1. The slope of the transformation curve dX_1/dX_2 expresses the opportunity cost of producing an additional unit of X_1 in terms of X_2. The movement of the transformation curve (over time) in the direction of the arrow – that is, the decline in the slope of T – implies that the cost of producing X_1 climbs when expressed in terms of the number of

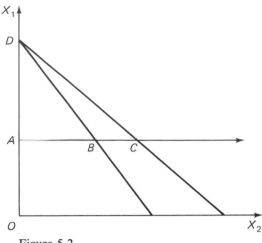

Figure 5.2

units of X_2 that must be sacrificed to secure the production of an additional unit of X_1.

Baumol discussed four characteristics of an economic system of this type:

1. In the course of time the unit costs of production in the static sector grow without limit relative to those in the progressive sector.
2. If the ratio of nominal expenditures for the two goods $X_1 P_1/X_2 P_2$ remains constant, the allocation of labor between the two sectors will not change; however, the static sector's share of real output will decrease continuously.
3. If the shares of the progressive and static sectors in the total real output remain constant, then in the long run the entire labor force will transfer from the progressive to the static sector.
4. The attempt to maintain balanced growth (constant sectoral shares in real output) despite unequal rates of growth of labor productivity ultimately leads to a zero rate of growth in output per worker.

Theorem 2 requires a word of explanation. From the constancy of the expenditure ratio ($X_i P_i/XP$ = constant), it follows that the division of the physical units of labor between the two sectors will remain constant. In addition, if one accepts Baumol's simplifying

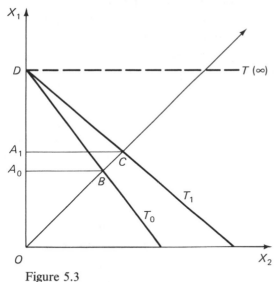

Figure 5.3

assumption that prices equal unit labor costs, then one may conclude as follows:

$$A = \frac{P_1 X_1}{P_2 X_2} = \frac{W N_1}{X_1} \cdot \frac{X_2}{W N_2} \left(\frac{X_1}{X_2} \right) = \frac{N_1}{N_2} \tag{6}$$

where A is a constant.

The second part of theorem 2 is depicted in Figure 5.2. In the first or static sector, labor productivity remains constant, so that the portion of the labor force employed in sector 1 may be calculated according to the relationship $X_1 = a N_1$. Note that the maximum output of X_1 is obtained when the entire labor force works in the first sector ($\bar{X}_1 = a\bar{N}$). The share of the labor force in the static sector can be read from Figure 5.2 as the ratio of the distances OA/OD. The growth path of the entire system is shown by the line ABC. Because the output of X_1 stays constant at OA, whereas that of X_2 grows continuously at a rate g, the ratio X_1/X_2 declines steadily over time.

In a similar fashion theorem 3 is illustrated in Figure 5.3. As mentioned, the actual employment of labor in the static sector can be read from the ratio of the distances OA/OD. According to theorem 3 the sectoral shares in real output remain constant, so that the ray OBC is the expansion path of the model. One can see in Figure 5.3 the growth in employment in the static sector as the ratio increases from OA_0/OD to OA_1/OD. As $t \to \infty$ the transformation curve tends to become parallel to the abscissa, and one can see from the diagram that (at infinity) the entire labor force will have entered the static sector. Finally, from Figure 5.3 one can immediately discern the validity of theorem 4, according to which the rate of increase in output per head (the rotation of the transformation curve upward and to the right) declines absolutely as T_t approaches $T(\infty)$.

Although the Baumol model of unbalanced growth is not really a model of inflation, it does have implications for inflation. Whereas prices in the progressive sector remain constant, because money wages increase at the same rate as labor productivity does, prices in the static sector increase at the same rate as money wages.

For simplicity, prices in the Baumol model are set equal to unit labor costs.

$$P_1 = \frac{WN_1}{X_1} = \frac{W_0 e^{gt}}{\Lambda_1} = \frac{W_0 e^{gt}}{a} \tag{7}$$

Unit labor costs can also be expressed as the ratio of the money wage rate W to labor productivity Λ_1, which is constant and equal to a in the static sector. Through the logarithmic differentiation of equation (7), we can show that the price of the static sector's output rises at the rate g. Therefore,

$$\frac{dP_1}{P_1} = g \tag{8}$$

In contrast, the price of the output of the progressive sector remains constant, since unit labor costs do not change.

$$P_2 = \frac{WN_2}{X_2} = \frac{W}{\Lambda_2} = \frac{W_0}{b} = \text{constant} \tag{9}$$

From equation (9), it follows that the rate of change in the price of the progressive sector's output equals zero ($dP_2/P_2 = 0$).

If one measures price changes in the Baumol model according to the Laspeyres Index formula, one obtains a theorem about the change in the general price level: As time proceeds, the general price level rises at a rate proportional to the rate of increase in the price of the static sector's output.

Let us construct a Laspeyres price index P_L by adding the weighted average of price increases of goods in the market basket to the general price level in a fixed basis period. For simplicity let the general price level in the basis period equal unity. For weights in the price index, take the share of each good of total expenditures during the basis period. Formally, the definition reads

$$P_L(t) = \sum_i \frac{P_i(t)X_i(0)}{\sum_j P_j(0)X_j(0)} = \sum_i \frac{P_i(0)X_i(0)}{\sum_j P_j(0)X_j(0)} \cdot \frac{P_i(t)}{P_i(0)}$$

$$= \sum_i \frac{P_i(0)X_i(0)}{\sum_j P_j(0)X_j(0)} \cdot \left[\frac{P_i(t) - P_i(0)}{P_i(0)} + 1 \right]$$

$$= 1 + \sum_i \frac{P_i(0)X_i(0)}{\sum_j P_j(0)X_j(0)} \cdot \frac{P_i(t) - P_i(0)}{P_i(0)}$$

In the simple case of a two-good economy, the Laspeyres Index is:

$$P_L(t) = 1 + \frac{P_1(0)X_1(0)}{\sum_{j=1}^{2} P_j(0)X_j(0)} \cdot \frac{P_1(t) - P_1(0)}{P_1(0)}$$

$$+ \frac{P_2(0)X_2(0)}{\sum_{j=1}^{2} P_j(0)X_j(0)} \cdot \frac{P_2(t) - P_2(0)}{P_2(0)}$$

In the Baumol model $P_2(t) - P_2(0) = 0$. Therefore, the rate of change in the general price level is determined solely by the rate of the price increase of the first good weighted by its share of the total expenditures.

5.1 The Hicks–Tobin theory of labor supply

Central to the structural model of inflation is the assumption that money wages grow at a *uniform* rate, whereas labor productivity in the progressive and static sectors changes at different rates. One may view this phenomenon as a special case of the more general problem that deals with the rigidity or limited flexibility of money wages.[1] The behavior of money wages in the Scandinavian model is adequately described by theories of the labor market based on contracts, in particular those of J. Tobin (1972) and J. Hicks (1974). Both theories share a fundamental axiom: In a modern industrial society one cannot analyze the goods and the labor markets according to the same economic principle. In the goods market the contact between two parties ends the moment the transaction (a sale or purchase) is completed. In contrast, the demand for or the supply of labor implies that both market participants expect to have a lasting relationship, at least for a certain time, similar to that expressed in rental or lease contracts.[2] Workers as well as firms have an interest in seeing that the labor contract is fulfilled in accordance with the agreed conditions, since changes give rise to adjustment costs for both sides (Poole, 1976). According to Hicks, continuity is the principle that differentiates the labor market from the auction market for goods. The wage contract regulates the relationship between the two participants in the labor market for a certain period of time. At least temporarily, the contract either eliminates

---

[1] R.M. Solow (1980, p. 8) recently listed six concepts to explain the "stickiness" of money wages: (a) Keynes's idea that wage earners defend traditional wage differentials; (b) reluctance of employers to cut wages because of adverse effects on labor productivity; (c) the notion of fairness, enforced by social pressure and legislation; (d) risk aversion on the part of wage earners (Azariadis–Baily–Gordon implicit contract theory); (e) monopoly elements in the collective bargaining process; and (f) wage changes seen by both market participants in the labor market as hard to reverse.

[2] Compare in this context Tobin's remark: "The market for labor service is not like a market for fresh produce where the entire current supply is auctioned daily. It is more like a rental housing market, in which most existing tenancies are the continuations of long-term relationships governed by contracts or less formal understandings" (1972, p. 12).

the power of the market to force adjustments in wages or weakens that power significantly. The principle of continuity leads to a lagged response of money wages to changes in market forces. An excess demand for labor leads only slowly to an increase in wages; similarly, an increase in unemployment does not lead to a decrease in money wages. Both partners in the labor market seek continuity in the labor contract. As a precondition for continuity, Hicks emphasized that the contract must be "fair." In particular, workers must perceive the wage contract as "fair." Although Hicks did not define the term "fairness," a significant element must be the relative wage rate. A worker, or a group of workers, always observes his wage rate in relation to that of a reference group. He considers his situation to be fair if he views his wage rate or the change in his wage rate as appropriate relative to the wage rate or the change in the wage rate of the reference group.

The contract theory of the labor market therefore explains the limited flexibility of money wages, not through money illusion on the part of workers or unions, but through the principle of fairness as expressed by the efforts of workers and employers to maintain the continuity implied in the wage contract.[3] However, the effort to achieve continuity explains only the limited flexibility of money wages; it does not explain which factors determine real wages or relative money wages and which factors change real wages. In the long run, market forces such as excess demand or excess supply as well as changes in labor productivity undoubtedly lead to changes in relative real wages. In the short run, the empirically given structure of wages is assumed to be fixed by the proponents of the contract theory. Because the labor market lacks an auctioneer to establish an equilibrium price, different groups of workers act in an entirely rational manner when they orient their behavior to wage differentials (i.e., to their rank in the wage hierarchy) and when they attempt to maintain these differ-

---

[3] "Employers [will be] reluctant to raise wages, simply because of labor scarcity; for to offer higher wages to particular grades of labor that had become scarce would upset established differentials. They are reluctant to cut wages, simply because of unemployment; for if they did so they would alienate those whom they continued to employ" (Hicks, 1974, p. 66).

entials. Workers therefore judge their compensation more on the basis of wage differentials and less by the absolute level of their real wage (Tobin, 1972, p. 3). If a general decline in real wages occurs, then, according to the Hicks–Tobin hypothesis, workers will attempt to defend not their real wage but their wage differential – that is, their relative real wage. This concept is central to the Keynesian theory of the supply of labor. For example, Keynes wrote: "Any individual or group of individuals, who consent to a reduction of money wages relatively to others, will suffer a *relative* reduction in real wages, which is a sufficient justification for them to resist it" (1936, p. 14). As long as each group accepts the decline in real wages and does not demand a compensating adjustment in nominal wages, wage differentials remain constant and thus the relative supply of labor remains constant. If one group attempts to raise money wages in an effort to stabilize its real wage, however, then other groups will follow in order to maintain the pattern of income differentials. The result is cost-push inflation.

An analogous situation exists for rising real wages in a growing economy. In this case individual groups attempt to maintain their standing in the income hierarchy. As long as all groups obtain the same percent increase in their money wages, then wage differentials remain constant and there is no shift in the supply of labor among sectors. Tobin summarized the Keynesian theory of labor supply as follows:

> Rigidities in the path of money wage rates can be explained by workers' preoccupation with relative wages and the absence of any central economy-wide mechanism for altering all money wages together [1972, p. 5].

The Hicks–Tobin contract theory of wages makes more precise the Keynesian theory of labor supply: The relative supply of labor is a function of the relative real wage. Let W_i be the money wage rate of group i and $\bar{W}$ be the average wage (Trevithick, 1976). Then

$$\frac{N_i^S}{N^S} = f\left(\frac{W_i}{\bar{W}}\right) \qquad f' > 0$$

The supply of labor to the ith sector N_i^S relative to the total supply of labor N^S increases, decreases, or remains constant as the money wage in sector i relative to the average wage rate increases, decreases, or remains constant. It should be noted that the Hicks–Tobin theory of labor supply particularly emphasizes social interdependence in income formation – that is, the relative position of a group in the income pyramid.

The Hicks–Tobin theory of labor supply can be summarized in the following three points:

a. In place of the determination of real wages through the market stands the principle of continuity embedded in contract theory.
b. Workers orient themselves in wage negotiations to income differentials relative to a reference group and they attempt to hold these differentials constant.
c. In the short run the historically given structure of income differentials is regarded as fair. A uniform rate of growth of money wages that maintains the existing pattern of income differentials, therefore, corresponds to the Hicksian principle of "fairness." "Wages rise in the non-expanding industries, not because of labour scarcity, but because of unfairness; because the workers in the non-expanding industries feel that they are getting left behind" (Hicks, 1974, p. 71).

In summary, the Hicks–Tobin hypothesis explains one assumption that is central to the model of structural inflation: the uniform rate of growth of wages.

5.2 The Scandinavian model of inflation

A bridge between Baumol's model of disequilibrium growth and the Scandinavian model of inflation is the important contribution of Bela Balassa (1964). He formulated a model of an open economy with two sectors: the progressive sector, which produces traded goods, and the static sector, which makes nontraded goods. This division into traded and nontraded goods is not a trivial matter, so perhaps a word of explanation is in order. The theory of international trade is based on a division of output into export and import goods as well as the analysis of the terms of trade, or the relative prices of these two categories of commodities. If a country is a price taker in the world markets for its exports as well as for its imports, then an increase in the world price level affects the country's export and import prices equally, so that the country's terms of trade are unaffected. One can therefore combine the prices of export and import goods into an index with fixed weights (Claassen, 1978, p. 120). In Balassa's model this composite traded good is contrasted with a similar index for nontraded goods. Shifts in relative prices can therefore occur only between traded and nontraded goods. Other changes in relative prices are not considered to be of interest in this approach.

The creators of the Scandinavian model, such as Odd Aukrust (1977) and the team of Gösta Edgren, Karl-Olof Faxén, and Clas-Erik Odhner (EFO) (1973), formulated an inflation model for a small, open economy, in which they linked the fundamental principles of the structural model with the small-country assumption. One may define a small, open economy as one that faces infinitely elastic supply and demand curves for its traded goods in the world markets (Calmfors, 1977, p. 501). Neither through its supply of export goods to the world market nor through its demand for import goods from that market can it influence the world market price. Like a firm in the model of perfect competition, a small, open economy is a pure price taker in the world market. As suggested, one can therefore aggregate export and import goods into an "exposed" (E) sector and nontraded goods into a "sheltered" (S) sector. More precisely, the E sector includes all those goods (and services) subject to international competition, whereas the S sector represents those goods and services completely protected from international competition. Empirically, the E sector includes industries that produce export goods as well as firms that produce goods for the domestic market that are subject to competition from imported substitutes. In contrast, the S sector comprises all firms that produce for the domestic market *and* are not exposed to international competition, such as most service industries, the construction industry, agriculture, and government activity.

In the Scandinavian model the E and S sectors differ through specific assumptions about technical progress and the price be-

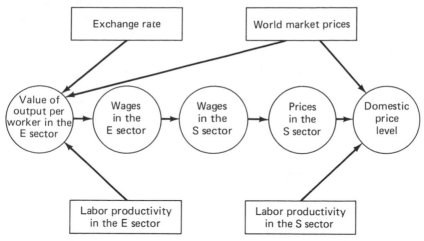

Figure 5.4. The structure of the Aukrust–EFO model.

havior of suppliers. First, it is assumed that technical progress is biased toward the E sector, where labor productivity expands at a faster rate than in the S sector. Thus, $\lambda_E > \lambda_S$, where λ_i denotes the rate of change in labor productivity in the ith sector. The differences in the degree of market competition lead to different pricing strategies by firms in each of the two sectors. In the E sector firms are pure price takers in accordance with the model of pure competition; they adjust the quantities they produce to the given, fixed world market price. Whereas world market conditions determine product prices in the E sector (or the rate of increases in prices in the E sector), firms in the S sector form prices on the basis of total costs. Specifically, we assume that prices in the S sector reflect unit labor costs and a fixed profit margin or markup. In contrast to the E sector, prices in the S sector change when unit labor costs change. Therefore, prices in the E sector are determined in the world market, whereas prices in the S sector are determined through the development of domestic costs.

We now discuss the structure of the Scandinavian model with reference to Figure 5.4. The arrows show the causal structure of the model. Rectangles denote exogenous variables and circles, endogenous variables. The Scandinavian model of inflation is characterized by the following five points:

1. World market prices for the output of the E sector together with the prevailing exchange rate determine the supply price of the E industry in domestic currency. Since the Scandinavian model assumes a fixed exchange rate, the model implies that the inflation rate in the E sector π_E is equal to the world rate of inflation π_w. The rate of growth of labor productivity in the E sector λ_E is assumed to be given exogenously. Together with the inflation rate π_E, this determines the rate of growth of the value of output per worker in the E sector ($\pi_E + \lambda_E$).

2. The rate of growth of the value of output (per worker) in the E sector determines the rate of growth of money wages in the E sector. In the long run, aside from short-term disturbances, it is assumed in this model that the rate of growth of money wages w_E equals the sum of the inflation rate π_E and the rate of growth of labor productivity λ_E. This implies a constant distribution of income.

3. Between the development of money wages in the E sector and that in the S sector there is a relationship that one can call a "spillover effect." Market forces as well as the wage policies of unions (the solidarity principle in wage negotiations) lead to money wages in the sheltered sector growing at the same rate as those in the external sector. Through this spillover effect the ratio of real wages in the E sector to those in the S sector remains unchanged.

4. Together with the rate of growth of labor productivity in the S sector λ_S, the rate of growth of money wages in the S sector w_S determines the rate of inflation π_S. Because a constant percent markup is added to unit labor costs to allow for profits in the S sector, the inflation rate equals the difference between the rate of growth of money wages w_S and the rate of growth of labor productivity λ_S.

5. The inflation rate in the E sector and the inflation rate in the S sector – multiplied by the appropriate weights – determine the domestic rate of inflation.

In summary, the Scandinavian model explains the three domestic rates of inflation π_E, π_S, and π as well as the increases in domestic money wages w_S and w_E through the exogenously given rate of increase in the foreign price level π_w and through the development of labor productivity in the E and S sectors. It should be stressed that the model assumes that the exchange rate is constant.

It is not difficult to formulate the Scandinavian model in algebraic terms. For convenience we use the following variables: The endogenous variables are π_E, the inflation rate in the E sector; π_S, the inflation rate in the S sector; π, the domestic rate of inflation; w_S, the percent change in money wages in the S sector; and w_E, the percent change in money wages in the E sector. The exogenous variables are π_w, the rate of increase in the price of internationally traded goods (world inflation rate); λ_S, the percent change of labor productivity in the S sector; λ_E, the percent change in labor productivity in the E sector; α_E, the weight of π_E in the definition of π, the domestic inflation rate; and α_S, the weight of π_S in the definition of π, the domestic inflation rate.

We can now formulate the Aukrust–EFO model as follows:

Direct impact of international inflation:

$$\pi_E = \pi_w \tag{1}$$

Development of money wages in the E sector:

$$w_E = \lambda_E + \pi_E \tag{2}$$

Wage spillover relationship: $w_E = w_S \tag{3}$

Markup pricing in the S sector: $\pi_S = w_S - \lambda_S \tag{4}$

Definition of the domestic inflation rate:

$$\pi = \alpha_E \pi_E + \alpha_S \pi_S \qquad \alpha_E + \alpha_S = 1 \tag{5}$$

The domestic inflation rate is a weighted average of the rates of inflation in the E and S sectors. The weights α_E and α_S correspond to the percent shares of expenditures for E goods and S goods of total expenditures; thus, $\alpha_E = X_E P_E / XP$ and $\alpha_S = X_S P_S / XP$.

The authors of the Scandinavian model assume that the expenditure ratios α_E and α_S remain constant. By solving equations (1)–(5) recursively, we get the Aukrust–EFO equation, the Scandinavian model's explanation of inflation.

$$\pi = \pi_w + \alpha_S(\lambda_E - \lambda_S) \qquad (6)$$

All variables on the right-hand side of equation (6) are exogenous. The inflation rate of a small, open economy is therefore determined through international price developments (the world inflation rate π_w) as well as the difference between the rates of growth of labor productivity in the two sectors, weighted by the sheltered sector's share of total expenditures.

As its distinguishing feature, the Scandinavian model traces the deviation of the domestic rate of inflation from the world inflation rate for internationally traded goods ($\pi - \pi_w$) to the structural component $\alpha_S(\lambda_E - \lambda_S)$. G. Maynard and W. van Ryckeghem (1976, pp. 162–182) spoke of the structural hypothesis as an explanation of inflation, since the rate of inflation is independent of excess demand. Moreover, as a result of a uniform rate of growth of money wages, the domestic rate of inflation according to the structural hypothesis depends only on the difference between the rates of growth in labor productivity in the two sectors. The greater is α_S, the sheltered sector's share of total expenditures, the larger is the deviation of the domestic rate of inflation from the world rate.

5.3. The constant distribution of income in the Scandinavian model

The Aukrust–EFO equation has been proposed as a guide to a long-run policy for national income distribution. If money wages rise at the same rate as the value of output per worker-hour, $\pi_E + \lambda_E$, then the relationship of the share of wages to the share of profits in the E sector remains constant. If, in addition, exchange rates are fixed, then the economy under consideration will retain its ability to compete in world markets. Here we would like to discuss the second aspect of the Scandinavian model: the constant distribution of income. The share of wages is defined as

$$L_i = \frac{W_i N_i}{P_i X_i} \qquad i = E, S \tag{1}$$

We can transform this expression into rates of growth, where lowercase letters denote percent changes (e.g., $x_i = dX_i/X_i$).

$$l_i = w_i - \pi_i - \lambda_i \tag{2}$$

where $\lambda_i = x_i - n_i$ denotes the percent change in labor productivity in the ith sector. If, as the Scandinavian model assumes, the wages in the E sector increase at a rate $w_E = \pi_E + \lambda_E$, then the wage share remains constant – that is, $l_E = 0$. The rate of growth of the value of output per worker-hour in the E sector therefore provides the leeway for a rate of growth of money wages that is neutral with respect to the distribution of income.

The Scandinavian model further implies a constant distribution of income in the sheltered sector. There the following identity holds:

$$l_S = w_S - \pi_S - \lambda_S = 0 \tag{3}$$

The constant distribution of income in this sector results from the adjustment of the inflation rate to the rate of growth of money wages in this sector. For a given rate of growth of money wages $w_E = w_S$ and a given rate of growth of labor productivity λ_S, the price of S goods rises at precisely the rate $w_S - \lambda_S$, since firms in the S sector follow a markup pricing rule. The wage share, therefore, remains constant and $l_S = 0$.

Another method of deriving the Aukrust–EFO equation under these conditions for the distribution of income starts from the following identity:

$$w_E - \pi_E - \lambda_E - l_E = w_S - \pi_S - \lambda_S - l_S = 0 \tag{4}$$

We can transform this equation to yield

$$\pi_S = \pi_E + (\lambda_E - \lambda_S) + (w_S - w_E) - (l_S - l_E) \tag{5}$$

According to the assumptions of the Scandinavian model, $w_E = w_S$ and $l_S = l_E = 0$, so that equation (5) becomes

$$\pi_S = \pi_E + (\lambda_E - \lambda_S) \tag{6}$$

or

$$\pi_S - \pi_E = \lambda_E - \lambda_S$$

Equation (6) expresses a concept of neoclassical production theory: The relative prices of two goods move in inverse proportion to the relative labor productivity in the industries that produce these goods. More precisely, the difference in the rates of price increase in the two sectors results from the difference in the rates of growth of labor productivity in the two sectors. If we substitute equation (6) into the definition of the inflation rate, we get

$$\pi = \alpha_S[\pi_E + (\lambda_E - \lambda_S)] + (1 - \alpha_S)\pi_E$$
$$= \pi_E + \alpha_S(\lambda_E - \lambda_S)$$

or precisely the Aukrust–EFO equation.

A constant income distribution is a long-run property of the Aukrust model. In the short run it is entirely possible that the growth of money wages may deviate from the neutral leeway described earlier. If, for example, w_E and therefore w_S increase more slowly than the rate at which the value of output per worker-hour in the E sector grows, then the share of profits will rise in the E sector, whereas the share of profits in the S sector will remain constant. In this case, the rate of inflation will decrease. In contrast, if w_E and w_S increase at a rate greater than $\pi_E + \lambda_E$, the neutral leeway, then the share of wages increases in the E sector and that of profits falls.

Are there mechanisms that correct the short-run deviations in the rate of growth of money wages from the rate of growth of the value of output per worker-hour and restore the long-run constancy of the share of wages? Aukrust discusses three such mechanisms.

a. Negotiations concerning wage rates for standard job classifications are in general conducted with an eye toward correcting any deviations. An increase in the share of profits in the E sector ($l_E < 0$) leads to higher wage demands and simultaneously to less resistance by firms to wage increases, so that for a certain time wages may rise at an above-average rate and the wage share will rise to its old level. In contrast, if the share of profits falls, this mechanism operates in the opposite direction, leading to less increase in money wages and to an increase in the share of profits.

b. In the same way, excess demand in the labor market leads to a stabilization of the share of wages. If the share of profits rises, then the demand for labor increases and this results in wage drift, or an increase in money wages above the agreed contract levels. This in turn reduces the share of profits. Conversely, if profits fall to less than their "normal" level as a result of a reduction of excess demand in the labor market, then money wages will tend to increase more slowly than stipulated in wage contracts. Negative wage drift occurs and the share of profits increases.

c. Finally, Aukrust assumes that economic policy in a small, open economy is generally directed at keeping the share of profits in the E sector at or above a certain level so that it can maintain its competitiveness in international markets. If money wages rise at a rate greater than the neutral leeway, then the government will bring profits back up to their normal level by restricting government expenditures or devaluing the domestic currency.

5.4 Demand conditions in the Scandinavian model

The Scandinavian model is a long-run supply model with implicit demand conditions. Real growth in both sectors is exogenously explained by the rate of growth of productivity and employment. To ensure that the goods produced will actually be sold, however, one must make special assumptions regarding demand conditions. To clarify the fundamental structure of this implicit demand system within the model, we use an approach adapted from W.H. Branson and J. Myhrman (1976).

We will study the demand in each sector separately. The sheltered sector produces nontraded goods exclusively and only domestic residents demand these goods. Less simple is the situation in the open sector, which produces internationally traded goods. Demand here consists of three components: the demand of domestic and foreign residents for domestically produced tradeable goods and the demand of domestic residents for foreign-produced tradeable goods. The following analysis assumes that the current account is in balance; that is, the portion of domestically produced tradeable goods that is not demanded by domestic residents always equals the value of imports. Because the demand of the rest of the world for the tradeable goods of the domestic country is assumed to be infinitely elastic (the small-country assumption), the difference between domestic production and domestic demand for goods produced in the open sector can always be sold at the prevailing world market price.

Let us first observe the demand for nontraded goods produced in the sheltered sector. This is homogeneous to degree zero in the prices P_E and P_S and in the nominal income Y; that is, for a equiproportional increase in all prices and money income, the real demand for S goods remains constant.

$$X_S = f(v,R) \qquad \frac{\partial f}{\partial v} < 0; \frac{\partial f}{\partial R} > 0 \tag{1}$$

$$v = \frac{P_S}{P_E} \qquad R = \frac{Y}{P_E} \tag{2}$$

By reason of the assumed homogeneity property, the real demand for S goods is determined by their relative price P_S/P_E and real income R. Real income is defined in a special way, as nominal income deflated by the price of the internationally traded good P_E. The partial derivatives of the demand function show the usual negative price and positive income effects.

We now turn to a formulation of this demand function in terms of its rate of growth. After totally differentiating the function and performing some elementary transformations, we obtain

$$\frac{dX_S}{dt} = \frac{\partial f}{\partial v} \cdot \frac{dv}{dt} + \frac{\partial f}{\partial R} \cdot \frac{dR}{dt} \tag{3}$$

$$\frac{dv}{dt} = \frac{P_S}{P_E} (\pi_S - \pi_E) \tag{2'}$$

$$\frac{dX_S}{dt} = \frac{\partial f}{\partial v} v(\pi_S - \pi_E) + \frac{\partial f}{\partial R} \cdot \frac{dR}{dt} \bigg| \frac{1}{X_S} \tag{3'}$$

$$\frac{dX_S}{X_S} = \frac{\partial f}{\partial v} \cdot \frac{v}{X_S} (\pi_S - \pi_E) + \frac{\partial f}{\partial R} \cdot \frac{R}{X_S} \left(\frac{dR}{R}\right) \tag{4}$$

In addition, we use the following definitions:

$$\eta_S = \frac{\partial X_S}{\partial v} \cdot \frac{v}{X_S} < 0 \qquad \text{(own price elasticity)} \tag{5.1}$$

$$\bar{\eta}_S = \frac{\partial X_E}{\partial v} \cdot \frac{v}{X_E} > 0 \qquad \text{(cross price elasticity)} \tag{5.2}$$

$$\varepsilon_S = \frac{\partial X_S}{\partial R} \cdot \frac{R}{X_S} > 0 \qquad \text{(income elasticity)} \tag{5.3}$$

$$\varepsilon_E = \frac{\partial X_E}{\partial R} \cdot \frac{R}{X_E} > 0$$

The own price elasticity denotes the percent change in the demand for S goods when the relative price P_S/P_E changes by 1 percent. The cross price elasticity shows the percent change in the demand for E goods when the price of nontraded goods relative to the price of traded goods changes by 1 percent. Since we assume that there is substitutability in demand between traded and nontraded goods, this cross elasticity is positive.

With the aid of equations (5.1) and (5.3), we can rewrite equation (4) as

$$x_S^d = \frac{dX_S}{X_S} = \eta_S(\pi_S - \pi_E) + \varepsilon_S(y - \pi_E) \tag{6}$$

The rate of growth of demand for nontraded goods depends on an inflation and an income component. The own price elasticity of demand is negative, whereas the difference in the rates of price increases in the two sectors is positive because, in the Scandinavian model, the relative price P_S/P_E rises continuously. As a result the first component has a negative impact on the rate of growth of demand for nontraded goods. In contrast, the rate of growth of real income $(y - \pi_E)$, weighted by the income elasticity of demand, has a positive effect on dX_S/X_S.

The demand for traded goods is analogous to the demand for nontraded goods. It too is homogeneous of degree zero in prices and nominal income Y.

$$X_E = g(v,R) \qquad \frac{\partial g}{\partial v} > 0; \frac{\partial g}{\partial R} > 0 \tag{7}$$

The positive partial derivative $\partial g/\partial v > 0$ expresses the negative substitution effect. As a relative price P_S/P_E rises, the demand for traded goods rises. An increase in real income leads to an increase in the demand for traded goods. As in the discussion of the demand for nontraded goods, we turn from equation (7) to a presentation of the rate of growth of the demand for traded goods.

$$\frac{dX_E}{X_E} = \frac{\partial g}{\partial v} \cdot \frac{v}{X_E} (\pi_S - \pi_E) + \frac{\partial g}{\partial R} \cdot \frac{R}{X_E} (y - \pi_E) \tag{8}$$

Using the definitions of elasticities given earlier, we obtain

$$x_E^d = \bar{\eta}_S(\pi_S - \pi_E) + \varepsilon_E(y - \pi_E) \tag{9}$$

An increase in the relative price P_S/P_E increases the demand for traded goods by reason of the substitution effect. In fact, the demand for traded goods must increase because the difference in the rates of price increases $(\pi_S - \pi_E)$ is positive in the Scandinavian model and real income is growing $(y - \pi_E > 0)$.

The Scandinavian model formulated by Aukrust assumes constant real income shares. This implies that the real rates of growth of demand for S goods and E goods must be identical. This common value is assumed to be positive and is denoted x.

$$x_S^d = x_E^d = x \tag{10}$$

Finally, we must consider the budget restraint. If we transform the definition of nominal income into rates of growth, we get

$$y = \alpha_S(x_S + \pi_S) + \alpha_E(x_E + \pi_E) \tag{11}$$

For the case of constant shares, it follows as a result of equation (10) that

$$y = \alpha_S\pi_S + \alpha_E\pi_E + x \tag{12}$$

The condition of constant real shares implies that

$$x_S^d - x_E^d = (\eta_S - \bar{\eta}_S)(\pi_S - \pi_E) + (\varepsilon_S - \varepsilon_E)(y - \pi_E) = 0 \quad (13)$$

By substituting equation (12) and taking into account the relationship $\pi_S - \pi_E = \lambda_E - \lambda_S > 0$ developed in the section on distribution in the Scandinavian model, we get after the appropriate transformations

$$\bar{\eta}_S - \eta_S = (\varepsilon_S - \varepsilon_E)\left(\alpha_S + \frac{x}{\lambda_E - \lambda_S}\right) \quad (14)$$

The factor $\alpha_S + x/(\lambda_E - \lambda_S)$ in equation (14) is determined by exogenous variables. Under the typical assumptions that $\eta_S < 0$ and $\bar{\eta}_S > 0$, equation (14) shows that the income elasticity of demand for nontraded goods must exceed that for traded goods if the constancy of real shares of the two sectors is to be simultaneously maintained when supply and demand are in balance. The economic reasoning behind this condition is relatively simple. Given that $\eta_S < 0$ and $\bar{\eta}_S > 0$, a continual rise in the relative price of the nontraded good P_S/P_E leads to a relative decline in the demand for nontraded goods. With balanced growth in production, this decline must be compensated by a higher income elasticity of demand for nontraded goods.

5.5 The generalized Scandinavian model

The Scandinavian model interprets inflation as a phenomenon determined by "costs." The domestic rate of inflation results from "imported" inflation as well as from the differential between the rates of productivity growth in the traded and nontraded goods sectors. The inflation process is associated with a continual increase in unit labor costs and in the relative price P_S/P_E. In contrast, the Phillips–Lipsey model, which was discussed in Chapter 3, interprets inflation as a demand-determined phenomenon, where the level of excess aggregate demand explains the level of the inflation rate. One may therefore raise the question whether these two concepts (the Scandinavian model and the Phillips curve) provide two completely incompatible explanations of inflation or whether they can be combined into an economically consistent "synthetic" model.[4] Two attempts to do so have been made; however, they differ fundamentally in their reasoning. We will examine both these synthetic models more closely; however, our comments merely sketch the two theories without fully developing the complete model.

The Aukrust–Calmfors interpretation

At the start of the discussion we postulate the following two equations:

$$\pi_A = \pi_w + \alpha_S(\lambda_E - \lambda_S) \tag{1}$$

$$\pi = \phi\pi^* - b(u - u^*) \tag{2}$$

where π_A is the inflation rate determined by the Aukrust–EFO equation, π_w is the world rate of inflation, π is the actual domestic rate of inflation, π^* is the expected rate of inflation, u is the actual unemployment rate, and u^* is the natural unemployment rate.

Equation (1) is the Aukrust–EFO equation, which we have already discussed. Equation (2) expands the Scandinavian model by adding a demand component in the form of the Phillips curve. The parameter $\phi \leq 1$ determines the extent to which the expected rate of inflation π^* affects the actual rate of inflation.

At the start two observations are in order:

    a. Central to the interpretation of O. Aukrust (1977) and L. Calmfors (1977) is the assumption that the weights α_S and α_E in the definition of the inflation rate remain constant. The relaxation of this assumption forms the starting point for the second interpretation of the generalized Scandinavian model by W. Branson and J. Myhrman.

    b. The Aukrust–EFO equation is valid as written in equation (1) only if the relationship $w_i = \pi_i + \lambda_i$ ($i = E, S$) holds in both the traded and the nontraded goods sectors.

Figure 5.5 depicts the two equations. The point G_0 represents a long-run equilibrium for a small, open economy; the inflation rate

---

[4] For a review of different approaches to generalize the Scandinavian model, especially to bring in a demand component via the Phillips curve, see Lindbeck (1979, pp. 13–40).

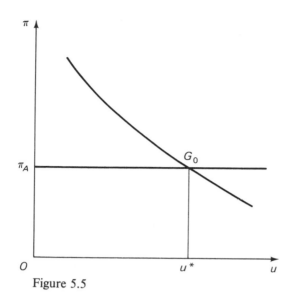

Figure 5.5

π_A is fully anticipated; and the unemployment rate corresponds to the natural rate u^*.[5] The position of the Phillips curve reflects the expected rate of inflation π^*. Because the actual inflation rate π equals the inflation rate π_A derived from the Aukrust–EFO equation, observation b holds. From this it follows that the distribution of income in the two sectors remains constant. In addition, at point G_0 the country's traded goods remain competitive in international markets, because money wages in the traded goods sector increase at a rate within the limits permitted by the Aukrust–EFO model.

We now assume that an unexpected increase in the world rate of inflation disturbs this equilibrium. From the rest of the world there is an excess demand for the country's traded goods as a result of the increase in π_w. The effect of such a change on the Aukrust–EFO equation is relatively simple. The line A_0 in Figure 5.6 shifts upward to A_1 because π_w increases and α_S, λ_S, and λ_E

[5] The underlying assumption of the following analysis is the NR hypothesis ($\phi = 1$).

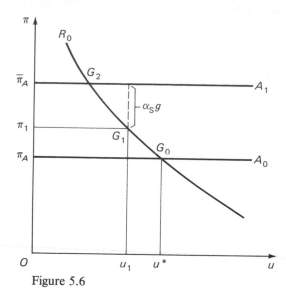

Figure 5.6

remain constant. However, some further remarks are necessary to establish the effect of an increase in the world rate of inflation on the Phillips curve.

The upward shift in the Aukrust–EFO equation expresses the increase in foreign demand, which confronts firms in the traded goods sector with the possibility of greater sales volumes. Simultaneously, a more favorable price situation develops. Therefore, the traded goods sector will increase its demand for labor, with the result that the rate of the wage increase will exceed the level that originally occurred at point G_0. The increased rate of growth of wages at a constant rate of growth of labor productivity leads to an increase in unit labor costs and an increase in the actual rate of inflation. This situation corresponds to a point such as G_1 on the Phillips curve R_0 in Figure 5.6. The unemployment rate u has fallen and the actual rate of inflation has increased. What does the point G_1 signify?

While income distribution in the nontraded goods sector has

remained constant because of its markup pricing rule, in the traded goods sector this distribution has shifted in favor of profits. To be sure, at the point G_1 money wages have risen but their rate of growth has been less than that of the value of the product ($w_E < \lambda_E + \pi_E$). This holds true as long as $\bar{\pi}_A$, the tolerance limit of the Aukrust–EFO equation, is greater than the actual rate of inflation π_1 (distance $\alpha_S g$ in Figure 5.6).

If we designate the higher rate of world inflation as π_w^1, then we can write the actual rate of inflation at point G_1 as

$$\pi_E = \pi_w^1 = w_E^1 - \lambda_E + g \tag{3}$$

This equation shows that the tolerance limit of the Aukrust–EFO equation has not been fully exhausted. The parameter g remains positive in the first phase of an unexpected price increase in the E sector. Recall the definition of the inflation rate

$$\pi = \alpha_S \pi_S + \alpha_E \pi_E \tag{4}$$

as well as the following assumptions:

$$w_E^1 = w_S^1 \tag{5}$$

$$\pi_S^1 = w_S^1 - \lambda_S \tag{6}$$

By substituting in equation (4) the actual rate of inflation becomes

$$\pi = \pi_w^1 + \alpha_S(\lambda_E - \lambda_S) - \alpha_S g \tag{7}$$

The actual rate of inflation is therefore less than the one determined by the Aukrust–EFO equation. As long as g remains positive, firms in the traded goods sector have an incentive to expand production and to increase employment. This leads to additional increases in money wages and the progressive exhaustion of the tolerance limit – in other words, to a movement of G_1 toward the point G_2 along the Phillips curve R_0. Because of the wage spillover effect in the Scandinavian model, wages in the nontraded goods sector also rise, and because of this sector's markup pricing rule, so do prices. Increased incomes in the traded goods sector lead, according to the demand conditions of the Scandina-

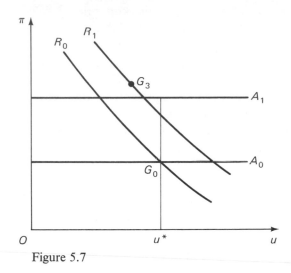

Figure 5.7

vian model, to increases in output and employment in the non-traded goods sector. (Increases in income have a stronger impact on the demand for nontraded goods.)

At point G_2 there is a new short-run equilibrium, at which the tolerance limit arising from the unexpected acceleration in the rate of world inflation is fully exhausted. Again at this point the distribution of income remains constant because money wages in the traded goods sector increase at the rate $w_E = \lambda_E + \pi_w^1$. The excess demand present at G_2 (u is below the natural rate of unemployment u^*) does not diminish the sector's competitiveness in world markets, since money wages increase at a rate within the tolerance limits of the Aukrust–EFO equation.

The preceding comments assume that the Phillips curve does not shift – that is, that the expected rate of inflation π^* does not change. However, the increase in inflation to a rate above its expected level induces an adjustment of the expected rate of inflation. The Phillips curve therefore shifts upward, say from R_0 to R_1 (Figure 5.7). As equation (7) shows, at points along the short-run Phillips curve under the Aukrust–EFO line (e.g., in Figure 5.6 the points on the Phillips curve R_0 under the line A_1)

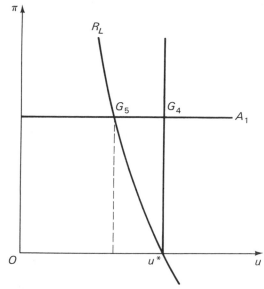

Figure 5.8

the distribution of income shifts in favor of employers. To compensate for the decline in the share of labor arising from the unanticipated inflation, workers must reach agreements for wage increases that exceed the tolerance limit $w_E = \pi_w^1 + \lambda_E$. Here starts the first of Aukrust's three mechanisms of correcting a deviation of labor's share of income from its long-run level. For a certain length of time wages will increase at an above-average rate, so that the actual rate of inflation will exceed that called for by the Aukrust–EFO equation (e.g., point G_3 in Figure 5.7).

Now we raise the question of where the new long-run equilibrium corresponding to the higher world rate of inflation π_w^1 will occur. In the new long-run equilibrium the distribution of income between the two sectors must remain constant. Only points along the line A_1 in Figure 5.8 fulfill this condition.

If the natural rate of unemployment hypothesis is valid [$\phi = 1$ in the Phillips curve equation (2)], then the long-run equilibrium can occur only at the intersection G_4 of the Aukrust–EFO equation with the vertical line $u = u^*$. If $\phi < 1$, then there is a long-run Phillips curve with a negative slope. This can be derived by substituting the condition $\pi = \pi^*$ in equation (2). From this it follows that the equation for the long-run Phillips curve is

$$\pi = \frac{-b}{1 - \phi} (u - u^*)$$

In this case an increase in inflation produces not merely a temporary employment effect but a permanent reduction in the rate of unemployment. The new equilibrium point then lies on the line A_1 to the left of u^* and on the long-run Phillips curve R_L (point G_5 in Figure 5.8).[6]

In conclusion we can summarize the Calmfors–Aukrust interpretation of the synthetic model of the relationship of the Aukrust–EFO equation and the Phillips curve as follows:

1. The Aukrust–EFO equation determines the movement of the price level or the rate of inflation in the long run.
2. The long-run Phillips curve determines the extent of excess demand (rate of unemployment) that is compatible with the Aukrust–EFO equation.

The interpretation of W. Branson and J. Myhrman

W. Branson and J. Myhrman (1976) criticized the assumptions underlying the first interpretation of the generalized Scandinavian model, particularly the constancy of α_S and α_E, the shares of the S and E sectors of total income. They assumed that

---

[6] Empirical research indicates that for small countries such as Austria or Sweden the hypothesis of the existence of a long-run Phillips curve might not be rejected. L. Calmfors's estimate for Sweden for the period 1958–73 shows the following Phillips relationship for the E sector:

$$w_E = 6.25 + 0.08(V - U) + 0.31\pi_E^{-1} + 0.18(\pi_E + \gamma_E) \qquad R^2 = 0.7;$$
$$\qquad\quad (3.53) \qquad\quad (2.44) \qquad\quad (2.13) \qquad\qquad DW = 1.98$$

The variable $(V - U)$ stands for the difference between the number of vacancies and the number of unemployed; "demand pressure" variable π_E^{-1} is the lagged rate of international inflation. This equation suggests that in the long run only half of a change in the international rate of inflation π_E is transmitted to the rate of change of money wages. The long-run coefficient of the "transmission" of international inflation into the domestic inflation is $(0.31 + 0.18 = 0.49)$ (Calmfors, 1977, p. 516). A similar result for Austria can be found in Frisch (1977a).

economic policy makers succeed in controlling aggregate demand with the help of fiscal and monetary policy. The authorities thereby achieve the desired level of employment and a certain unemployment rate. Whereas the inflation rate is exogenously determined in the Aukrust–Calmfors interpretation, in the Branson–Myhrman version the unemployment rate is exogenous. Through demand management the government achieves a certain rate of unemployment and, therefore, it implicitly chooses a certain rate of inflation according to the Phillips curve relationship. If the actual rate of inflation deviates from the distributionally neutral rate π_A of the Aukrust–EFO equation, then according to Branson and Myhrman an adjustment process sets in, which leads to a shift in the shares of the sectors of total real output. If the actual rate of inflation is higher than the tolerance level permitted by the Aukrust–EFO equation, then the share of the S sector (as expressed by the parameter α_S) increases at the expense of the E sector, and vice versa.

In the following discussion we again use the two equations of the generalized Scandinavian model:

$$\pi_A = \pi_w + \alpha_S(\lambda_E - \lambda_S) \tag{1}$$

$$\pi = \phi\pi^* - b(u - u^*) \tag{2}$$

Figure 5.9 is a graphic presentation of the two equations. As a starting point we again take the equilibrium position G_0. Let us assume that the government raises the demand for goods and services in both sectors through expansive fiscal and monetary policies and that it therefore brings the economy to the point G_1 on the Phillips curve R_0 in Figure 5.9. According to the Phillips curve analysis, at this point the unemployment rate is lower and the inflation rate is higher than at the equilibrium G_0.

To satisfy the unexpected additional demand, firms in both sectors will attempt to increase employment through an increase in the rate of growth of wages. In the S sector this occurs without a problem, since firms follow a markup pricing rule and increase their supply price in accordance with the increase in money

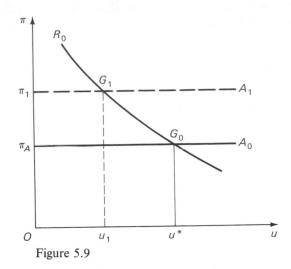

Figure 5.9

wages. In the E sector, however, higher money wages lead to a decline in profitability, because product prices (or their rate of increase) are determined in the world market. The decline in the share of profits in the E sector can be seen directly in Figure 5.9 because the inflation rate corresponding to point G_1 lies above the distribution-neutral Aukrust–EFO line A_0.

One should note that at G_1 the actual output exceeds the desired level ($u < u^*$) and therefore a higher real and nominal income is produced and spent. According to the demand conditions of the Scandinavian model, especially the higher income elasticity for S goods, the demand for S goods increases.

Because the share of profits in the S sector remains constant, firms attempt to satisfy the increase in demand by increasing employment and expanding capacity. This raises the real rate of growth in the S sector. The decline in the profit share in the E sector prevents marginal firms in the industry from undertaking the investments needed to maintain their competitiveness in international markets. The failure of these uncompetitive firms leads to a reduction in the rates of growth of output and of employment in the E sector. This is the core of the Branson–Myhr-

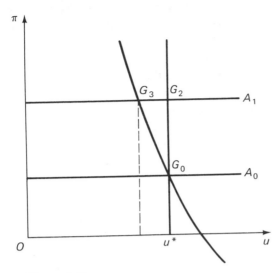

Figure 5.10

man adjustment mechanism. Whereas real growth accelerates in the S sector, it decelerates in the E sector, thereby leading to a shift in the shares of the two sectors. The share of the S sector increases, and that of the E sector declines. The process of shifting output shares is linked, of course, to a shift in the distribution of employment. Workers transfer from the E sector to the S sector.

In equation (1) this result implies an increase in the parameter α_S. An increasing α_S leads to an upward shift in Figure 5.9 of the Aukrust–EFO line. If the expected rate of inflation remains unchanged, then the process of shifting shares ends at point G_1 in Figure 5.9. (The new Aukrust–EFO line is at A_1; the share of the S sector has increased relative to the starting point G_0.)

However, at point G_1 the actual rate of inflation exceeds the expected rate ($\pi_1 > \pi^*$), so that the expected rate of inflation will be revised. This is expressed by an upward shift in the Phillips curve, implying a deceleration of output growth in both sectors and a consequent increase in the overall rate of unemployment. It is possible that further shifts in sectoral output shares will subsequently occur. If so, this would bring about further movements in the Aukrust–EFO line. An exact analysis of this possibility goes beyond the sketch of the model presented here, however.

We can nonetheless investigate the question of a long-run equilibrium. The parameter ϕ in the Phillips curve again plays a decisive role. Under the assumption that $\phi = 1$, the relationship $u = u^*$ must hold in a long-run equilibrium. For example, the economy will reach a point such as G_2 in Figure 5.10. In contrast, when $\phi < 1$, economic policy makers have the opportunity to keep the unemployment rate permanently below the natural rate u^* (point G_3 in Figure 5.10). At G_2 as well as at G_3 the real share of the S sector has increased relative to the starting point G_0 (as has the parameter α_S), while the world rate of inflation has remained constant.

In conclusion, we can summarize the Branson–Myhrman interpretation of the generalized Scandinavian model as follows:

1. The Phillips curve determines the rate of inflation as a function of excess demand.
2. In contrast, the Aukrust–EFO equation determines the real shares of the two sectors.

6

Stagflation

6.1. Definition and basic concepts

Stagflation is a condition of the economy that is as inconvenient as the word itself is inelegant. The widely accepted definitions of stagflation define the phenomenon by its symptoms. M. Bronfenbrenner stated: "Stagflation is a condition in which the price level is rising despite the existence of substantial unemployment. (Indeed, the unemployment level may be rising at the same time)" (1979, p. 226). A.S. Blinder started his investigation of stagflation with the definition: "*Stagflation* . . . connote(s) the simultaneous occurrence of economic *stag*nation and comparatively high rates of in*flation*" (1979, p. 1). Although stagflation problems were well known in the 1960s, stagflation became an international problem after the world recession of 1974–5.

In this chapter we will consider stagflation in the context of a neoclassical macroeconomic model. After a brief explanation of the basic elements of this model, we will develop the model of a demand-induced stagflation and the core of the stagflation analysis, the supply-inflation model. Stagflation in relation to the 1974–5 world recession is discussed at the end of the chapter.

In general we can distinguish two types of stagflation.

1. Stagflation as an adjustment process following a previous demand inflation

187

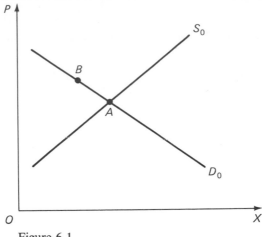

Figure 6.1

2. Stagflation resulting from an autonomous shift in the supply
   function ("supply inflation")

1. Stagflation as an adjustment process following a demand inflation can be understood as a business-cycle phenomenon that
appears in the later phase of the cycle. It is generally accepted
that in this phase prices and costs continue to rise, whereas real
output fails to increase or begins to decline.

2. Stagflation as supply inflation is explained by an upward
shift of the supply function that was not induced by a preceding
increase in aggregate demand. This supply shock can, as we will
see, have different causes.

One can differentiate the two types of stagflation by using a
well-known geometric representation. The tools of this analysis
are the macroeconomic demand function D_0 and the macroeconomic supply function S_0. In Figure 6.1 real output is plotted on
the abscissa and the price level on the ordinate. It is intuitively
plausible that the aggregate demand curve slopes downward and
the aggregate supply curve slopes upward. The functions under
discussion are macroeconomic or aggregate functions, however;
they do not refer to individual markets.

The aggregate demand curve

Since the demand curve D_0 is derived from a complete macroeconomic system, it is an equilibrium curve. Each point on D_0 corresponds to a possible equilibrium in the goods and money markets – in other words, to an intersection of the IS and LM curves. For example, a movement from A to B along D_0 should be interpreted as follows: If the price level rises for a given supply of money, then the money market moves into disequilibrium and excess demand for money results. This will increase the rate of interest, which eliminates the disequilibrium in the money market and reduces the interest-sensitive components of consumption and investment demand. Point B differs from point A because at B the goods and money markets are again in equilibrium but at a higher rate of interest and a higher general price level.

The aggregate supply curve

Because the shift in the supply curve is the core of the stagflation analysis, let us examine the construction of the aggregate supply function in more detail. This function is determined by the labor market equilibrium and the production function. The production function relates the level of output to the level of inputs; for example, $X = F(N,K)$, where N and K represent the quantity of labor and capital, respectively. Because we are only interested in analyzing short-run changes in the economy, we can treat the stock of capital as being fixed. Thus, we can write $X = F(N,\bar{K})$, where $\bar{K}$ is constant. Given any level of employment N, the production function shows the level of output the economy will produce for some given stock of capital $\bar{K}$.

Figure 6.2 depicts a typical short-run neoclassical production function. To determine the level of employment and consequently the level of output, we have to look at the labor market.

The labor market

We use a neoclassical model of the labor market. For the demand for labor, we assume that firms in the economy will hire

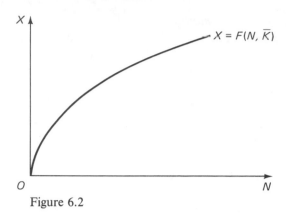

Figure 6.2

labor up to the point at which the real wage rate is equal to the marginal product of labor. Because the marginal product of labor diminishes as more labor is hired, the demand for labor is a decreasing function of the real wage. [This relationship is represented graphically as $f(N,\bar{K})$ in Figure 6.4.]

In the standard neoclassical model the supply curve of labor is postulated as an upward-sloping schedule of the real wage rate. More recent contributions include the distinction between the actual price level P and the expected price level P^*. According to a well-known theory, the supply of labor $h(N)$ is an upward-sloping function of the "expected real wage" (Branson, 1979). This is expressed in equation (1).

$$\frac{W}{P^*} = h(N) \qquad h'(N) > 0 \tag{1}$$

where W/P^* denotes the expected real wage, and $h(N)$ describes the labor–leisure preference of workers. Instead of equation (1) we can write

$$W = P^* \cdot h(N) \tag{2}$$

Now we can convert equation (2) into a relationship between the actual real wage W/P (rather than the expected real wage) and the level of employment N. Multiplying equation (2) by $1/P$, we

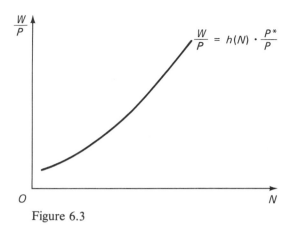

$$\frac{W}{P} = h(N) \cdot \frac{P^*}{P}$$

Figure 6.3

get the relationship

$$\frac{W}{P} = h(N) \cdot \frac{P^*}{P} \qquad (3)$$

which is plotted in Figure 6.3. The labor supply curve in the figure is identical with the labor supply curve as usually drawn in the $(W/P, N)$ space if we assume that the quotient P^*/P is one – that is, that workers correctly anticipate the actual price level. This means that workers have no "money illusion" and the labor supply depends only on the real wage rate W/P.[1] The equations for the demand for and the supply of labor, therefore, are

$$\frac{W}{P} = f(N) \qquad \text{(demand for labor)}$$

$$\frac{W}{P} = h(N) \cdot \frac{P^*}{P} \qquad \text{(supply of labor)}$$

The two equations are graphically represented in Figure 6.4. This formulation implies that employers always have correct expectations, whereas workers may be mistaken. The main argument for this assumption is that firms have to predict only their

[1] If the quotient P^*/P is less than one, the price expectation P^* does not fully adapt to changes in P. This is called "money illusion" (Branson, 1979, pp. 110, 113).

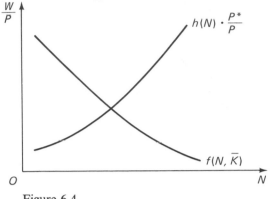

Figure 6.4

own prices (which they set), whereas workers have to predict a weighted average of all prices – that is, the purchasing power of their wages.[2]

The equilibrium condition in the labor market is

$$f(N) = h(N) \cdot \frac{P^*}{P} \tag{4}$$

The labor market equilibrium is represented by the intersection of the two curves at point A in Figure 6.5a. For given values of the actual price level P_0 and the expected price level P_0^*, equilibrium employment is N_0 and the real wage rate is W_0/P_0.

From the production function in Figure 6.5b we can derive the level of output X_0 that corresponds to employment N_0. Combining Figures 6.5a and b we can plot point A on the supply curve in the (P,X) space in Figure 6.5c. Let us assume that the price expectation P^* is fixed and the price level rises exogenously from P_0 and P_1. This implies that the ratio P^*/P decreases and the aggregate labor supply curve shifts outward to the right in Figure

---

[2] This argument was developed in M. Friedman's Nobel lecture. He argued that the real wage that matters to the employer "is the wage in terms of the price of his product." To workers, however, the situation is different. "What matters to them is the purchasing power of wages not over the particular good they produce but over all goods in general" (Friedman, 1977, p. 457).

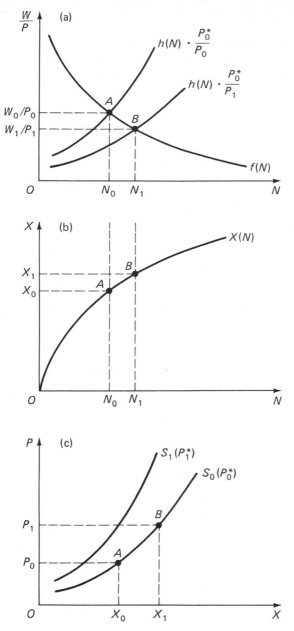

Figure 6.5. (a) Labor market; (b) production function; (c) supply function.

6.5a while the demand curve for labor remains fixed. As one can readily see, employment rises from N_0 to N_1 and output from X_0 to X_1 in Figure 6.5b (point B). When we combine the increasing price level in Figure 6.5a with the increasing output in Figure 6.5b, we find a positive relationship between the price level and real output, the aggregate supply curve $S_0(P_0^*)$ in Figure 6.5c.

This analysis is based on the assumption of a given price expectation P^*. If workers realize that the general price level has increased, they correct their expectation of the price level and set it higher according to the price increase (from P_0 to P_1 in Figure 6.5c). Therefore, the labor supply curve shifts upward in Figure 6.5a because the index P^*/P increases again. In the (P, X) space this upward shift manifests itself in an upward shift of the aggregate supply curve from $S_0(P_0^*)$ to $S_1(P_1^*)$ in Figure 6.5c.

The aggregate supply curve depicts the production of goods planned by firms at alternative price levels under the assumption of a given price expectation of workers.

Employment–unemployment

At the beginning of this chapter stagflation was defined in terms of inflation and high (or increasing) unemployment. The following analysis, however, is in terms of levels of employment rather than rates of unemployment. A shift in the demand curve or the supply curve of labor will shift the employment equilibrium in the labor market. In Figure 6.5a, for example, the increase in the labor supply increases employment from N_0 to N_1. Implicit in this analysis is the assumption of the existence of a labor force L, defined as that level of employment at which the labor supply curve becomes vertical. The difference between the total labor force L and the level of employment in Figure 6.6 is defined as the level of unemployment U_0.

A shift in either the supply curve or the demand curve of labor leads to an expansion or contraction of employment and therefore to a contraction or expansion of the level of unemployment. The problem with this analysis is that in a strict sense unemployment is "voluntary," since the workers are always *on* their supply

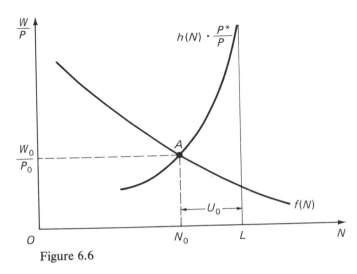

Figure 6.6

curve (see point A in Figure 6.6). In this context it might be reasonable to take a pragmatic view and distinguish between "normal" and "abnormal" levels of unemployment. With this distinction, stagflation can be redefined as a condition in which the price level is rising despite the existence of an abnormal level of unemployment – that is, an abnormally low level of employment. The larger part of the following discussion, especially the wage-push model, is based on this interpretation of the rate of unemployment.

In the later discussion of the "oil shock" model, the notion of rigid real wages is introduced. When labor demand falls (as a result of the energy price increase) real wages do not fall so that actual employment in the labor market is off the labor supply curve (point A' in Figure 6.17a). In this case "involuntary" unemployment in a strict sense develops and can be measured by the difference $N_0 - N_1$ in Figure 6.17a.

6.2 Demand-induced stagflation

Let us start with the first model, demand-induced stagflation. The story should begin with a business cycle upswing, trig-

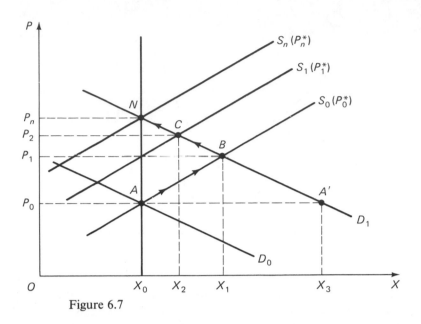

Figure 6.7

gered by an increase in aggregate demand from D_0 to D_1 (Figure 6.7). Such an autonomous shift in the demand function can arise from any factor that shifts either the IS curve or the LM curve or both. These factors include, for example,

1. An increase in the propensity to consume and/or a change in autonomous expenditures of the private sector
2. An increase in the money supply
3. An increase in government expenditures
4. A combination of 2 and 3
5. An increase in exports in an open economy

The increase in aggregate demand leads to a goods gap $\overline{AA}'$ in Figure 6.7. Point A', however, is not feasible because it is off the short-run supply curve S_0. Firms are willing to produce a higher output (at lower real wages) only on the short-run supply curve S_0. A short-run equilibrium of the economy is found at point B, the intersection of D_1 and S_0, characterized by a higher price level and a higher real output. But point B cannot be a long-run equilibrium. Remember that the short-run supply curve is drawn under the assumption that the expected price level is P_0^*. As one can see, position B implies an actual price level P_1 that is higher than P_0^*. At a short-run equilibrium, firms are satisfied but workers are not. When workers realize that the actual price level has risen to P_1, which is higher than the expected level P_0^*, they correct their expectations upward to $P_1^* = P_1$.[3] Since the position of the S curve depends on the expected price level, the supply curve shifts upward in Figure 6.7 from S_0 (implying P_0^*) to the new position S_1 drawn for the new price expectation P_1^*. The new intersection of D_1 and S_1 is point C, which is marked by a higher price level and a fall in the output rate to X_2. But again, the actual price level P_2 exceeds the expected price level P_1^* at position C of the economy. And as soon as workers learn that they have been fooled again, they correct their expectations of the price level and set it higher in accordance with the price increase. Therefore, nominal wages increase (to restore the real wage), which again shifts the aggregate supply curve upward to the left. Whenever the intersection of S and D (i.e., a short-run equilibrium) is to the right of the X_0 line, the actual price level is higher than the expected price level and the aggregate supply curve shifts upward.[4] The only place where the economy can be on the demand curve D and where workers are not fooled is point N, the intersection of $S_n(P_n^*)$ and D_1. The supply curve S_n reflects the full adjustment of money wages to the higher price level. In the new (long-run) equilibrium N the same real wage exists as at A, but both nominal wages and the price level have risen.

Thus, demand inflation occurs in two distinct phases:

1. An expansive phase $\overline{AB}$, in which an increase in demand manifests itself in (temporarily) greater output and employment and an increase in the price level.

---

[3] As one can see, this mechanism implies an expectations-formation process in its simplest form: $\Delta P^* = P_{-1} - P_{-1}^*$. The change in the price expectation ΔP^* is always equal to the difference between the actual price level and the expected price level of the last period.

[4] Points on the vertical line $X = X_0$ represent positions of long-run equilibrium with $P^* = P$. If D and S intersect at the $X = X_0$ line, the conditions of a long-run equilibrium are satisfied. The actual price level P is exactly what individuals expect.

2. A stagflation phase $\overline{BN}$, in which there is a further increase in the price level and an adjustment of the supply function to higher costs. Output and therefore employment fall, whereas prices continue to rise as indicated by the path BN.

6.3 Supply inflation and stagflation

Let us turn to the second possibility: Inflation is initiated by an autonomous upward shift in the supply curve. Such a supply shift could be caused by a variety of events, including the following (Blinder, 1979, p. 14):

   a. Natural disaster
   b. Monopoly of natural resources [Organization of Petroleum-Exporting Countries (OPEC) control of crude oil]
   c. Adverse changes in the terms of trade
   d. Decrease of labor productivity
   e. Aggressive wage or profit increase

A natural disaster such as an earthquake, a flood, or simply bad weather could lead to a scarcity of agricultural products or other commodities. Monopoly control of some natural resource (such as the OPEC cartel fixing the price of crude oil) could raise its price. A deterioration in the terms of trade means that a country has to give up a larger volume of its domestic product in exchange for the same volume of imports. (The increase in the oil price, for example, worsened the terms of trade in the industrial world.) Higher prices of raw agricultural products, intermediate goods, and/or crude oil are cost increases in the industrial sector.

At higher costs firms are willing to continue to supply their old levels of output only at a higher price. The aggregate supply curve shifts upward. A fall in the marginal productivity of labor – that is, a downward shift in the labor demand function – can also initiate an adverse shift of the supply curve in the goods market.

A considerable amount of literature is devoted to explaining the shift in the supply curve by "administered" prices and wages. Administered price increases by industries that produce intermediate and investment goods as well as wage increases due to collective bargaining cause the supply curve to shift upward. The cost increases in this context have to be autonomous in the sense that they would not have occurred merely as a result of competitive markets in the absence of monopoly power. Cost-push models are relatively simple as long as they contain only a single impulse. It is customary to distinguish a "pure" wage-push model and a "pure" price-push model. The former results from attempts to increase real wages; the latter from attempts to raise profit margins.

We will now take a closer look at the stagflation process indicated by administrative wage policy. This pure wage-push model is widely accepted. We will then present a model of stagflation that tries to take into account the price policy of the OPEC cartel and the scenario of the world recession in 1974–5.

6.4 The role of demand policy in the stagflation process

Important for the analysis of stagflation is understanding the role of monetary policy or, more generally, of the government's demand management policy. It is useful to distinguish between "accommodating" and "nonaccommodating" demand policy. Stagflation develops when the supply function shifts upward – due to one or more of the causes mentioned earlier – but the demand function remains unchanged because the money supply does not increase at the same time. If, on the other hand, the supply shift is followed by an increase in the nominal money supply (for instance, as a consequence of expansive fiscal measures), then the government validates the previous wage and price increase by increasing demand and "reflating" the economy. In the latter case stagflation will disappear and real output (and employment) will approach its previous level.

Supply-shift inflation without accommodating
demand policy

Let us begin with the standard case of stagflation analysis: a one-time increase in money wages due to the wage-raising power of a strong trade union. First, assume no validating increase in the money supply or government expenditure. We shall develop this stagflation model in two steps:

1. Model I assumes a given (fixed) price expectation P^*.
2. Model II allows for an adjustment of price expectations to changes in the price level.

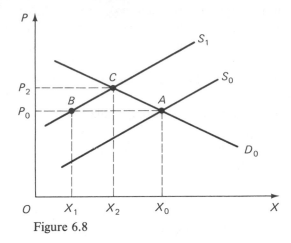

Figure 6.8

Model I: fixed price expectations. The wage increase pushes the aggregate supply function upward and to the left from S_0 to S_1, whereas the demand curve remains at the initial position D_0 (Figure 6.8). The new intersection C of D_0 and S_1 is characterized by a smaller real output X_2 and a higher price level P_2. To understand the background of the situation we have to take a closer look at the labor market.

We can use the graphic apparatus introduced at the beginning of this section. In Figure 6.9a the aggregate demand for labor $f(N)$ represents the marginal productivity of labor schedule; the function $h_0(N)$ denotes the aggregate supply of labor for a given labor–leisure preference of workers; and the ratio P^*/P is a measure of the money illusion of workers. A cost-push effect in this context is initiated by an exogenous upward shift in the labor supply function $h(N)$, which can result from (a) an increase in wage demands as a result of collective bargaining or (b) a shift in the taste of the workers for leisure.

The demand for an increase in real wages (in a highly unionized economy) shifts the labor supply function from the initial position $h_0(N)$ to $h_1(N)$ in Figure 6.9a. This shift in the labor supply function reduces equilibrium employment to N_1 and equilibrium out-

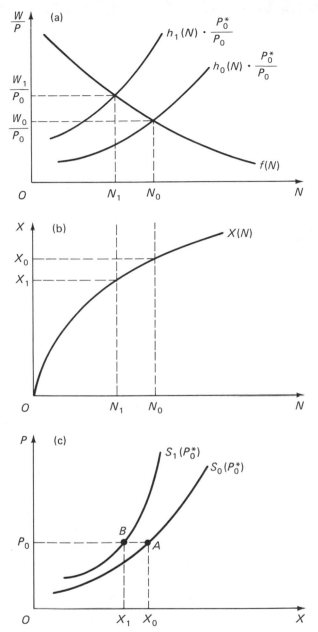

Figure 6.9. (a) Labor market; (b) production function; (c) supply function.

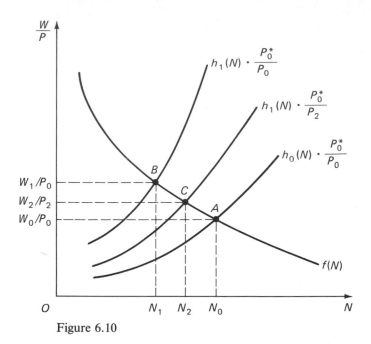

Figure 6.10

put to X_1 at the initial price level P_0. In other words, the macro-economic supply curve shifts upward to $S_1(P_0^*)$ in Figure 6.9c.

Let us return to the situation in the goods market shown in Figure 6.8. The shift of the supply curve from S_0 to S_1 creates excess demand measured by $\overline{X_0 X_1}$ at the original price level P_0. Firms want to supply X_1, but consumers and the government want to buy X_0. This excess demand causes prices to rise to P_2. As we can see in Figure 6.8, the rise in the price level increases the supply of real output along the new supply curve S_1 (from B to C) and at the same time reduces the equilibrium output demanded along the demand curve D_0 (from A to C).

The price increase in the goods market to P_2 changes the index of price expectation in the labor market to P_0^*/P_2. Because the price expectation remains unchanged throughout this analysis, a price increase will reduce this ratio. In Figure 6.10 the labor demand curve remains fixed, whereas the labor supply curve shifts to the right to the position $h_1(N)(P_0^*/P_2)$, thus increasing employment to N_2. Equilibrium is restored in the goods market at a price level P_2 where excess demand has disappeared and output has fallen to X_2. Note that points A, B, and C in Figure 6.8 (the goods market) correspond with points A, B, and C in Figure 6.10 (the labor market). The increase in wage demands represented by an upward shift in the labor supply curve raises costs and causes firms to reduce output and increase prices.

Model II: adaptive price expectations. Model I does not tell the full story because of the assumption of fixed price expectations. In model II we introduce an adaptive price expectation mechanism of the form $\Delta P^* = P_{-1} - P_{-1}^*$, which was used in the section on demand-induced stagflation. The change in the price expectation ΔP_t^* equals the difference between the actual price level and the expected price level of the previous period. It is the task of model II to examine the influence of the adjustment of price expectations on the supply curve. The result will be rather cheerless in that the increase in price expectations (as a consequence of the increased price level) will further aggravate stagflation. We can begin with the short-run equilibrium at point C in Figure 6.11, the intersection of D_0 and the supply curve $S_1(P_0^*)$. As soon as we allow for an adjustment of price expectations, this position cannot be stable. Point C implies an actual price level P_2 that is higher than the underlying price expectation $P_0^* = P_0$. We appeal to the same argument used in Section 6.2: At a short-run equilibrium, firms are satisfied but workers are not because the unexpected price increase reduces their real wage. Therefore workers correct their price expectations and adjust the expected price level upward to $P_2^* = P_2$. Since the position of the S curve depends on the expected price level, the supply curve shifts upward in Figure 6.11 from $S_1(P_0^*)$ to $S_2(P_2^*)$. Along the new supply curve $S_2(P_2^*)$, there is only one long-run equilibrium at point D, where the expected price level P_2^* is exactly the same as the actual price level P_2. The new supply curve $S_2(P_2^*)$ intersects the demand curve D_0 at point E, which is characterized by a higher

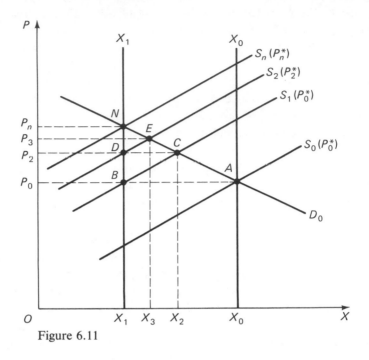

Figure 6.11

price level P_3 and a lower real output level X_3. But again at this intersection the actual price level P_3 exceeds the expected price level P_2^*. When workers learn that the price level has risen again, they adjust their price expectation P^* upward. As mentioned, whenever the intersection of the S and D curves is to the right of the X_1X_1 line,[5] the actual price level is higher than the expected price level and the aggregate supply curve shifts upward along the vertical line X_1X_1. The supply curve will remain stable when the crossing point of $S_n(P_n^*)$ and D_0 is reached. At this point the price expectations of the workers are correct – that is, $P_n^* = P_n$ – and there is no stimulus to change P^* further.

Consider the same process in the labor market. The initial wage push leads in Figure 6.12 to a shift in the supply function to

---

[5] Points on this line represent positions of long-run equilibrium with correct price expectations $P^* = P$.

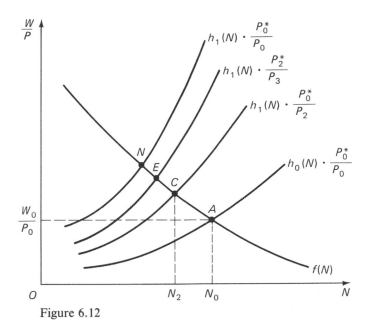

Figure 6.12

$h_1(N)(P_0^*/P_0)$. Because the price in the goods market rises to P_2, the index of money illusion P_0^*/P_2 is reduced and the labor supply function moves back to the position $h_1(N)(P_0^*/P_2)$. The result is point C in the labor market (with employment N_2), which corresponds to point C in the goods market (Figure 6.11). Similarly, point E in the labor market (in which the index of money illusion is P_2^*/P_3) corresponds to point E in the goods market. While the S curve moves upward to S_n in Figure 6.11, the labor supply function shifts in the direction of $h_1(N)(P_0^*/P_0)$. At N we reach a position in which there is no money illusion in the labor market and the actual price level is equal to the expected price level (that is, $P^*/P = P_0^*/P_0 = 1$). The labor supply curve is in an equilibrium position; it corresponds to the long-run supply curve X_1X_1 in the goods market.

To sum up, the stagflation process initiated by a wage-push can be analyzed in two steps. In the first step (without considering the adjustment of price expectations) the wage-push leads to a short-run equilibrium with an increased price level, a smaller output, and a reduced level of employment. In the second step the adjustment of price expectations to the increased price level strengthens the stagflation phenomenon; prices increase further and employment shrinks until a new long-run equilibrium is attained. An additional increase in the wage level has been reached, but at the cost of a lower level of employment.

Supply-shift inflation with accommodating demand policy

With this model, accommodating demand policy in a situation of stagflation can be analyzed only with additional simplifications. In particular one must specify exactly the degree to which the expectation adjustment process can develop before the government starts to intervene with expansionary monetary and fiscal measures.[6]

In Figure 6.13 our starting point is the intersection of D_0 and S_0 at the full-employment level X_0. Full employment implies tightness in the labor and goods markets (Bronfenbrenner, 1979, p. 227). By assumption organized trade unions take advantage of this situation and secure an increase in real wages, which shifts the aggregate supply curve to $S_1(P_0^*)$ in Figure 6.13. The new intersection of D_0 and S_1 (point C) is marked by a real output that is less than the initial output X_0 (i.e., the actual rate of employment is now less than the rate at X_0) and a higher price level. Up to this point the analysis is not different from the analysis of the first type of stagflation.

But now let us assume – in contrast to the former case – that the government (and/or the central bank) is under political pressure (especially in election years) to increase aggregate demand to raise the level of employment. The authorities initiate an expansive monetary and fiscal policy to increase aggregate demand

---

[6] For example, the government increases autonomous expenditures and simultaneously raises the money supply. In terms of the IS-LM analysis, both the IS curve and the LM curve will shift to the right.

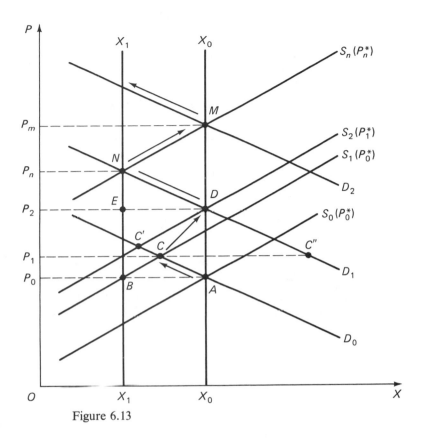

Figure 6.13

to D_1 in Figure 6.13. At the same time the price expectations rise to P_1^*, which implies that the supply curve shifts to $S_2(P_1^*)$. In the absence of any accommodating monetary and fiscal policy, a new short-run equilibrium would come into existence at point C', the intersection of the original demand curve D_0 and $S_2(P_1^*)$. If the government pursues policies designed to move the economy back to the previous equilibrium at X_0, the demand curve must be shifted upward along the path depicted by the arrow (from point C to D).

At point C and price level P_1 there is a goods gap in the commodity market. The excess demand for goods leads to a rise in the price level, which makes producers willing to produce a higher output along the short-run supply curve $S_2(P_1^*)$. The previous equilibrium position is restored at D, the crossing point of the demand curve D_1 and the new supply curve $S_2(P_1^*)$.

There is, however, an important difference compared with the initial position: At point D the price expectations are not correct. The actual price level P_2 is higher than the expected price level P_1^*. Therefore, workers correct their price expectations and revise the expected price level upward to P_2^* through point E (see Figure 6.13). Provided the demand function remains fixed at the position D_1 and expectations adjust as discussed earlier, the supply curve shifts continuously upward and to the left along D_1 over the interval $\overline{DN}$. The new intersection N of the demand curve D_1 and the supply curve $S_n(P_n^*)$ is a new long-run equilibrium because the expected price level equals the actual price level ($P_n = P_n^*$). However, at N stagflation is fully developed; there is not only a higher price level but also a lower rate of employment compared with point C. This position of stagflation cannot be accepted politically by the government, which answers with additional government purchases accommodated by an increase in the money supply. This fiscal and monetary policy mix will shift the demand curve to D_2 and move the economy again to the initial output position at point M. We have now duplicated the situation that characterized point D. The economy has returned to the higher initial employment position but the workers suffer from money illusion: The actual price level P_m exceeds the expected price level P_n^*. The adjustment of price expectations to the new reality of higher actual prices shifts the supply curve again upward and to the left (in the direction of the arrow) and the developments already analyzed at points C and D will repeat themselves.

If one follows the arrows in Figure 6.13 one can observe stagflation periods over the ranges $\overline{AC}$ and $\overline{DN}$ followed by expansive episodes over the ranges $\overline{CD}$ and $\overline{NM}$. This analysis can be interpreted as an "aggressive" wage-push model (Machlup,

1969), in which the increase in real wages is repeatedly eroded through the resulting inflation because of an accommodating monetary and fiscal policy. M. Bronfenbrenner (1979) related both types of stagflation with the political system. Under American conditions the first type of stagflation (without accommodating demand policy) is associated most frequently with the Republican party. The upward movement of the aggregate supply curve (particularly the full adjustment of price expectations) will come to a standstill or even reverse itself if the government refuses to support the expansion of aggregate demand and convinces the public that it will adhere to the "hard line." Trade unions will eventually realize that the resulting abnormal unemployment rate is too high a price for the increased real wage. The basic idea of a nonaccommodating strategy is to try to give the responsibility for maintaining high employment to the trade unions (Lindbeck, 1980, p. 82). Traces of such policy were found in the U.S. Republican party during the Eisenhower administration (1953–61) and the first years of the Nixon administration (1969–71).

The second type of stagflation process is associated more frequently with the Democratic party because of its stronger commitment to full employment. At the low-employment position (point *C* in Figure 6.13) the Democrats are more likely to adopt an expansive demand policy to validate the previous increase in wages and prices. Under these political conditions a time path of the economy will develop (*ACDNM* in Figure 6.13) in which stagflation episodes alternate with expansive periods.

6.5 The "oil shock"

Using this model we can now investigate the stagflation phenomena that were set off by the so-called oil shock. As is well known, the OPEC cartel reduced the supply of raw oil and simultaneously quadrupled its price in 1973–4. If we want to analyze the supply shock in the framework of the previous model, we have to introduce two further assumptions.

a. The production function has to be modified by introducing an additional production factor E (energy) that cooperates with labor N and capital K. The production function now reads

$$X = F(N, E, \bar{K}) \tag{1}$$

Again we are only interested in analyzing short-run changes in the economy; we can treat the stock of capital as being fixed: $K = \bar{K}$. We assume that the production function (1) has the neoclassical properties – that is, that the marginal products of the two variable production factors N and E are positive (1.1) but decreasing (1.2):

Marginal product of labor (MPL)	Marginal product of energy (MPE)	
$\dfrac{\partial F}{\partial N} = F_N > 0$	$\dfrac{\partial F}{\partial E} = F_E > 0$	(1.1)

and

Decreasing MPL	Decreasing MPE	
$\dfrac{\partial^2 F}{\partial N^2} = F_{NN} < 0$	$\dfrac{\partial^2 F}{\partial E^2} = F_{EE} < 0$	(1.2)

b. For simplicity we assume that the OPEC cartel has sufficient monopoly power to determine the relative price of energy $P_E/P = \pi_E$. This might be considered an intermediate-run rather than a short-run assumption, but the main results will not change if we understand it as strictly short run.

Under the assumption that firms in the economy maximize their profits, the following two conditions hold:

$$\frac{W}{P} = F_N(N, E, \bar{K}) \tag{2}$$

$$\pi_E = \frac{P_E}{P} = F_E(N, E, \bar{K}) \tag{3}$$

Relation (2) states that labor is hired up to the point at which the real wage equals the marginal product of labor $F_N(N, E, \bar{K})$. Relation (3) says that energy is used up to the point where its relative price P_E/P equals the marginal product of energy $F_E(N, E, \bar{K})$.

Solving equation (3) for E results in the relationship

$$E = g(N,\pi_E) \qquad g_N > 0; \, g_{\pi_E} < 0 \tag{4}$$

This is a demand function for energy. The demand for energy depends on the relative factor price π_E and on the amount of labor used in the production process. An increase in π_E decreases the demand for energy, whereas an increase in N increases the input demand for E because production factors tend to be complementary.

To make the analysis comparable to the model of the previous part we substitute equation (4) into equations (1) and (2). We can now represent the production function and the labor demand function in the following way:

$$X = F[N, \bar{K}, g(N,\pi_E)] = F(N,\pi_E,\bar{K}) \tag{1.3}$$

$$\frac{W}{P} = F_N[N, \bar{K}, g(N,\pi_E)] = f(N,\pi_E,\bar{K}) \tag{2.1}$$

Figure 6.14 portrays the production function (1.3) in the $(N - X)$ space. It differs from the production function in Figure 6.2 by the parameter π_E, the fixed energy price. The production function (1.3) shows the output level X for different values of N given the relative price of energy π_E. This modified production function is drawn under the assumption that for a given π_E and N, firms use their optimal amount of energy according to the profit-maximization condition (3). A higher energy price leads to a reduction in the amount of energy used and to a downward shift in the production function. In Figure 6.14a there are two production functions for two different energy prices with $\pi_E^1 > \pi_E^0$.

In Figure 6.14b the labor demand curve $f(N,\pi_E,\bar{K})$ is drawn. It also takes into consideration the profit-maximizing condition (3) on the energy side. It differs from the labor demand function in Figure 6.4 only through the additional parameter π_E. An increase in π_E will shift $f(N,\pi_E,\bar{K})$ to the origin, implying that the firms now demand less labor at any real wage.

In Figure 6.14 we consider the effect of an exogenous rise in the price of energy. If the OPEC cartel increases π_E^0 to π_E^1, the pro-

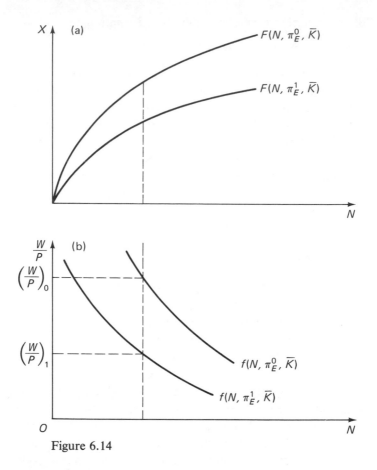

Figure 6.14

duction function shifts downward to $F(N, \pi_E^1, \bar{K})$ in Figure 6.14a; the labor demand curve shifts to $f(N, \pi_E^1, \bar{K})$ in Figure 6.14b. This means that at a higher energy price firms are willing to hold the same number of workers only if the real wage drops from $(W/P)_0$ to $(W/P)_1$.

Let us consider Figure 6.14b in more detail and complete the analysis by introducing the labor supply curve developed in the previous model.

$$\frac{W}{P} = h(N) \cdot \frac{P^*}{P} \qquad \text{(supply of labor)}$$

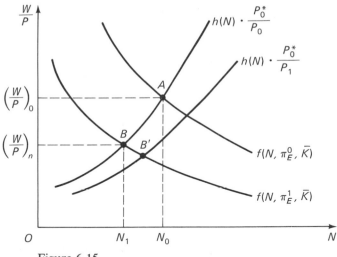

Figure 6.15

The initial situation in the labor market is represented by point A in Figure 6.15. The OPEC increase in π_E shifts the demand for labor curve down to $f(N, \pi_E^1, \bar{K})$, which reduces equilibrium employment from N_0 to N_1. The new equilibrium position is B.

But this is not the end of the story. We have to go back to the goods market. In Figure 6.16 two effects, the downward shift of the production function and of the labor demand function in Figure 6.14, cause the supply curve to move upward from $S_0(\pi_E^0, P_0^*)$ to $S_1(\pi_E^1, P_0^*)$. At the initial price level P_0, firms are willing to produce only $O\bar{X}_1$ units of output. At P_0 excess demand in the goods market, measured by the distance $\overline{AB}$, develops and forces the price level to move upward until point B' with (P_1, X_1) is reached. (Points B and B' in Figures 6.15 and 6.16 correspond to each other.)

A question now arises: Why can the output level X_1 be produced only at the higher price level P_1? The answer can be found in the developments in the labor market. With given price expectations P_0^*, the labor supply curve shifts to the right in Figure 6.15 to the position $h(N)(P_0^*/P_1)$. Point B' in Figures 6.15 and 6.16 shows the short-run realization of the system. This point cannot

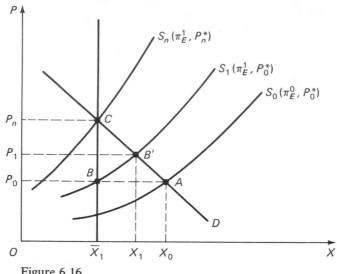

Figure 6.16

be stable because $P_1 > P_0^*$. The expectations adjustment process starts to work and leads to a further upward shift of the supply curve in Figure 6.16. The details of the adjustment process will not be repeated here because the argument was developed in the previous section on Model II. In the absence of any demand management policy, the aggregate demand curve D in Figure 6.16 remains stable. A new long-run equilibrium will be attained when the supply function reaches its final position $S_n(\pi_E^1, P_n^*)$ with the price level P_n and the output level $\bar{X}_1$ (point C). At this position the price expectations are correct – that is, $P_n^* = P_n$ – and there is no further stimulus to adjust P^*.

In the labor market, the labor supply function moves back to the initial position $h(N)(P_0^*/P_0) = h(N)(P_n^*/P_n)$, implying $P_n^* = P_n$, so that point B in Figure 6.15 corresponds to the new long-run equilibrium (point C in Figure 6.16).

According to this analysis the main results of an autonomous increase in π_E by the OPEC cartel are

a. An output drop from X_0 to $\bar{X}_1$ (Figure 6.16)
b. An increase in the price level from P_0 to P_n (Figure 6.16)
c. A decrease in equilibrium employment from N_0 to N_1 (Figure 6.15)

Some authors such as M. Bruno and J. Sachs (1979a,b) have tried to explain the stagflation episodes in the context of the world recession of 1974–5 by the following assumptions:

1. The OPEC cartel has the monopoly power to determine π_E.
2. Money illusion has disappeared in the labor market in almost all industrial countries. In the context of this model they postulate $P = P^*$. This means that the labor supply function is stable in the $(W/P, N)$ space.
3. Real wages are rigid downward.

Assumptions 2 and 3 have major consequences for the supply side of the economy.

The model is depicted in Figure 6.17. Let us start with the labor market (Figure 6.17a). The initial equilibrium is A, with employment N_0 and real wage rate $(W/P)_0$. The equilibrium employment N_0 inserted into the production function $F(N, \pi_E^0, \bar{K})$ (Figure 6.17b) results in a real output X_0. The salient point of this analysis is that a price change does not change anything in Figures 6.17a and b. The real output X_0 will be produced at all price levels P, since by assumption both relative prices W/P and π_E are fixed. Therefore, output is independent of the price level. In the (P, X) space the supply function will become a vertical line S_0 on the horizontal axis (Figure 6.17c).

The oil shock – that is, the increase in the relative price π_E^0 to π_E^1 – shifts the production function downward to $F(N, \pi_E^1, \bar{K})$ in Figure 6.17b and the labor demand function to $f(N, \pi_E^1, \bar{K})$ in Figure 6.17a.

Because the real wages are rigid and firms are profit-maximizing (i.e., firms always operate along their labor demand curve), point A' in Figure 6.17a will result. Employment will fall from N_0 to N_1 and output from $X_0 = F(N_0, \pi_E^0, \bar{K})$ to $X_1 = F(N_1, \pi_E^1, \bar{K})$ (Figure 6.17b). The new position on the production function is A' with a real output X_1. The corresponding supply curve is S_1 in

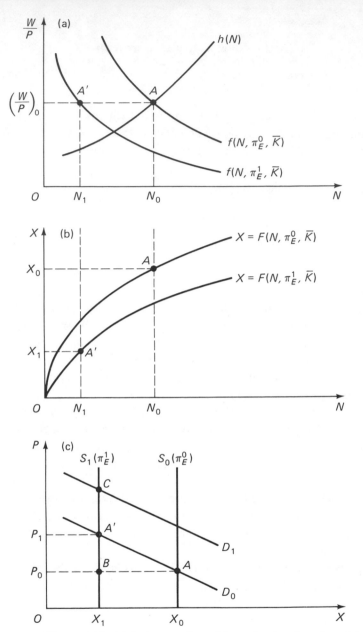

Figure 6.17. (a) Labor market; (b) production function; (c) goods market.

Figure 6.17c. At A' output is again independent of the price level, and the supply function is therefore vertical (S_1 in Figure 6.17c). With constant real wages the increase in the price of energy from π_E^0 to π_E^1 shifts the supply curve to the left and initiates a drop in real output by the amount $X_0 - X_1$. The leftward shift of the supply function generates excess demand at the original price level P_0 to the extent $\overline{AB}$ in the goods market. The latter is removed by a rise in the price level to P_1 in Figure 6.17c.

In this model we can explicitly show the rate of unemployment in Figure 6.17a. The amount of employment that the workers in the economy want to obtain is $\overline{ON_0}$, whereas the amount effectively employed by firms is $\overline{ON_1}$ (point A' on the labor demand curve). Thus, the number of workers who are involuntarily unemployed is $N_0 - N_1$. This model shows that stagflation phenomena develop as a result of the shift in the supply function. In the labor market involuntary unemployment has been created, while excess demand in the goods market increases the general price level (Figure 6.17c). Because the real wages are fixed, at this point a wage-price spiral develops. The price rise has no effect on real wages because it is fully compensated for by an increase in nominal wages.

What will happen if an attempt is made to boost demand, to validate an increase in the price of energy by an expansive fiscal and monetary policy? The answer is straightforward: An accommodative fiscal and monetary policy will shift the demand curve D_0 to D_1 in Figure 6.17c. All that would happen is a further rise in the price level (without any change in real output), a move from point A' to C. Why? The price rise is fully offset by a simultaneous wage increase (wages are "indexed") and an increase in the price of energy P_E. Therefore, both relative prices – the real wage and π_E – remain constant. If the output is determined by supply, as in this case, an increase in real output can come about only as a result of a fall in real wages or a rise in the capital stock.

7

Some traditional explanations of inflation

7.1 The quantity theory

The quantity theory is often characterized as the classical or neoclassical theory of inflation.[1] Recent work, however, has shown that the quantity theory plays a role in neoclassical theory different from its function in classical theory (O'Brien, 1975, pp. 159–65).

We will begin with a short presentation of the quantity theory, then discuss it in the context of a neoclassical model, and conclude with a short sketch of the difference from the classical model. The quantity theory will be presented in two forms:

1. The "transactions" equation formulated by I. Fisher (1920)
2. The "cash balance" equation of the Cambridge school

Irving Fisher's transactions equation

Fisher sought a macroeconomic approach that would enable him to formulate the relationship between the money supply and the general price level. The transactions equation served him well because it described a relationship between the money sup-

[1] By "classical" economics we generally mean the work of A. Smith (1723–90), D. Ricardo (1772–1823), and J.S. Mill (1806–73); "neoclassical" refers to the work of L. Walras (1834–1910), A. Marshall (1842–1924), and A.C. Pigou (1877–1959).

ply M, the velocity of money V, the real volume of transactions T, and the price level P:

$$P \cdot T = M \cdot V \tag{1}$$

In fact this relationship is an identity from which one cannot draw any further conclusions. Because each purchase corresponds to a sale, the value of all sales (the volume of transactions times the average price) must necessarily equal the value of all purchases. The latter must again equal the existing supply of money times the "average" frequency with which that money changes hands. However, one can further assume, along with Fisher, that the velocity of money is determined by institutional developments in the monetary sector and that it remains constant in the short run ($V = \bar{V}$). One can also assume that the real sector determines the volume of transactions and that the latter is also fixed at a predetermined level ($T = \bar{T}$). Under these assumptions, the transactions equation can be interpreted as determining the general price level.

$$P = (\bar{V}/\bar{T})M \tag{2}$$

The price level is proportional to the money supply M; the constant of proportionality is the ratio $\bar{V}/\bar{T}$ (Friedman, 1970a, p. 196).

In the literature one also frequently finds a second presentation of the transactions equation:

$$P \cdot \bar{X} = \bar{V}_x \cdot M \tag{3}$$

In place of the volume of transactions $\bar{T}$, the "real" net national product $\bar{X}$ appears in equation (3). Underlying this substitution is the assumption that the real net national product is proportionately related to the real volume of transactions. In equation (3) the income velocity V_x replaces the transactions velocity V in equation (2).[2]

---

[2] Distinguish the transactions velocity of money V, the number of times a unit of money physically turns over, and V_x, the income velocity of money, the rate of circulation of money relative to the rate of production of real income (Laidler, 1977, p. 62).

The Cambridge equation

In contrast to Fisher's equation, the Cambridge equation uses a microeconomic approach. As formulated by A. Marshall and A.C. Pigou, the question is: What determines the amount of money an economic agent (households and firms) would wish to hold when he needs cash to conduct transactions (Laidler, 1977, p. 59)?

Because money competes with alternative forms of investment, the division of wealth into money and other financial assets is optimal only if the marginal utility yielded by the last unit of cash balances equals the marginal utility derivable from an investment in an alternative asset. Pigou simplified this approach by assuming that the economic agent would not alter the relationship among his wealth, his volume of transactions, and his income in the short run. In this way individuals' demand for money can be aggregated into a macroeconomic demand for money M^D that is proportional to the nominal level of income XP.

$$M^D = k \cdot XP$$

For example, if households and firms hold an average cash balance equal to one-tenth of their nominal income, then the desired coefficient of cash balances k is 0.1. If we add to the money demand function a money supply function and assume that the money market is in equilibrium, then

$$M^D = M^S = M$$

We can establish the following relationship between the Fisher and Cambridge equations:

$$M \cdot \frac{1}{k} = M\bar{V}_x = P\bar{X} \tag{4}$$

where $\bar{V}_x = 1/k$, that is, where the income velocity of money equals the reciprocal of the cash balances coefficient. Relationship (4) is a formal equation, as is the Fisher identity (3). As we have seen, however, the economic interpretations of the two approaches differ considerably.

We now turn to an important implication of the theory of inflation. From the assumption that $\bar{V}/\bar{T}$ or $\bar{V}_x/\bar{X}$ is constant, it follows that the elasticity of the general price level with respect to a change in the supply of money equals unity. This result forms the core of the quantity theory. The elasticity of P with respect to M is

$$\eta_{P \cdot M} = \frac{dP}{dM} \cdot \frac{M}{P} \tag{5}$$

From equation (4) we can derive

$$\frac{dP}{dM} = \frac{\bar{V}_x}{\bar{X}} \tag{6}$$

By substituting in equation (5), we get

$$\eta_{P \cdot M} = \frac{\bar{V}_x}{\bar{X}} \cdot \frac{M}{P} \tag{7}$$

This result may be transformed with the use of the definition of V_x to

$$\eta_{P \cdot M} = \frac{\bar{X} P}{M \bar{X}} \cdot \frac{M}{P} = 1 \tag{8}$$

From equation (3) we can also derive a relationship that the monetarist model uses. By differentiating equation (3),

$$X \, dp + P \, dX = M \, dV_x + V_x dM \tag{9}$$

Dividing both sides of the equation by $1/XP$,

$$\frac{dP}{P} + \frac{dX}{X} = \frac{M}{XP} \, dV_x + \frac{V_x}{XP} \, dM \tag{10}$$

If we use the definition of income velocity $V_x = PX/M$, then we can transform equation (10) into

$$\frac{dP}{P} + \frac{dX}{X} = \frac{dM}{M} + \frac{dV_x}{V_x} \tag{11}$$

Equation (11) presents the income version of the transactions equation in the form of rates of growth. The rate of growth of nominal income (the sum of the terms on the left-hand side) is defined to be equal to the rate of growth of the money supply and the rate of change of the income velocity of money. Under the assumption made by neoclassical theory that the income velocity of money is constant ($dV_x/V_x = 0$), equation (11) may be simplified to

$$\frac{dM}{M} = \frac{dP}{P} + \frac{dX}{X} \quad \text{or} \quad m = \pi + x \tag{12}$$

In other words, the rate of growth of the money supply equals the sum of the rate of growth of the real national product x and the rate of inflation π.

The neoclassical model. The neoclassical model is characterized by a dichotomy in the economic system. Relative prices and the quantities of goods supplied and demanded are determined in the real sector; in contrast, the general price level is determined in the monetary sector. This dichotomy permits one to discuss the real and monetary sectors separately.

We begin with a graphic analysis of the real sector.

$$X = X(N) \qquad \text{(neoclassical production function)} \tag{13}$$

$$\frac{W}{P} = \frac{dX}{dN} \qquad \text{(profit-maximization condition)} \tag{14}$$

$$N^S = N^S \left(\frac{W}{P}\right) \qquad \text{(labor supply function)} \tag{15}$$

Figure 7.1a depicts the well-known neoclassical production function.[3] An increase in the use of labor, the variable factor of production, leads to a less than proportional increase in output; the marginal product of labor dX/dN falls. Figure 7.1b presents the supply N^S of and the demand N^D for labor. The supply of labor is an increasing function of the real wage. The demand function for labor is derived from the firm's profit-maximization condition (price equals marginal cost).

[3] The discussion of the neoclassical model follows the lines of Ackley (1961, pp. 125–37).

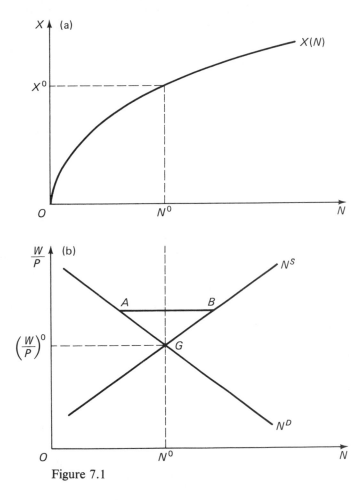

Figure 7.1

The firm's marginal cost of production is defined as the additional costs incurred to produce an additional unit of output. If labor is the only variable input, then the marginal cost equals the ratio $W/(dX/dN)$, or the money wage rate divided by the marginal product of labor. Under the assumption of perfect competition, profits are maximized when

$$\frac{W}{dX/dN} = P \qquad \text{or} \qquad \frac{W}{P} = \frac{dX}{dN}$$

In this case, the profit-maximization condition can also be interpreted as the firm's demand function for labor. Since the marginal product of labor $(dX/dN)(N)$ decreases as N increases, the demand for labor is negatively related to the real wage. Point G in Figure 7.1b $[(W/P)^0, N^0]$ represents equilibrium in the labor market. Flexible real wages guarantee that an equilibrium point such as G will always exist. An excess supply of labor such as $\overline{AB}$ in Figure 7.1b will be eliminated by competition on the labor market so that the real wage falls.

An excess demand for labor will lead to an increase in real wages. If we substitute the level of employment N^0 in the production function of Figure 7.1a, we obtain the level of full-employment output X^0. Therefore, employment, production, and the model's relative price, the real wage rate $W/P,$ are completely determined. Figure 7.1a also shows the equilibrium in the goods market that prevails at X^0. At this point the total expenditures of firms and households equal the total value of production, independent of the general price level. How can we make this statement without a further investigation of demand conditions?

In the neoclassical model, Say's law (J.B. Say, 1767–1832) remains valid in equilibrium. The law holds that in an exchange economy, the sum of excess demands in all goods and factor markets is equal to zero. Assume there are n markets, of which $n - 1$ are in equilibrium (i.e., excess demand in these markets is zero). Then the nth market is automatically also in equilibrium. Applied to our model with two markets – namely, the goods market and the labor market – Say's law reads

$$P \left[D \left(\frac{W}{P} \right) - S \left(\frac{W}{P} \right) \right] + W \left[N^D \left(\frac{W}{P} \right) - N^S \left(\frac{W}{P} \right) \right] = 0$$

The first expression in brackets is the excess demand in the goods market; the second, the excess supply in the labor market. In Figure 7.1b it is shown that equilibrium prevails in the labor market $[N^D((W/P)^0) - N^S((W/P)^0) = 0]$ at a real wage rate of $(W/P)^0$. From Say's law we can now conclude that the goods market is also in equilibrium $[D((W/P)^0) - S((W/P)^0) = 0]$.

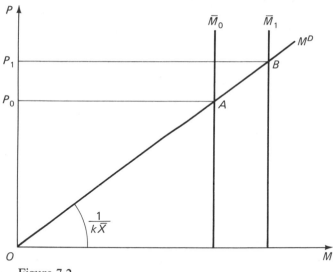

Figure 7.2

We complete the neoclassical model by introducing the money market. The demand for money M^D is expressed by the Cambridge equation; the supply of money is exogenous.

$$M^D = k\bar{X}P \quad \text{(money demand)} \tag{16}$$

$$M^S = \bar{M} \quad \text{(money supply)} \tag{17}$$

In Figure 7.2 the demand for money is depicted as a ray through the origin. The equation for this line results from solving equation (16) for P and from the assumption that the level of real output is given by $\bar{X}$:

$$P = \frac{1}{k\bar{X}} \cdot M^D \tag{18}$$

The slope of the line is determined by the ratio $1/k\bar{X}$ or $\bar{V}_x/X$. The slope is smaller, the larger is $\bar{X}$ and the smaller is $\bar{V}_x$, the income velocity of money. The intersection of the vertical money supply function with the money demand line determines the general price level P_0. Therefore, the money market determines the absolute level of prices. A higher supply of money $\bar{M}_1$ corresponds with the given slope of the money demand function to a higher price level P_1. (To see this, compare points A and B in Figure 7.2.)

Let us summarize the preceding results. The neoclassical model is characterized by a dichotomy between two systems of price determination. Relative prices (in this presentation there is only one relative price, the real wage) result from supply and demand conditions in the real sector. They are independent of the level of the money supply. In contrast, nominal prices or the general price level is a function of the supply of money. The quantity equation records this relationship. Doubling the money supply doubles all nominal prices but leaves relative prices unaffected, therefore, the volumes of goods demanded and supplied remain constant. This property of the neoclassical model – that a change in the supply of money influences only the general price level and leaves relative prices and therefore production and unemployment unchanged – is known as the "neutrality of money."[4]

Classical economists such as Smith, Ricardo, and Mill did not endow money with the property of neutrality, however. As O'Brien emphasized, D. Hume's essay "Of Money" (1752) was a common reference for classical theorists in their formulation of the quantity theory. According to Hume an increase in the supply of money does increase the general price level; however, it does not do so directly, but only through a complex transmission process. The increase in the cash balances of economic actors leads to higher expenditures and in a first round to real effects – namely, to an increase in production and employment. Price ad-

---

[4] In the neoclassical model the demand and supply for good j are functions of all the money prices in the economy. It is assumed that supply and demand functions are homogeneous of degree zero in all prices. The demand function for good j can, for instance, be written as: $D_j = D_j(p_1, p_2, \cdots, p_n) = D_j[(p_1/p_n),(p_2/p_n), \cdots, (p_{n-1}/p_n), 1]$. If all money prices are doubled, relative prices (p_i/p_j) are in fact unchanged and so are the quantities supplied and demanded. A more extensive presentation of the "dichotomy of the price system" is found in Niehans (1978, p. 7), Claassen (1970, p. 227), and Hansen (1970a, p. 31).

justment follows only with a time lag. In addition, Hume does not assume full employment as in the neoclassical analysis. Finally, the positive impact of an increase in the money supply on production and employment lasts only until the general price level has risen to a point corresponding to a higher supply of money. In the classical system, therefore, money is not neutral at all; changes in the supply of money induce changes in output and employment as well as in the general price level (O'Brien, 1975, p. 162).

Finally, in the monetarist model of inflation, the quantity theory of money plays a very different role from the one it has in the neoclassical model. The quantity theory is a theory of comparative statics, which yields alternative general price levels for alternative levels of the money supply insofar as the real sector is in equilibrium. In the framework of the monetarist model the quantity theory can be interpreted as a theory of nominal income that maintains "that changes in the money stock are the dominant determinant of changes in money income" (Mayer et al., 1978, p. 5). Changes in the supply of money (or in the rate of growth of the money supply) alter at least in the short run both the general price level and real variables. Therefore, the quantity of money is not neutral. If one observes long-run equilibrium conditions in which all adjustments have taken place, however, then the neoclassical dichotomy of the price system is again valid, and the results of the neoclassical quantity theory are identical with those of the monetarist theory.

7.2 The inflation gap model

In November 1939 J.M. Keynes published two long articles in *The Times* (London) discussing English war finance. Modified and extended, they formed the basis for his famous essay *How to Pay for the War* (Keynes, 1972, pp. 367–439), in which he investigated the relationship among inflation, taxation, and the distribution of income that results from an unanticipated increase in nonconsumption expenditures. The aspect of this analysis that deals with inflation later became known as the "inflation gap model." The model was expressly developed for the problem of war finance, which is particularly apparent from its special hypothesis concerning the relationship between wages and prices. More generally, one may express the problem Keynes handled as follows: Assume that one component of aggregate demand in a fully employed economy increases unexpectedly. In what way does the resulting inflation reduce the real share of the other components of total aggregate demand?

Keynes addressed his essay not to a narrow circle of professional economists but to the broad public. Nonetheless, the essay remains an exemplary exercise in macroeconomic thought that considerably promoted the "scientific" discussion of inflation. Recently S. Maital (1972) and J.A. Trevithick (1975) have revived interest in the model, particularly in its implications for the theory of income distribution.

Perhaps it is of interest to replicate the numerical example that Keynes developed in his essay. Then we will present one of the well-known formulations of the model. Keynes's numerical example reads:

		£ in million
X	level of real output (at prices prevailing before beginning of inflation)	5.500
E	private income (including transfer payments)	6.000
T	direct taxes	1.400
E^d	private disposable income $= E - T$	4.600

Keynes assumes that the government (including private investors) is in a position to purchase £2.250 million of goods and services G necessary to conduct the war at the "old" set of prices. The proportion of national income that remains available to private households is therefore

$$X - G = 5.500 - 2.250 = 3.250$$

Therefore, real disposable private income of £4.600 million compares with a volume of goods and services available for private consumption of only £3.250 million.

To determine the extent of the inflationary gap one must con-

sider the level of private saving. In Keynes's example the private
sector saves £700 million. Effective aggregate demand E^f therefore amounts to £3.900 million (4.600 − 700). This yields the
following result:

		£ in million
E^f	effective aggregate demand	3.900
$X - G$	volume of goods and services available for private consumption	3.250
	inflationary gap	650

The inflationary gap is therefore the excess demand in the market for consumption goods and services. In Keynes's example
this increases the general price level by 20 percent. Real output
amounting to £3.250 at the "old" prices is sold at current prices
for £3.900. This leads to windfall profits – that is, to unanticipated
profits by firms amounting to £650 million – which subsequently
induces excess demand in the goods market and leads to inflationary effects.

The higher marginal tax rates of firms under the progressive tax
system as well as the entrepreneur's higher propensity to save
ensure that only a portion of the windfall profits will have an
inflationary impact, however. For example, Keynes assumed that
a second round of price increases amounting to 2–3 percent
would be sufficient to eliminate the real excess demand and bring
the inflation process to an end.

This analysis is valid only under the assumption of constant
money wages; however, excess demand in the goods market will
produce demand pressure in the labor market under the original
assumption of full employment. Together with the favorable
profit picture among entrepreneurs, this will lead to an increase in
money wages to the full extent of the previous increase in the
general price level. Once restored to their original level, real
wages will create a new inflationary gap in the goods market,
which again will lead to an increase in prices. If money wages
follow suit in the next round, this will induce further price increases. A spiral results.

Central to Keynes's argument in *How to Pay for the War* is the wage-lag hypothesis: that wages adjust to changes in the general price level with a temporal lag. Price increases always run ahead of wage increases, which follow with a distinct lag so that real wages are constantly depressed below the level that prevailed before the start of the inflation process. Keynes is quite clear on this point: "Wages and other costs will chase prices upwards, but nevertheless prices will always (on the above assumptions) keep 20 percent ahead. However much wages are increased, the act of spending these wages will always push prices this much in advance" (1972, p. 420).

The inflation process in *How to Pay for the War* is basically a redistribution process. Inflation acts like a pump that transfers income from wage earners who have a low propensity to save and a low marginal tax rate to the entrepreneurial sector with a higher propensity to save and a higher marginal tax rate. The inflationary gap is therefore financed by the inflation process itself in which real wages are depressed through a lagged adjustment of money wages.

Neo-Keynesian authors such as A. Smithies (1942), G. Ackley (1961), and H. Scherf (1967) transformed the verbal analysis of Keynes into a strict, formal model. We will follow the presentation of Smithies and Ackley, who adhere closely to Keynes's verbal version. The model consists of the following eight equations:

$$A = \bar{A} \tag{1}$$

The variable A remains constant. It represents real government expenditures and private and public investment, exogenously given.

$$C_{ut} = m + c_u \frac{R_t}{P_t} \tag{2}$$

where C_{ut} is the real consumption of the entrepreneurs, m is autonomous real consumption, c_u is the marginal propensity of the entrepreneur to consume, R_t is the nominal profits of the entrepreneur, and P_t is the general price level.

$$C_{wt} = c_w \frac{Q_t}{P_t} \tag{3}$$

where C_{wt} is the real consumption of the wage earners, c_w is the marginal propensity of the wage earners to consume, and Q_t is the workers' nominal amount of wage income.

$$Q_t = W_t N_0 \tag{4}$$

where W_t is the money wage rate and N_0 is the exogenously given level of employment at full employment.

$$Y_t = P_t X_0 \tag{5}$$

where Y_t is the nominal gross national product and X_0 is the full-employment level of real output (exogenously given).

$$Y_t = Q_t + R_t \tag{6}$$

This equation is an identity that defines the nominal gross national product as the sum of factor incomes.

$$X_t = X_0 = C_{wt} + C_{ut} + A \tag{7}$$

This equation defines real output as the sum of the categories of real expenditure.

$$W_t = \varphi P_{t-1} \tag{8}$$

Equation (8) describes the relationship between wages and prices according to the wage-lag hypothesis.

The central assumption of the model, on which the entire neo-Keynesian school of distribution theory is based, is that there is a difference in the marginal propensities to consume: That of wage earners exceeds that of entrepreneurs: $c_w - c_u > 0$ (Kaldor, 1955/6).

Assume that before the start of war financing equilibrium prevails, so that the inflationary gap IG is zero and the price level remains constant ($P_t = P_{t-1} = P_0$). From equation (8) it follows that the parameter φ must correspond to the equilibrium real wage of the prewar period.

Let us examine the inflationary gap more closely. It is defined as the excess demand in the goods market for a given supply of full-employment output.

$$IG_t = (C_{wt} + C_{ut} + A) - X_0$$

$$= (m + A) + c_u \frac{R_t}{P_t} + c_w \frac{Q_t}{P_t} - X_0$$

$$= (m + A) + (c_w - c_u) \frac{W_t N_0}{P_t} - (1 - c_u)X_0 \qquad (9)$$

At the prewar level of autonomous expenditures A and at prewar wages W_0 and prices P_0, IG_t equals zero. War expenditures increase A by an amount ΔA. This increase produces, for a given W_0 and P_0, a positive inflationary gap (a goods gap), as one can recognize from equation (9). Because wages are fixed for the period under consideration ($W_1 = \varphi P_0$), the gap in the goods market can be closed only by an increase in prices. The price increase from P_0 to P_1 necessary to accomplish this can be calculated by means of equation (9) under the consideration that $W_1 = \varphi P_0$ and $IG_1 = 0$.

$$(m + A + \Delta A) + (c_w - c_u)\varphi \frac{P_0 N_0}{P_1} - (1 - c_u)X_0 = 0$$

$$\frac{P_1}{P_0} = \frac{(c_w - c_u)\varphi N_0}{X_0(1 - c_u) - (m + A + \Delta A)} \qquad (10)$$

This result shows that the rate of inflation (more precisely the ratio of the price level in period 1 to that in period 0) depends positively on the difference $c_w - c_u$ as well as on ΔA. The greater is the marginal propensity of wage earners to consume relative to that of entrepreneurs, and the greater is the increase in real autonomous expenditures ΔA, the greater will be the increase in prices. In contrast, the inflation rate correlates negatively with the full-employment supply of real output X_0.

Equation (10) expresses the inflation rate during the transition from time t_0 to t_1. What occurs during later periods? To find out, we must use the wage-lag hypothesis. The increase in the price level from P_0 to P_1 closes the gap in the goods market, but in period 2 it pulls nominal wages upward to $W_2 = \varphi P_1$ and therefore restores the original level of real wages. Equation (9) shows that this upward readjustment in nominal wages again induces a gap in the goods market that can be eliminated only by another round of price increases of the magnitude determined by equation (10). The inflation process continues as long as the exogenously given rate of autonomous expenditures exceeds the original equilibrium level. The point of the model is really the following: Through the first round of price increases from P_0 to P_1 the real wage is depressed. The subsequent inflation is necessary to prevent the real wage from climbing back to its original level. This is successful only because money wages adjust with a temporal lag to changes in the general price level.

This formulation remained for a long time the standard interpretation of Keynes's text *How to Pay for the War*. However, the paper of Maital (1972) and the criticism of Trevithick (1975) activated the discussion of the model. Maital posed two questions that are relevant in this context:

    a. What distribution of income into wages and profits corresponds to a given rate of investment $g = A/X_0$?

    b. What rate of inflation is necessary to produce the "functional" distribution of income corresponding to a certain g?

It is not necessary to discuss the specific Maital model because the Smithies–Ackley version of Keynes's model provides direct and indirect answers to these questions. With respect to the first question, Maital showed that each rate of investment A/X_0 corresponds to a certain share of labor income for given marginal propensities to consume c_u and c_w. At this rate of investment, planned savings equal nonconsumption expenditures A, which implies $IG_t = 0$. This equilibrium wage share can be derived from equation (9) of the Smithies–Ackley model if one sets $IG = 0$ and solves for the wage share.

$$\frac{W_t \cdot N_0}{P_t \cdot X_0} = \frac{1 - c_u}{c_w - c_u} - \frac{m + A}{X_0(c_w - c_u)} \tag{11}$$

If the rate of investment A/X_0 rises 1 percent, then the share of labor income must fall by $1/(c_w - c_u)$ percentage points. This exactly reproduces the result derived by Maital (1972, p. 159). For example, set $c_w = 0.9$ and $c_u = 0.4$. Then $c_w - c_u = 0.5$. To raise the rate of investment by 1 percent, the share of labor income must fall by 1.0/0.5, or 2 percent.

Let us now turn to the second question. How high must the increase in the general price level be to reduce the share of income going to wages (or the real wage rate) that corresponds to an increase in the rate of investment? This is answered in equation (10). The increase in autonomous expenditures ΔA leads to an increase in the general price level and thus to the necessary reduction in the real wage or labor's share via the lagged-wage adjustment process.

7.3 Bent Hansen's model of the double inflationary gap

Bent Hansen's inflation model (1951, 1970a) can be regarded as a further development of the inflationary gap model just discussed. Whereas Keynes considered only the goods gap in *How to Pay for the War,* Hansen considered both the goods market and the labor market. He differentiated between a goods gap and a factor gap. The model rests on two important assumptions:

    a. The quantity of labor is exogenously given and is fixed. The output obtainable through the use of the entire supply of available labor (full-employment output $\bar{X}$) cannot be exceeded.
    b. Prices and money wages are completely flexible.

Hansen's model consists of three behavioral equations (1)–(3) and two price reaction functions (4) and (5).

$$X = \bar{X} \tag{1}$$

where $\bar{X}$ is a constant representing full capacity.

$$X = g\left(\frac{P}{W}\right) \qquad g' > 0 \tag{2}$$

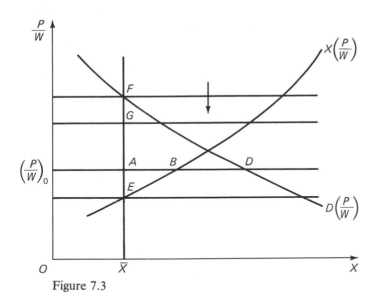

Figure 7.3

This is an equation of the planned supply of output.

$$D = h \left(\frac{P}{W}\right) \qquad h' < 0 \tag{3}$$

This equation represents the planned demand for output.

Equation (2) may be understood as an aggregate supply function for the economy. As the ratio of prices to wages increases (as real wages fall), entrepreneurs increase the amount of output they plan to supply. In contrast, private demand for goods falls as P/W rises (as the real wage falls). This results from the fact that an increase in P/W leads to an increase in the share of profits in a constant, full-employment real income and to a decline in the wage share. Following Keynes, Hansen further assumed that the marginal propensity of entrepreneurs to consume is lower than that of workers. Hence, planned demand decreases as P/W rises.

Figure 7.3 presents the Hansen model in a graphic form. On the abscissa is real output X; on the ordinate, the ratio of prices to wages. Let us examine the situation at $(P/W)_0$, where there is a factor gap measured by the distance AB. The factor gap $X - \bar{X} =$

AB represents the amount of output planned for production in excess of the realizable maximum – namely, full-employment output $\bar{X}$. Hansen considered this factor gap to be an index of the excess demand in the labor market. Under the assumption of flexible money wages, this excess demand leads to an increase in money wages. Hansen therefore extended the model to include a labor market, wage-reaction function.

$$\frac{dW}{dt} = F(X - \bar{X}) \qquad F(0) = 0; F' > 0 \tag{4}$$

This represents the well-known neoclassical wage-reaction function according to which the change in the money wage rate is positively related to the level of excess demand in the labor market.

The distance *AD* represents the amount of excess demand in the goods market at $(P/W)_0$, the goods gap. The planned demand for goods exceeds the maximum obtainable supply by the amount *AD*. Under the assumption of a neoclassical price-reaction function, this leads to an increase in goods prices.

$$\frac{dP}{dt} = f(D - \bar{X}) \qquad f(0) = 0; f' > 0 \tag{5}$$

As a starting point for a further consideration of the model, we take the point *F*, where $D - \bar{X}$ equals zero but $X - \bar{X}$ exceeds zero. Although equilibrium prevails in the goods market, there is excess demand in the labor market. From this it follows that the real wage rises because goods prices remain constant while money wages increase. The price–wage ratio moves in the direction of the arrow. At a lower price–wage ratio (a higher real wage) excess demand develops in the goods market so that the price level also begins to rise. At point *G*, for example, $D - \bar{X} > 0$ and $X - \bar{X} > 0$, which implies that $\dot{W} > 0$ and $\dot{P} > 0$.

We could also begin the discussion at point *E*, where there is an equilibrium in the labor market ($X - \bar{X} = 0$) but excess demand in the goods market ($D - \bar{X} > 0$). According to the wage and price reaction functions of equations (4) and (5), P/W begins to rise and the real wage starts to fall. One may assume that this process would take the economy to point *A*, where the real wage has declined to the extent that excess demand in the labor market develops along with excess demand in the goods market, so that both goods prices and money wages begin to rise.

These deliberations lead to the conclusion that in the interval *EF* there must be a "quasiequilibrium" in which prices and wages are increasing at the same rate, so that the real wage remains constant. The proof can be clearly stated as follows: At *F* the change in money wages dW/dt is positive; dW/dt declines as P/W falls and $dW/dt = 0$ at point *E*. However, at point *E* the change in prices dP/dt is positive. As P/W rises in value, dP/dt falls and $dP/dt = 0$ at point *F*. From this it follows that there must be a point P/W between *E* and *F*, such as $(P/W)_0$, with the property that prices and wages are increasing at the same rate.

In this quasiequilibrium the following analytical relationship holds:

$$\frac{d}{dt}\left(\frac{P}{W}\right) = \frac{W\frac{dP}{dt} - P\frac{dW}{dt}}{W^2} = \frac{f(D - \bar{X}) - \frac{P}{W}F(X - \bar{X})}{W} = 0 \quad (6)$$

The real wage is therefore constant if the following holds:

$$\frac{P}{W} = \frac{f(D - \bar{X})}{F(X - \bar{X})} \quad (7)$$

The point of quasiequilibrium can be determined from the following four equations with the unknowns $\bar{X}$, X, D, and P/W:

$$\bar{X} = \text{constant} \quad (1)$$

$$X = g\left(\frac{P}{W}\right) \quad (2)$$

$$D = h\left(\frac{P}{W}\right) \quad (3)$$

$$\frac{P}{W} = \frac{f(D - \bar{X})}{F(X - \bar{X})} \quad (7)$$

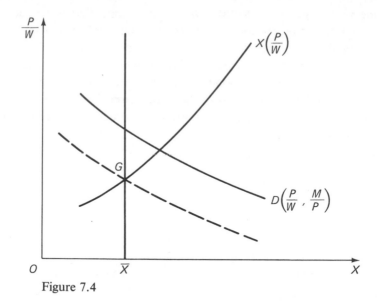

Figure 7.4

The point of Hansen's model is to prove by simple means that there can be an inflationary equilibrium with excess demand simultaneously existing in both the goods and factor markets. From the perspective of recent theoretical developments, however, the model has a series of faults.

1. The model fails to consider the role of expectations in the goods and factor markets. This shortcoming is common to all the older inflation models, however.
2. Hansen postulated an absolute upper limit for capacity $\bar{X}$, the maximum output of full employment. From this assumption the model is left to pose only a sterile question. For this it has often been criticized. One cannot discuss Friedman's problem of the division of the impact of a monetary impulse into inflation and output effects.
3. Suppose we assume that the demand function is specified in the form used by Patinkin so that it contains real cash balances M/P as well as the relative price of goods and labor.

$$D = D\left(\frac{P}{W}, \frac{M}{P}\right) \qquad D_{(M/P)} > 0$$

In this case the quasiequilibrium can be maintained over time only if the money supply increases at the same rate as the rate of inflation so that real cash balances M/P remain constant. If the nominal supply of money were to remain constant, then the quasiequilibrium would not be stable because the falling real cash balances would shift the demand function to the left (Figure 7.4). This real balance effect (the Patinkin effect) could shift the demand function so far to the left that the excess demand vanishes and a stationary equilibrium at G (with $X - \bar{X} = 0$ and $D - \bar{X} = 0$) replaces the inflationary quasiequilibrium.

7.4 Demand-pull and cost-push inflation

A central theme in the discussion of inflation in the 1960s was the classification of inflation into two types: demand-pull and cost-push. The literature distinguished between them on the basis of two factors.

1. It sought to determine the cause or the springboard for the inflation process already under way.
2. It sought to offer a basis for economic policy actions. Here, the literature sought to determine whether the inflation process could be arrested by a restriction of monetary demand without an increase in the rate of unemployment.

By means of a well-known analysis we now attempt to differentiate between the two types of inflation (Branson, 1979, pp. 375–96.)[5] The tools used in this analysis are the macroeconomic demand function D_0 and the macroeconomic supply function S_0. (In Figure 7.5 real national product X is on the abscissa and the price level P is on the ordinate.) It is intuitively plausible that the aggregate demand curve is a declining function of the price level and that the supply curve is a rising function. One should not forget, however, that the functions under discussion are macroeconomic, or aggregate, functions and they do not refer to individual markets. If one derives the demand function D_0 from a complete macroeconomic system, then one should interpret it as an equilibrium curve. Each point on D corresponds to a possible

---

[5] This analysis is also used in: Bronfenbrenner and Holzmann (1963), Bronfenbrenner, (1976, 1979), and Gordon (1977, 1978, pt. III, pp. 171–200).

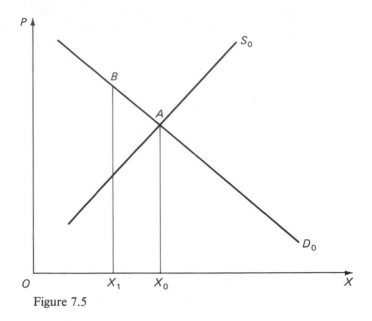

Figure 7.5

equilibrium in the goods and money markets – in other words, to an intersection of the IS and LM curves.[6] For example, a movement from A to B along D_0 should be interpreted as follows: If the price level rises for a given supply of money, then the money market moves into disequilibrium; an excess demand for money results. This induces an increase in the interest rate, which eliminates the disequilibrium in the money market and reduces the interest-sensitive components of consumption and investment demand. Point B differs from point A because at B the goods and money markets are again in equilibrium at a higher rate of interest and a higher general price level.

The aggregate supply curve depicts the supply of goods planned by firms at alternative general price levels under the assumption that the labor market remains in equilibrium. The

[6] A thorough investigation of the relationship of a macroeconomic supply and demand system to the macroeconomic IS-LM system is found in Branson (1979).

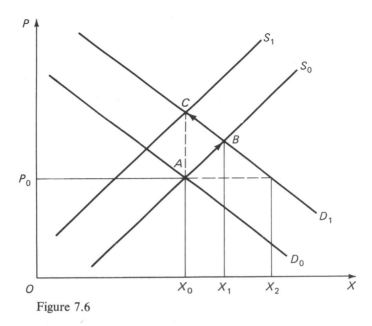

Figure 7.6

intersection of D_0 and S_0 is therefore a general equilibrium point for the entire economy. Assume that the aggregate demand function shifts from D_0 to D_1, as is shown in Figure 7.6. Such an autonomous shift in the demand function can arise from any factor that shifts either the IS curve or the LM curve or both curves simultaneously. These factors include, for example,

1. An increase in the propensity to consume and/or a change in the autonomous investment expenditures of the private sector
2. An increase in government expenditures
3. An increase in the money supply
4. A combination of 2 and 3
5. An increase in exports in an open economy

We assume that the aggregate demand curve shifts from D_0 to D_1 as a consequence of an increase in government expenditures, which the government finances through an increase in the money supply by reducing its cash balances (point 4).

The increase in aggregate demand leads to a goods gap of $X_0 X_2$

(Figure 7.6) and an increase in the general price level corresponding to the concept of excess demand. The consequences for the
real sector and for inflation occur in a process that the literature
of the 1960s does not analyze thoroughly. However, we can interpret demand-pull inflation in a more modern fashion according to
the New Microeconomics, as developed in Section 3.5 of this
book.

Firms will attempt to employ new workers in the labor market
by raising the wage they offer. Workers base their decision concerning labor supply on the expected real wage W/P^*, where W is
the nominal wage rate and P^* is the expected price level. Because
their price expectation P^* will be adjusted only with a temporal
lag to the change in the general price level, they misread the
increase in money wages as an increase in the real wage. This
leads to an increase in employment and an increase in real output
along the aggregate supply curve S_0 in the direction AB. In the
demand-pull model the increase in aggregate demand leads in
general to an expansion of output X beyond X_0 or, correspondingly, to an increase in employment N above its original level N_0.
R.J. Gordon remarked that the concept of demand-pull inflation
was proposed in the 1960s by two schools of thought: the Keynesian school, which traces the excess demand to nonmonetary im-
pulses such as autonomous increases in the expenditures of the
government or of the private sector, and the quantity theory,
which considers the change in the money supply as the cause of
the shift in the aggregate demand function (Gordon, 1977, p. 43).

If we consider the recent work on the adjustment of expectations (Chapter 2), however, it is impossible to conclude the discussion of a demand inflation at this point. Let us examine point B
in Figure 7.6. This cannot be a stable position. After a certain
period of time workers will realize that their real wage had not
risen because the general price level also increased. They correct
their expectation of the general price level and set it higher in
accordance with the increase in prices. Therefore, an increase in
nominal wages occurs to restore the real wage to its equilibrium
level; the aggregate supply curve shifts to the left (Gordon, 1978,

pt. III). The supply curve S_1 in Figure 7.6 reflects the full adjustment of money wages to the increase in the expected price level. At the new equilibrium point C the same real wage exists as at A, but with the difference that both the nominal wage and the general price level have risen.

Demand-pull inflation thus occurs in two distinct phases (Figure 7.6):

1. AB, characterized by an increase in the general price level and a temporary increase in production and employment
2. BC, a further increase in the general price level and an adjustment of the supply function to the higher costs

In his analysis of demand inflation, F. Machlup stated, "Autonomous expansions of demand (government spending, business spending, consumer spending) are followed by responsive (competitive) price and wage increases" (1960, p. 131).

The standard case of cost-push inflation in a closed economy is an autonomous, one-time increase in money wages without any prior increase in labor productivity or in the general price level. This can result from false expectations of inflation or from the goal of unions to change the distribution of income. Not only wage increases but also increases in the prices of other input factors resulting from monopolistic market practices can lead to cost-push inflation (Bronfenbrenner, 1976, p. 5).

An autonomous increase in costs shifts the aggregate supply curve from S_0 to S_1; each level of output X is produced at a higher level of costs (general price level). In Figure 7.7 an excess demand for goods of $X_1 X_0$ occurs at the old price level P_0. This leads to an increase in the general price level from P_0 to P_2. Assume for the moment that the increase in costs, the cost-push, is not accommodated by an increase in the money supply. Then the position of the D_0 curve remains unchanged. The cost inflation leads to a reduction in real cash balances from M_0/P_0 to M_0/P_2. At this point the interplay between the money and goods markets sets in; the interest rate mechanism begins to operate as mentioned earlier. The excess demand for money leads to an increase in the interest rate, which in turn results in a crowding-

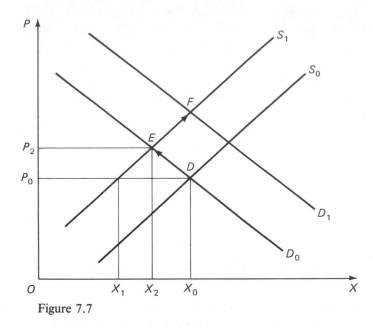

Figure 7.7

out effect in the goods market; in other words, the interest-sensitive components of private demand are reduced. The fall in aggregate demand induces a decline in production and output (point *E* in Figure 7.7). The immediate reaction to an autonomous cost-push, therefore, is a reduction in output and employment combined with an increase in the general price level. As was the case in the type of demand-pull inflation discussed earlier, it is doubtful that the initial reaction to a cost-push (point *E* in Figure 7.7) will prove to be a stable equilibrium point. For example, if stagflation is regarded as unacceptable and the central bank increases the money supply or accommodates the previous autonomous wage and/or price increases, then the demand curve shifts to the right to D_1. Now production and output increase and the price level rises further until a new equilibrium is reached at point *F*. The complete adjustment path in the case of cost-push inflation with a lagged increase in the money supply lies in the direction of the arrows from *D* to *E* and from *E* to *F*.

F. Machlup (1960, p. 129) improved the analysis of cost-push and demand-pull inflation by further differentiating these two types of inflation. Demand-pull inflation may be autonomous, induced, or supportive. *Autonomous* demand inflation arises from shifts in the aggregate demand function that are independent of realized or anticipated increases in costs. *Induced* demand inflation results from shifts in the aggregate demand function that are a consequence of cost increases. The latter lead to increases in income or wages that induce higher consumption expenditures. Cost increases that lead to shifts in the aggregate demand function are linked with an increase in the money supply because the affected firms must either reduce their cash balances or draw down a larger amount of bank credit. A *supportive* (accommodating) increase in aggregate demand occurs if the government attempts to use fiscal or monetary policy measures to increase demand or to compensate the decline in aggregate demand caused by the inflation in costs. In either case, the aggregate demand function will shift in response to policy.

With the aid of Machlup's taxonomy, we can interpret the shifts in the aggregate demand function depicted in Figures 7.6 and 7.7 more exactly. The movement in the aggregate demand function from *A* to *B* along the supply curve in Figure 7.6 represents an autonomous shift; it depicts an instance of autonomous demand-pull inflation. In contrast, Figure 7.7 depicts an instance of supportive demand inflation, because the increase in the money supply by the central bank caused the shift in the aggregate demand curve.

According to Machlup, cost-push inflation results from changes in administered prices and wages. In contrast to market wages and prices, they are the product of collective bargaining and are uniformly applied. Cost inflation occurs in two forms: aggressive and defensive cost-push inflation. The former results from attempts to increase real wages for a given level of labor productivity; the latter arises from attempts to restore a previous equilibrium level of real wages.

This classification is applicable not only to wage costs but also to the costs of other important inputs (such as energy). In Figure 7.7 the shift in the supply curve from S_0 to S_1 corresponds to "aggressive" cost-push inflation as defined by Machlup. In contrast, the shift in the supply curve in Figure 7.6 is of a "defensive" nature. It results from the adjustment of money wages to the higher general price level P_1 brought about by the demand-pull inflation.

A. Lindbeck (1980) recently refined the analysis of cost-push inflation by subdividing the latter into three types:

1. Exogenous cost inflation
2. Relative price or income claims inflation
3. "Inertia" inflation

Causes for the first type may be exogenous cost increases in higher import prices for intermediate goods (the oil shock), "unexplained" higher profit markups by firms, and "unexplained" higher wage rates brought about by collective bargaining between unions and employers. This type of inflation might explain a one-time increase in the price level.

The second type of cost inflation is caused by the attempt of various economic agents or groups of agents with market power over relative prices or wage rates to change their relative price or relative income shares. The agents relate their product (or factor prices) to the products (or factor prices) of other agents. A special case of this situation is a behavior pattern in which an agent i (or a group of agents) tries to keep a fixed price (or wage) relationship to a specific reference group j. This relationship may then be written as

$$\frac{P_i}{P_j} = \lambda \qquad \lambda \text{ is constant}$$

Why does this behavior pattern imply a cost-push effect? The basic concept is that on a macroeconomic level such a pattern may create income claims that exceed the produced real income at the existing price level and induce an upward move in the general price level.

The third type of cost inflation is based on the fact that economic agents expect an increase in the future price level. A cost inflation develops when households and firms try to protect their desired real income by adjusting their wage rates and their prices to the expected future inflation. In contrast to the "relative price" cost inflation, agents do not try to improve their relative position; they only attempt to prevent an expected fall in the real value of their own prices and wages. To the extent that the increase in the price level is the result of an attempt to protect the real income of agents or a group of agents, this inflation can be called "inertia inflation."

It is easily seen that Lindbeck's autonomous cost inflation and relative price inflation are included in Machlup's aggressive cost inflation, whereas inertia inflation corresponds to Machlup's defensive cost inflation.

Although the distinction between cost inflation and demand inflation is not obsolete, recent developments in inflation theory – as discussed in the first part of this book – have not followed this distinction. One important reason for this is that this difference has remained only theoretical. No one has developed an empirical method to classify actual inflationary episodes. Can one determine whether a process in which both wages and prices rise represents cost-push or demand-pull inflation? If so, how?

An attempt to check whether prices or money wages are the first to increase resembles the chicken and the egg problem. According to the base period chosen, a wage increase may be interpreted either as an autonomous wage push or as an adjustment to a previous increase in the general price level. A similar problem applies to prices. Exactly this objection may also be made to the attempt of the monetarists to explain inflation by a previous acceleration in the growth of the money supply (see Chapter 4). According to the base period chosen, the increase in the money supply may also be understood as an accommodating measure that an inflationary development has induced the monetary authorities to take.

In popular treatments of inflation one speaks of wage-cost inflation when money wages increase more rapidly than labor productivity. However, a moment's thought should be enough to convince anyone that money wages must also grow more rapidly than labor productivity in a demand inflation.

Finally, one cannot use the statement that the increase in nominal expenditures exceeds the increase in real national product as a criterion for demand inflation. The statement is tautological because it must hold in any type of inflation.

Of greater interest is the test proposed by Machlup, which observes the change in the distribution of income brought about by inflation. If the share of profits increases as a result of the inflation process, then demand inflation is occurring; if the share of wages rises, this points toward cost-push inflation. This test would break down for the same reason cited earlier, however; the choice of a reference period influences the measurement of changes in the distributional shares of income.

To complete our discussion we should briefly examine the experiment proposed by P.A. Samuelson and R.M. Solow (1960). If a small reduction in aggregate demand markedly slows down the rate of increase of wage (and other input) costs and it raises the unemployment rate only slightly, then one can conclude that inflation is of the demand-pull type. On the other hand, if a small reduction in aggregate demand has no dampening effect on the increase in prices and wages – in other words, if substantial unemployment were necessary to prevent a rise in prices – then inflation may be classified as cost-push. This experiment loses its predictive power when demand or cost inflation is in an adjustment phase, however (*BC* in Figure 7.6 and *EF* in Figure 7.7, respectively). For this case Samuelson and Solow (1960) created a third type of inflation, the mixed type, which contains both cost and demand elements.

Aside from the impossibility of uniquely identifying a concrete case of inflation by empirical methods, the cost-push/demand-pull concept suffers from an additional shortcoming: It is inherently static. It can explain a one-time increase in the general price level as a consequence of a shift in the demand curve or in the supply curve. In both cases the resulting excess demand is dissipated by an increase in the general price level. If one attempts to use this model to explain inflation – that is, a continuous increase in the general price level – then one must assume that the demand and supply curves continuously shift upward. The static model is appropriate to explain a one-time increase in the general price level but not for the analysis of continuous price increases, such as characterize the inflation process.

BIBLIOGRAPHY

Journal abbreviations

AEJ	*Atlantic Economic Journal*
AER	*American Economic Review*
BPEA	*Brookings Papers on Economic Activity*
EC	*Econometrica*
EER	*European Economic Review*
EJ	*Economic Journal*
IEA	*Institute of Economic Affairs*
IER	*International Economic Review*
JEL	*Journal of Economic Literature*
JET	*Journal of Economic Theory*
JF	*Journal of Finance*
JMCB	*Journal of Money, Credit, and Banking*
JME	*Journal of Monetary Economics*
JPE	*Journal of Political Economy*
QJE	*Quarterly Journal of Economics*
ReSt	*Review of Economic Studies*
WWA	*Weltwirtschaftliches Archiv*
ZfgS	*Zeitschrift für die gesamte Staatswissenschaft*
ZfN	*Zeitschrift für Nationalökonomie*

Ackley, G. 1961. *Macroeconomic Theory*. New York: Macmillan.

Alchian, A.A. 1971. "Information Costs, Pricing and Resource Unemployment," in *Microeconomic Foundations of Employment and Inflation Theory*, edited by E.S. Phelps et al. London: Macmillan, pp. 27–52.

Alexander, S. 1952. "The Effects of Devaluation on a Trade Balance," *International Monetary Fund Staff Papers*, (April)II(2):263–78.

250

Allen, R.G.D. 1975. *Index Numbers in Theory and Practice.* London: Macmillan.

Aukrust, O. 1977. "Inflation in the Open Economy: A Norwegian Model," in *Worldwide Inflation,* edited by L.B. Krause and W.S. Salant. Washington, D.C.: The Brookings Institution, pp. 107–53.

Balassa, B. 1964. "The Purchasing-Power Parity Doctrine: A Reappraisal," *JPE,* (December)72(6):584–96.

Barro, R.J. 1976. "Rational Expectations and the Role of Monetary Policy," *JME,* (January)2:1–32.

Baumol, W. 1967. "Macroeconomics of Unbalanced Growth: The Anatomy of Urban Crises," *AER,* (June)57(3):415–26.

Bergstrom, A.R., et al., eds. 1978. *Stability and Inflation.* London: Wiley, 1978.

Blinder, A.S. 1979. *Economic Policy and the Great Stagflation.* New York: Academic Press.

Branson, W.H. 1979. *Macroeconomic Theory and Policy.* New York: Harper & Row.

Branson, W.H., and Myhrman, J. 1976. "Inflation in Open Economies: Supply-determined versus Demand-determined Models," *Inflation in Small Countries,* edited by H. Frisch. Berlin: Springer, pp. 17–46. Reprinted in *EER,* (January 1976)7(1):15–34.

Brinner, R.E. 1977. "The Death of the Phillips Curve Reconsidered," *QJE,* (August)91(3):389–418.

Bronfenbrenner, M. 1976. "Elements of Stagflation Theory," *ZfN* 36(1–2):1–8.

1979. *Macroeconomic Alternatives.* Arlington Heights, Ill.: AHM.

Bronfenbrenner, M., and Holzmann, F.D. 1963. "A Survey of Inflation Theory," *AER,* (September)53(4):593–661.

Brunner, K. 1970. "The 'Monetarist Revolution' in Monetary Theory," *WWA* 105(1):1–30.

Brunner, K., and Meltzer, A.H. 1976. "An Aggregative Theory for a Closed Economy," in *Monetarism,* edited by J.L. Stein. Amsterdam: North-Holland, pp. 69–103.

Bruno, M., and Sachs, J. 1979a. "Macroeconomic Adjustment with Import Price Shocks: Real Monetary Aspects," Seminar Paper no. 118. Stockholm: Institute for International Economic Studies, February.

1979b. "Supply versus Demand Approaches to the Problem of Stagflation," NBER Working Paper no. 382. Cambridge, Mass., August.

Buiter, W. 1980. "The Macroeconomics of Dr. Pangloss: A Critical Survey of the New Classical Macroeconomics," *EJ,* (March)90(357):34–50.

Cagan, P. 1956. "The Monetary Dynamics of Hyperinflation," in *Studies in the Quantity Theory of Money,* edited by M. Friedman. Chicago: University of Chicago Press, pp. 25–117.

Calmfors, L. 1977. "Inflation in Sweden," in *Worldwide Inflation,* edited by L.B. Krause and W.S. Salant. Washington, D.C.: The Brookings Institution, pp. 493–537.

Carter, C.F., and Ford, J.L., eds. 1972. *Uncertainty and Expectations in Economics.* Oxford: Basil Blackwell Publisher.

Claassen, E.-M. 1970. *Probleme der Geldtheorie.* Berlin: Springer.

1972. "Short-Period Fluctuations in Nominal and Real Income: A Monetarist

Model," *Stabilization Policies in Interdependent Economies,* edited by E.-M. Claassen and P. Salin. Amsterdam: North-Holland, pp. 44–61.

1976. "The Role of Economic Size in the Determination and Transmission of World Inflation," in *Inflation in Small Countries,* edited by H. Frisch. Berlin: Springer, pp. 91–119.

1978. *Weltinflation.* Munich: F. Vahlen.

Claassen, E.-M., and Salin, P., eds. 1972. *Stabilization Policies in Interdependent Economies.* Amsterdam: North-Holland.

1976. *Recent Issues in International Monetary Economics.* Amsterdam: North-Holland.

Clayton, G., Gilbert, J.C., and Sedgwick, R., eds. 1971. *Monetary Theory and Monetary Policy in the 1970's.* London: Oxford University Press.

Dornbusch, R. 1975. "Inflation, Growth and Unemployment: An Expository Framework" (mimeograph).

Dornbusch, R., and Fischer, St. 1978. *Macroeconomics.* New York: McGraw-Hill.

Eagly, R.V. 1965. "Market Power As an Intervening Mechanism in Phillips Curve Analyses," *Economica,* (February)32(125):48–64.

Earl, P.H., ed. 1975. *The Analysis of Inflation.* Lexington, Mass.: D.C. Heath.

Eckstein, O., ed. 1972. *The Economics of Price Determination,* Conference. Washington, D.C.: Board of Governers, Federal Reserve System.

Edgren, G., Faxén, K.-O., and Odhner, C.E. 1973. *Wage Formation and the Economy.* London: Allen & Unwin.

Fand, D. 1970. "A Monetarist Model of the Monetary Process," *JF* (May)25(2):275–89.

Feldstein, M. 1976. "Temporary Layoffs in the Theory of Unemployment," *JPE,* (October)84(5):937–58.

Fischer, St. 1977. "Long-Term Contracts, Rational Expectations, and the Optimal Money Supply Rule," *JPE,* (February)85(1):191–205.

Fisher, I. 1920. *The Purchasing Power of Money: Its Determination and Relation to Credit, Interest and Crisis.* New York: Macmillan.

Frenkel, J.A. 1976. "Adjustment Mechanisms and the Monetary Approach to the Balance of Payments: A Doctrinal Perspective," in *Recent Issues in International Monetary Economics,* edited by E.-M. Claassen and P. Salin. Amsterdam: North-Holland, pp. 29–48.

Frenkel, J.A., and Johnson, H.G. 1976. "Introductory Essay: The Monetary Approach to the Balance of Payments; Essential Concepts and Historical Origins," in *The Monetary Approach to the Balance of Payments,* edited by J.A. Frenkel and H.G. Johnson. London: Allen & Unwin, pp. 21–45.

Friedman, M. 1956. "The Quantity Theory of Money – A Restatement," in *Studies in the Quantity Theory of Money,* edited by M. Friedman. Chicago: University of Chicago Press, pp. 3–21.

1968. "The Role of Monetary Policy," *AER,* (March)58(1):1–17.

1969. *The Optimum Quantity of Money and Other Essays.* London: Macmillan.

1970a. "A Theoretical Framework for Monetary Analysis," *JPE,* (March/April)78(2):193–238.

1970b. "The Counter-Revolution in Monetary Theory," *IEA*, Occasional Paper 33.

1971. "A Monetary Theory of Nominal Income," *JPE*, (March/April) 79(2):323–37.

1974. "A Theoretical Framework for Monetary Analysis," in *Milton Friedman's Monetary Framework*, edited by R.J. Gordon. Chicago: University of Chicago Press, pp. 1–62.

1975. "Unemployment versus Inflation?" *IEA*, Lecture No. 2, Occasional Paper 44, London.

1977. "Nobel Lecture: Inflation and Unemployment," *JPE*, (June)85(3):451–72.

Frisch, H. 1977a. "The Scandinavian Model of Inflation: A Generalization and Empirical Evidence," *AEJ*, (December)5(3):1–14.

1977b. "The Role of Money in the Inflation Analysis," in *Inflation Theory and Anti-Inflation Policy*, edited by E. Lundberg. Macmillan, pp. 109–29.

1977c. "Inflation Theory 1963–1975: A Second-Generation Survey," *JEL*, (December)15(4):1289–317.

1980. *Die neue Inflationstheorie*. Göttingen: Vandenhoeck und Ruprecht.

Frisch, H., ed. 1976. *Inflation in Small Countries*. Berlin: Springer-Verlag.

Frisch, H., and Hof, F. 1981/2. "A 'Textbook'-Model of Inflation and Unemployment," *Kredit und Kapital*, pp. 159–76.

Frydman, R. 1981. "Sluggish Price Adjustments and the Effectiveness of Monetary Policy under Rational Expectations," *JMCB*, (February)13(1):94–102.

Gordon, R.J. 1976. "Recent Developments in the Theory of Inflation and Unemployment," *JME*, (April)2(2):185–219.

1977. "Recent Developments in the Theory of Inflation and Unemployment," in *Inflation Theory and Anti-Inflation Policy*, edited by E. Lundberg. London: Macmillan, pp. 42–71.

1978. *Macroeconomics*. Boston: Little, Brown.

1981. "Output Fluctuations and Gradual Price Adjustment," *JEL*, (June)XIX(2):493–530.

Gordon, R.J., ed. 1974. *Milton Friedman's Monetary Framework*. Chicago: University of Chicago Press.

Hahn, F.H. 1980. "Monetarism and Economic Theory," *EC*, (February) 47(185):1–17.

Hall, R.E. 1975. "The Rigidity of Wages and the Persistence of Unemployment," *BPEA* 2:301–35.

1980. "Employment Fluctuations and Wage Rigidity," *BPEA* 1:91–123.

Hansen, B. 1951. *A Study in the Theory of Inflation*. London: Allen & Unwin.

1970a. *A Survey of General Equilibrium Systems*. New York: McGraw-Hill.

1970b. "Excess Demand, Unemployment, Vacancies and Wages," *QJE*, (February)84(1):1–23.

Haslinger, F. 1978. *Volkswirtschaftliche Gesamtrechnung*. Munich: R. Oldenbourg.

Hicks, J.R. 1937. "Mr. Keynes and the Classics; A Suggested Interpretation," *Econometrica*, (April)5(2):147–59. Reprinted in M.G. Mueller, ed. 1971.

Readings in Macroeconomics. New York: Holt, Rinehart and Winston, pp. 137–45.

1946. *Value and Capital.* New York: Oxford University Press.

1974. *The Crisis in Keynesian Economics.* New York: Basic Books.

Hines, A.G. 1976. "The 'Microeconomic Foundations of Employment and Inflation Theory': Bad Old Wine in Elegant New Bottles," in *The Concept and Measurement of Involuntary Unemployment,* edited by G.D.N. Worswick. London: Allen & Unwin, pp. 58–79.

Holt, Ch.C. 1971. "Job Search, Phillips' Wage Relation, and Union Influence: Theory and Evidence," in *Microeconomic Foundations of Employment and Inflation Theory,* edited by E.S. Phelps et al. New York: Macmillan, pp. 53–123.

Johnson, H.G. 1972a. *Inflation and the Monetarist Controversy.* Amsterdam: North-Holland.

1972b. *Further Essays in Monetary Economics.* London: Allen & Unwin.

1976. "The Monetary Approach to Balance-of-Payments Theory," in *The Monetary Approach to the Balance of Payments,* edited by J.A. Frenkel and H.G. Johnson. London: Allen & Unwin, pp. 147–67.

Kahn, R. 1976. "Unemployment As Seen by the Keynesians," in *The Concept and Measurement of Involuntary Unemployment,* edited by G.D.N. Worswick. London: Allen & Unwin, pp. 19–34.

Kaldor, N. 1955/6. "Alternative Theories of Distribution," *ReSt* 23:83–100.

Keynes, J.M. 1936. *The General Theory of Employment, Interest and Money.* London: Macmillan.

1940. *How to Pay for the War.* London: Macmillan. Reprinted in Keynes, J.M. 1972. *Essays in Persuasion,* edited by E. Johnson and D. Moggridge. New York: Macmillan, pp. 367–439.

1972. *Essays in Persuasion,* Vol. IX of the collected writings of John Maynard Keynes, edited by E. Johnson and D. Moggridge. London: Macmillan, 1972.

Kierzkowski, H. 1976. "Theoretical Foundations of the Scandinavian Model of Inflation," *The Manchester School,* (September)44-232–46.

Klausinger, H. 1980. *Rationale Erwartungen und die Theorie der Stabilisierùngspolitik.* Bern: Peter Lang.

Klein, L.R. 1967. "Wage and Price Determination in Macroeconomics," in *Prices: Issues in Theory, Practice and Public Policy,* edited by A. Phillips and O.E. Williamson. Philadelphia: University of Pennsylvania Press, pp. 82–100.

1972. "The Treatment of Expectations in Econometrics," in *Uncertainty and Expectations in Economics,* edited by C.F. Carter and J.L. Ford. Oxford: Blackwell Publisher, pp. 175–90.

König, H. 1978. "Ein monetaristisches Modell zur Erklärung von Arbeitslosigkeit und Inflation: Modellprobleme und -implikationen für die BRD," *ZfN* 38(1–2):85–104.

1979. "Sucharbeitslosigkeit–ein Phänomen der siebziger Jahre," in *Ist Arbeitslosigkeit unvermeidlich?* edited by H. Seidel and F. Butschek. Stuttgart: Fischer, pp. 37–59.

Kyle, J.F. 1976. *The Balance of Payments in a Monetary Economy.* Princeton,

N.J.: Princeton University Press.

Laidler, D.E.W. 1969. *The Demand for Money.* New York: In text.

1971. "The Influence of Money on Economic Activity. – A Survey of Some Current Problems," in *Monetary Theory and Monetary Policy in the 1970's,* edited by G. Clayton, J.C. Gilbert, and R. Sedgwick. New York: Oxford University Press, pp. 73–135.

1975a. *Essays on Money and Inflation.* Chicago: University of Chicago Press.

1975b. "The Phillips Curve, Expectations and Incomes Policy," in *Essays on Money and Inflation.* Chicago: University of Chicago Press, pp. 82–100.

1976. "An Elementary Monetarist Model of Simultaneous Fluctuations in Prices and Output," in *Inflation in Small Countries,* edited by H. Frisch. Berlin: Springer-Verlag

1977. *The Demand for Money, Theories and Evidence,* 2nd ed. New York: Dun-Donnelley.

1981. "Monetarism, an Interpretation and an Assessment," *EJ* (March) 91(361):1–28.

Laidler, D.E.W., and Parkin, M.J. 1975. "Inflation – A Survey," *EJ,* (December)85(340):741–809.

Leijonhufvud, A. 1968. *On Keynesian Economics and the Economics of Keynes.* London: Oxford University Press.

1976. "Schools, 'Revolutions' and Research Programmes in Economic Theory," in *Method and Appraisal in Economics,* edited by S.J. Latsis. London: Cambridge University Press, pp. 65–108.

Lindbeck, A. 1979. "Imported and Structural Inflation and Aggregate Demand: The Scandinavian Model Reconstructed," in *Inflation and Employment in Open Economies,* edited by A. Lindbeck. Amsterdam: North-Holland, pp. 13–40.

1980. *Inflation, Global, International and National Aspects.* Leuven: Leuven University Press.

Lipsey, R.G. 1960. "The Relationship Between Unemployment and the Rate of Change of Money Wage Rates in the UK, 1862–1957: A Further Analysis," *Economica,* (February)27(105):1–32.

1974. "The Micro Theory of the Phillips Curve Reconsidered: A Reply to Holmes and Smyth," *Economica,* (February)41(191):62–70.

1978. "The Place of the Phillips Curve in Macroeconomic Models," in *Stability and Inflation,* edited by A.R. Bergstrom et al. New York: Wiley, pp. 49–75.

Löwe, H. 1970. *Einführung in die Lernpsychologie des Erwachsenenalters.* Berlin: Deutscher Verlag der Wissenschaften.

Lucas, R.E. 1972a. "Expectations and the Neutrality of Money," *JET,* (April)4(2):103–24.

1972b. "Econometric Testing of the Natural Rate Hypothesis," in *The Economics of Price Determination,* edited by O. Eckstein. Washington, D.C.: Board of Governors, Federal Reserve System, pp. 50–59.

1973. "Some International Evidence on Output–Inflation Tradeoffs," *AER,* (June)63(3):326–34.

1981. "Tobin and Monetarism: A Review Article," *JEL,* (June)XIX(2):558–67.

Lucas, R.E., and Rapping, L.A. 1971. "Real Wages, Employment, and Inflation," in *Microeconomic Foundations of Employment and Inflation Theory*, edited by E.S. Phelps et al. London: Macmillan.

McCallum, B.T. 1980. "Rational Expectations and Macroeconomic Stabilization Policy," *JMCB*, (February)12(4):716–46.

Machlup. F. 1960. "Another View of Cost-Push and Demand-Pull Inflation," *ReSt*, (May)42(2):125–39.

1969. "Cost Push and Demand Pull," in *Inflation*, edited by R.J. Ball and P. Doyle. Harmondsworth: Penguin.

Maddock, R., and Carter, M. 1982. "A Child's Guide to Rational Expectations," *JEL*, (March)XX:39–51.

Maital, S. 1972. "Inflation, Taxation and Equity," *EJ*, (March)82(325):158–67.

Malinvaud, E. 1977. *The Theory of Unemployment Reconsidered*. Oxford: Blackwell.

Mattila, J.P. 1974. "Job Quitting and Frictional Unemployment," *AER*, (March)64(1):235–9.

Mayer, Th., et al. 1978. *The Structure of Monetarism*. New York: Norton.

Maynard, G., and v. Ryckeghem, 1976. *A World of Inflation*. London: B.T. Batsford.

Meltzer, A. 1977. "Anticipated Inflation and Unanticipated Price Change," *JMCB*, (February)IX(2):182–205.

Morgan, B. 1978. *Monetarists and Keynesians – Their Contributions to Monetary Theory*. London: Macmillan.

Mortenson, D.T. 1971. "A Theory of Wage and Employment Dynamics." in *Microeconomic Foundations of Employment and Inflation Theory*, edited by E.S. Phelps et al. London: Macmillan, pp. 224–56.

Mundell, R.A. 1968. *International Economics*. New York: Macmillan.

1971. *Monetary Theory*. Pacific Palisades, Calif.: Goodyear.

Mussa, M. 1974. "A Monetary Approach to Balance of Payments Analysis," *JMCB*, (August)6(3):333–51.

Muth, J.F. 1961. "Rational Expectations and the Theory of Price Movements," *EC*, (July)29(3):315–35.

N.-Whitman, M. 1975. "Global Monetarism and the Monetary Approach to the Balance of Payments," *BPEA*, 3:491–536.

Niehans, J. 1978. *The Theory of Money*. Baltimore: John Hopkins University Press.

O'Brien, D.P. 1975. *The Classical Economists*. New York: Oxford University Press (Clarendon Press).

Okun, A.M. 1970. *The Political Economy of Prosperity*. Washington, D.C.: The Brookings Institution.

1974. "Unemployment and Output in 1974," *BPEA*, 2:495–505.

Otruba, H. 1974. "The Optimum Quantity of Money: A Delayed Criticism," *ZfN*, 34(1–2):125–36.

1981. *Wirtschaftliches Verhalten bei Ungleichgewicht*. Vienna: Verlag der Österreichischen Akademie der Wissenschaften.

Ozga, S.A. 1965. *Expectations in Economic Theory*. London: Weidenfeld and Nicolson.

Parkin, M.J. 1975. "The Causes of Inflation: Recent Contributions and Current

Controversies," Discussion Paper 7405. Manchester: University of Manchester.

Phelps, E.S. 1967. "Phillips Curves, Expectations of Inflation and Optimal Unemployment over Time." *Economica,* (August)34(135):254–81.

1971a. "Introduction: The New Microeconomics in Employment and Inflation Theory," in *Microeconomic, Foundations of Employment and Inflation Theory,* edited by E.S. Phelps et al. London: Macmillan, pp. 1–23.

1971b. "Money Wage Dynamics and Labour Market Equilibrium," *Microeconomic Foundations of Employment and Inflation Theory,* edited by E.S. Phelps et al. London: Macmillan, pp. 124–66.

1972. *Inflation Policy and Unemployment Theory: The Cost-Benefit Approach to Monetary Planning.* London: Macmillan.

Phelps, E.S., and Taylor, J.B. 1977. "Stabilizing Powers of Monetary Policy under Rational Expectations," *JPE,* (February)85(1):163–90.

Phelps, E.S., et al., eds. 1971. *Microeconomic Foundations of Employment and Inflation Theory.* London: Macmillan.

Phillips, A.W. 1958. "The Relation Between Unemployment and the Rate of Change of Money Wage Rates in the United Kingdom, 1861–1957," *Economica,* (November)22(100):283–99. Reprinted in Mueller, M.G., ed. 1971. *Readings in Macroeconomics.* New York: Holt, Rinehart and Winston, pp. 245–56.

Phillips, A., and Williamson, O.E., eds. 1967. *Prices: Issues in Theory, Practice and Public Policy.* Philadelphia: University of Pennsylvania Press.

Poole, W. 1976. "Rational Expectations in the Macro Model," *BPEA,* 2:463–505.

Ramser, H.J. 1978. "Rationale Erwartungen und Wirtschaftspolitik," *ZfgS,* (March)134(1):57–72.

Rose, K. 1976. *Theorie der Außenwirtschaft.* Munich: F. Vahlen.

Rothschild, K.W. 1978. "Arbeitslose: Gibt's die?" *Kyklos* 31(1):21–35.

Samuelson, P.A., and Solow, R.M. 1960. "The Problem of Achieving and Maintaining a Stable Price Level: Analytical Aspects of Anti-Inflation Policy," *AER,* (May)50(2):177–94. Reprinted in Mueller, M.G., ed. 1971. *Readings in Macroeconomics.* New York: Holt, Rinehart and Winston, pp. 372–85.

Samuelson, P.A., and Swamy, S. 1974. "Invariant Economic Index Numbers and Canonical Duality: Survey and Synthesis," *AER,* (September)64(4): 566–93.

Santomero, A.M., and Seater, J.J. 1978. "The Inflation-Unemployment Tradeoff: A Critique of the Literature," *JEL,* (June)16(2):499–544.

Sargent, T.J. 1973. "Rational Expectations, the Real Rate of Interest, and the Natural Rate of Unemployment," *BPEA* 21:429–72.

1976. "A Classical Macroeconomic Model for the United States," *JPE,* (April)84:207–38.

1979. *Macroeconomic Theory.* New York: Academic Press.

Sargent, T.J., and Wallace, N. 1973. "Rational Expectations and the Dynamics of Hyperinflation," *IER,* (June)14(2):328–50.

1975. "'Rational' Expectations, the Optimal Monetary Instrument, and the Optimal Money Supply Rule," *JPE,* (April)83(2):241–54.

1976. "Rational Expectations and the Theory of Economic Policy," *JME,* (April)2:169–83.

Scherf, H. 1967. *Untersuchungen zur Theorie der Inflation*. Tübingen: J.C.B. Mohr (Paul Siebeck).

Smithies, A. 1942. "The Behaviour of Money National Income under Inflationary Conditions," *QJE*, (November)57(4):113–28.

Solow, R.M. 1969. *Price Expectations and the Behavior of the Price Level*. Manchester: Manchester University Press, 1969.

1980. "On Theories of Unemployment," *AER*, (March)70(1):1–11.

Stein, J.L. 1976. "Introduction: The Monetarist Criticism of the New Economics," in *Monetarism*. Amsterdam: North-Holland, pp. 1–16.

Streeten, P. 1962. "Wages, Prices and Productivity," *Kyklos*, 15(4):723–31.

Swoboda, A.K. 1976. "Monetary Approaches to Balance-of-Payments Theory," in *Recent Issues in International Monetary Economics*, edited by E.-M. Claassen and P. Salin. Amsterdam: North-Holland, pp. 3–23.

1977. "Monetary Approaches to Worldwide Inflation," *Worldwide Inflation*, edited by L.B. Krause and W.S. Salant. Washington, D.C.: The Brookings Institution. pp. 9–62.

Taylor, J.B. 1979. Staggered Wage Setting in a Macro Model," *AER*, (May)69:108–13.

Teigen, R.L. 1972. "A Critical Look at Monetarist Economics," Rev. Federal Reserve Bank of St. Louis, Rep. Series 74, January.

Theil, H. 1970. *Economic Forecasts and Policy*. Amsterdam: North-Holland.

Tintner, G., Böhm, B., and Rieder, R. 1977. "Stabilitätskonzepte am Beispiel Österreichs," *Empirica* I:85–104.

Tobin, J. 1961. "Money, Capital and Other Stores of Value," *AER*, (May)51(2):26–37.

1972. "Inflation and Unemployment," *AER*, (March)62(1):1–18.

1974. "Friedman's Theoretical Framework," in *Milton Friedman's Monetary Framework*, edited by R.J. Gordon. Chicago: University of Chicago Press, pp. 77–89.

1977. "Comments," in *Worldwide Inflation*, edited by L.B. Krause and W.S. Salant. Washington, D.C.: The Brookings Institution, pp. 56–60.

1980. *Asset Accumulation and Economic Activity*. Oxford: Blackwell.

1981. "The Monetarist Counter-Revolution Today – An Appraisal," *EJ*, (March)91(361):29–42.

Trevithick, J.A. 1975. "Keynes, Inflation and Money Illusion," *EJ*, (March)85(337):101–13.

1976. "Money Wage Inflexibility and the Keynesian Labour Supply Function," *EJ*, (June)86(342):327–32.

Trevithick, J.A., and Mulvey, Ch. 1975. *The Economics of Inflation*. London: Martin Robertson.

Triplett, J.E. 1975. "The Measurement of Inflation: A Survey of Research on the Accuracy of Price Indexes," in *The Analysis of Inflation*, edited by P.H. Earl. Lexington, Mass.: Heath, pp. 19–82.

Vanderkamp, J. 1975. "Inflation: A Simple Friedman Theory with a Phillips Twist," *JME* 1:117–22.

Worswick, G.D.N., ed. 1976. *The Concept and Measurement of Involuntary Unemployment*. London: Allen & Unwin.

AUTHOR INDEX

SUBJECT INDEX